Blue Genes: Sharing and Conserving the World's Aquatic Biodiversity

Blue Genes: Sharing and Conserving the World's Aquatic Biodiversity

David Greer and Brian Harvey

London • Sterling, VA

International Development Research Centre

Ottawa • Cairo • Dakar • Montevideo • Nairobi • New Delhi • Singapore

First published in the UK, USA and Canada in 2004
by Earthscan and the International Development Research Centre (IDRC)

ISBN: 1–84407–106–5 paperback
         1–84407–105–7 hardback

Typesetting by Saxon Graphics, Derby, UK
Printed and bound in the UK by Cromwell Press, Trowbridge
Cover design by Gillian Harvey

For a full list of publications please contact:

Earthscan
8–12 Camden High Street
London, NW1 0JH, UK
Tel: +44 (0)20 7387 8558
Fax: +44 (0)20 7387 8998
Email: earthinfo@earthscan.co.uk
Web: **www.earthscan.co.uk**

22883 Quicksilver Drive, Sterling, VA 20166–2012, USA

Earthscan publishes in association with WWF-UK and the International Institute for Environment
and Development

International Development Research Centre
PO Box 8500, Ottawa, ON, Canada K1G 3H9
pub@idrc.ca/www.idrc.ca

A catalogue record for this book is available from the British Library

Library of Congress Cataloging-in-Publication Data

Greer, David (David Seton)

Blue genes: sharing and conserving the world's aquatic biodiversity / David Greer and Brian Harvey
        p. cm.
    Includes bibliographical references and index.
    ISBN 1–84407–106–5 (pbk.) – ISBN 1–84407–105–7 (hardback)
        1.   Aquatic genetic resources conservation–Government policy. 2. Aquatic genetic
    resources–Economic aspects. I. Harvey, Brian J. II. Title.

QH75.G7175 2004
333.95'16'0916–dc22

                            2003022768

Printed on elemental chlorine-free paper

Contents

List of Photographs, Figures and Boxes

PHOTOGRAPHS

FIGURE

BOXES

Preface

The impact of biotechnology can be compared to that of the Industrial Revolution two centuries ago. Nowhere is this more evident than in the food and drug industries. Genetic modification of crops has become so commonplace that a wide variety of products in an average supermarket now contains ingredients produced or affected by genetic engineering. The development of many pharmaceutical products results from biotechnological manipulation of the genetic codes for natural plant compounds.

The international trade in genetic resources is significant. The global market for pharmaceuticals alone is more than US$300 billion a year. Like the Industrial Revolution, the biotechnology revolution has created a demand by corporations for access to the resources of southern countries – with the difference that genetic resources (genetic material containing the fundamental units of heredity) rather than natural resources (timber, minerals, fish) are the prize today. For their part, countries providing genetic resources haven't forgotten the price paid by many southern countries during and before the Industrial Revolution: colonization by European countries. Control over access to plant genetic resources and sharing in the benefits from their use are extraordinarily sensitive issues.

In the rush to develop global policies that deal with access to genetic resources, aquatic animals and plants have largely been overlooked. International agreements such as the Convention on Biological Diversity (CBD) and the Agreement on Trade-related Aspects of Intellectual Property Rights (TRIPS) have been largely driven by agricultural and pharmaceutical agendas, and have tended to treat aquatic matters as an afterthought. The same trend appears to be occurring in the development of national strategies for biodiversity management and of laws regulating access to genetic resources.

Plant genetic resources have received far more press than aquatic ones for good reason: scientific understanding and commercial use of aquatic genetic resources lag decades behind their plant counterparts. But this situation is changing fast. Although industrial-scale aquaculture was virtually unknown 30 years ago, it's now predicted that more than 40 per cent of global food fish production will come from farms by 2020. Similarly, bioprospecting for marine organisms with value for pharmaceutical or industrial applications lags far behind terrestrial bioprospecting – but the quest for the holy grail of a cancer cure is a powerful incentive for increased activity. Meanwhile, the natural capital of aquatic genetic diversity is rapidly being eroded by overfishing and development, with species disappearing before they are even known to humans.

While it is true that certain aspects of biodiversity and genetic resources policy can apply equally to plants or fish, significant differences need to be taken into account as well. For example, whereas seed companies can collect their genetic resources from international gene banks, fish farmers generally rely on wild populations to replenish their broodstock. The very different nature of aquatic genetic resources (for example, hidden, migratory, publicly accessible) raises ownership issues that may be different from those known to the plant world. Communities in the areas where aquatic genetic resources are likely to be collected may have no traditional knowledge that is useful to fish farmers or pharmaceutical companies – yet some countries' laws make the sharing of useful traditional knowledge a prerequisite for a community's right to benefit from providing access to genetic resources.

These and many other distinctions between plant and aquatic genetic resources deserve consideration by policy makers. In addition, the vacuum in policies for the management and conservation of aquatic biodiversity needs to be addressed before countries begin to contemplate putting access regulations in place. This book offers an analysis of policy gaps and proposes approaches at the international, national and community levels to providing a foundation for the conservation and sharing of aquatic biodiversity.

Acknowledgements

Dedication

Blue Genes is dedicated to the memory of Chusa Gines, who worked indefatigably to promote the sustainable use of genetic resources from the developing world. Chusa agreed with us that aquatic genetic resources are as important as terrestrial ones, and she was a key figure in promoting and obtaining IDRC approval for the *Blue Genes* project. Chusa died in a plane crash in the Andes in 2002.

Acknowledgements

We would like to express our thanks to the International Development Research Centre in Ottawa for funding the research and writing of this book.

Every book needs a believer. *Blue Genes* could not have been completed without the unfailing support, encouragement and patience of IDRC's Brian Davy. Thanks, Brian.

Many people were generous in providing the information and assistance we needed to develop the case studies that illuminate the themes addressed by *Blue Genes*. We would particularly like to thank the following: William Aalsbersberg, University of the South Pacific; Ephraim Batungbacal, Tambuyog Development Center; Ning Labbish Chao, Universidade do Amazonas; Gisela Concepcion and Lourdes Cruz, Marine Science Institute, University of the Philippines; Elenita Dano, South East Asian Regional Institute for Community Education; Timothy Fleming, Icy Waters Ltd; Modadugu Gupta, World Fish Center; Sandy Johnson, Fisheries and Oceans Canada; Clarissa Marte, South East Asia Fisheries Development Center; Jiji Rodriguez, GIFT Foundation; Michael Tlusty and Scott Dowd, New England Aquarium; and Bill Vernon, Creative Salmon Ltd.

Others who provided invaluable information and advice include Yogi Carolsfeld, World Fisheries Trust; Keith Davenport, Ornamental Aquatic Trade Association; Fred Fortier, Shuswap Nation Fisheries Commission; Rainer Froese, World Fish Center; Lyle Glowka; Michael Halewood, Genetic Resources Policy Initiative; Paul Holthus, Marine Aquarium International; Steven King, Shaman Pharmaceuticals; Heather MacAndrew; Don McAllister, Ocean Voice International; Bob McFetridge, Canadian Biodiversity Convention Office; Jeff McNeely, IUCN; Anna Rosa Martinez Prat; Roger Pullin, formerly with the World Fish Center; Calvin Sandborn; Krystyna Swiderska, International Institute for Environment and Development; and Amanda Vincent, Project Seahorse.

We are also grateful to the participants of a workshop that we organized in British Columbia to discuss indigenous peoples' views on the use and sharing of aquatic genetic resources: Dennis Ableson, Carrier-Sekani Tribal Council; Robert Fritzchse, Gitxsan Hereditary Chiefs; Crystal Ross and Mark Bowler of the Haisla Nation Fisheries Commission; Glenn Barner, Nisga'a Tribal Council Fisheries Program; Dave Moore, Shuswap Nation Fisheries Commission; Carl Sidney, Yukon Salmon Committee; Juanita Sidney, Teslin-Tlingit Fisheries Program; and Joey Amos and Burton Ayles, Northwest Territories Fisheries Joint Management Commission.

We are indebted to Rob West, Ruth Mayo, Jennifer Poole and Camille Adamson of James & James/Earthscan and to Bill Carman of IDRC for their efforts in bringing *Blue Genes* to publication, and to Carmen Ross of World Fisheries Trust for formatting several drafts of the book.

David Greer
Brian Harvey

List of Acronyms and Abbreviations

AADIS	Aquatic Animal Diversity Information System
AKVAFORSK	Institute of Aquaculture Research of Norway
ASEAN	Association of South East Asian Nations
BGRRP	Biodiversity and Genetic Resources Research Programme (World Fish Centre)
CBD	Convention on Biological Diversity
CBFM	Community-based Fisheries Management
CGRFA	Commission on Genetic Resources for Food and Agriculture
CGIAR	Consultative Group on International Agricultural Research
CITES	Convention on International Trade in Endangered Species of Wild Flora and Fauna
COP	Conference of the Parties (to the Convention on Biological Diversity)
DADIS	Domestic Animal Diversity Information System
DFO	Department of Fisheries and Oceans, Canada
DNA	deoxyribonucleic acid
EEZ	Exclusive Economic Zone
ETC Group	Erosion, Technology and Concentration Group
FAMI	Fisherman's Association of Malalison Island
FARMC	Fisheries and Aquatic Resource Management Council
FAO	UN Food and Agriculture Organization
FINGER	Fisheries Information Network on Genetic Resources
FSC	Forest Stewardship council
GIFT	Genetic Improvement of Farmed Tilapia
GRAIN	Genetic Resources Action International
IACBGR	Inter-Agency Committee on Biological and Genetic Resources
IBAMA	Instituto Brasileiro do Meio Ambiente e dos Recursos Naturais Renováveis
ICLARM	International Center for Living Aquatic Resources Management
IDRC	International Development Research Centre
INGA	International Network on Genetics in Aquaculture
IPGRI	International Plant Genetic Resources Institute
IPRs	intellectual property rights
IRRC	International Rice Research Institute
IUCN	International Union for the Conservation of Nature
MAC	Marine Aquarium Council
MSC	Marine Stewardship Council
MSI	Marine Science Institute, Philippines
NBSAP	National Biodiversity Strategy and Action Plan

NGO	non-governmental organization
OAU	Organization of African Unity
SB	Smith Kline Beecham
SEAFDEC	South East Asia Fisheries Development Center
SEARICE	South East Asian Regional Institute for Community Education
SIDR	Strathclyde Institute of Drug Research
SPACHEE	South Pacific Action Committee for Human Ecology and Environment
SBSTTA	Subsidiary Body on Scientific, Technical and Technological Advice
TRIPS	Trade-related Aspects of Intellectual Property Rights
UNCED	United Nations Conference on Environment and Development
UNCLOS	United Nations Convention on the Law of the Sea
UPOV	International Union for the Protection of New Varieties of Plants
USP	University of the South Pacific
WFT	World Fisheries Trust
WIPO	World Intellectual Property Organization
WTO	World Trade Organization
WWF	World Wide Fund for Nature

Overview

Cardinal tetra fisherman, Rio Negro, Brazil (photo by David Greer)

THE GENE RUSH:
Finding new value in aquatic biodiversity

The genetic manipulation of underwater life represents a quantum leap forward in humans' use of aquatic biodiversity. Every year, scientists discover new ways and new reasons to transfer genes not only between different fish species, but also between much more distantly related organisms. The creators of the Super Salmon, a transgenic Atlantic salmon that contains the genes of an Arctic flounder and grows several times faster than wild stocks, have applied for US Food and Drug Administration approval to market their invention to American consumers (Moore, 2000). Fish genes have been transferred to fruits to make them more frost resistant (Specter, 2000), and insect genes have been inserted into fish in an effort to increase disease resistance (Fletcher et al, 1999). In 2003, an American company secured regulatory approval to market the GloFish – a vivid, artificially fluorescent ornamental fish created by injecting the eggs of zebra fish with a sea anemone gene (Gong et al, 2003).

The creation of transgenic varieties is the most dramatic of several types of use of genetic resources – genetic material containing functional units of heredity (eg eggs, sperm, DNA). Fish biologists also use more conventional selective breeding – combining the eggs and sperm from different populations of the same species – to improve farmed stocks. For example, genetically improved tilapias developed from broodstock collected in Africa are now widely farmed in Southeast Asia'. Government fisheries agencies, corporations and even some indigenous communities have started 'banks' of cryogenically frozen fish sperm to facilitate commercial breeding and stock rebuilding, and to provide insurance against extinctions.

Meanwhile, researchers hired by pharmaceutical companies continue to collect and analyse marine organisms whose chemical compounds could provide the clues needed for the invention of anti-cancer drugs, painkillers or a host of other medicinal products. Deep in the ocean recently discovered bacterial communities in hydrothermal vents are being tested for the ability of their enzymes to convert harmful chemicals to safer derivatives, enabling the clean up of oil spills and hazardous wastes (Glowka, 1998a).

The stakes are high. Global sales of pharmaceuticals exceed US$300 billion a year (Laird, 2002). The global share of food fish production from aquaculture is projected to rise to 41 per cent in 2020, up from 31 per cent in 1997 (Delgado et al, 2003). The interest among aquarium hobbyists in Europe, Japan and North America in cultured ornamental fish with never-before-seen colours and markings is huge.

The variety of raw material for genetic modification of aquatic life is vast, including fish germplasm and somatic cell DNA, tissue samples of marine organisms such as snails or sponges to be screened for useful chemical compounds, even aquatic plants and bacteria. In some cases, pharmaceutical companies have succeeded in reducing the amounts of raw materials needed through technologies such as chemical recombination, while the most common ornamental species such as neon tetras have been bred in captivity through so many generations that there is little if any need for wild broodstock. While it's not clear precisely how great the demand for aquatic genetic resources will be in the future, the explosion in new uses suggests that it will increase significantly.

What is clear is that the trade in aquatic genetic resources requires clear policy direction. There are many players with different and sometimes competing priorities. Commercial and academic researchers need to know the rules for obtaining access to the raw material in the wild, and so do the local communities where the resources may be found. Complicating the task of developing workable access policies is the fact that the real economic value of genetic resources lies not in the physical material but in the knowledge of how to use it. Users of genetic resources – a fish farmer who invents a new strain, a pharmaceutical company that develops a new drug – protect their knowledge with a patent. But who protects the knowledge of an indigenous community that a collector may need to speed the process of developing an 'invention'?

Should genetic resources and the traditional knowledge of their uses be valued separately in negotiations for access? If so, what's a fair price for each? Countries around the world are grappling with questions like these as they struggle to develop laws to regulate access to genetic resources. One question they usually overlook, but which is becoming more and more relevant as new uses of aquatic genetic resources proliferate, is: what differences between aquatic and plant genetic resources do access rules need to take into account?

GENE DRAIN: Halting the erosion of genetic diversity

To many of us, newly announced products of genetic engineering can seem miraculous, outlandish and sometimes frightening. All the developments described above have happened in the last 20 years, usually in the absence of clear regulatory frameworks. It's hard to properly regulate new practices without fully understanding their long-term consequences. Scientists studying biodiversity management repeatedly call for the application of the precautionary principle in the use of aquatic biodiversity (Bartley and Pullin, 1999), but it takes a lot to convince governments of the need for long-term risk assessment in the face of short-term economic pressures. Governments even shy away from making the small investment that it would take to bank fish germplasm as insurance against extinctions, fearful that such an initiative might imply that they don't adequately manage risks to fish populations (Harvey et al, 1998).

Genetic diversity within species is the foundation for aquaculture, pharmaceutical development and for all the other existing and potential uses of aquatic genetic resources, in addition to being valuable in its own right. The more genetic diversity there is within a species, the greater the likelihood of characteristics that may some day be invaluable for improvement of farmed stocks. For example, each of the six species of Pacific salmon contains several hundred stocks, a small number of which are currently considered commercially valuable. Salmon are sensitive to minute changes in ocean temperatures. A stock that is capable of adapting to warmer temperatures produced by climate change might be invaluable for aquaculture in the future – provided science knows of its existence and it doesn't join the hundreds of stocks that have already become extinct, unable to survive high-tech harvesting practices or the habitat impacts of logging, mining, damming, agricultural runoff or urban development.

'Sustainable development' has been a catchphrase for governments around the world since the United Nation's (UN) Brundtland report made it popular in the late 1980s (WCED, 1987). However, without concerted government action and corporate buy-in, the natural capital needed for biotechnology will continue to erode at an alarming rate. Many more marine species could be close to extinction by 2050 if more isn't done to stem the increasing impact of high-technology harvesting, especially in the deep sea (Pauly, 2003). One-fifth of freshwater fish species is considered to be extinct or endangered (Heywood, 1995). Science may have a better understanding today of the effects of human activities on aquatic life, but governments and other stakeholders still need to find the determination and resources to reduce those effects.

Somewhat ironically, the wide publicity given to advances in genetic sciences and to new inventions such as the GloFish stands in sharp contrast to the lack of knowledge about aquatic biodiversity. Aquatic science in general lags behind terrestrial sciences in identifying species, understanding ecosystem relationships and assessing potential uses for genetic resources. Communities of life on the ocean floor are the least-understood ecosystems on the planet. The deep sea alone may contain 10 million species that have yet to be described (Norse, 1993), and perhaps only 45,000 out of a million freshwater species have been identified (McAllister et al, 1997). Every year, some aquatic species become extinct before science has even become aware of their existence. Too often, the underwater world has been out of sight, out of mind when it comes to funding basic science and developing policies for biodiversity management and conservation. When a rain-forest is clear cut, the world takes notice; but when a trawler scours away all the seabed life in its path, there's no one to see.

CONSERVING AND SHARING AQUATIC BIODIVERSITY: Filling policy gaps

New uses of aquatic biodiversity require new policy approaches. The introduction or expansion of food fish aquaculture, for example, creates the need for policy makers to consider a wide variety of issues such as environmental impacts of fish farming, potential health risks to consumers of genetically modified products, access by fish farmers to wild broodstock and transfers of live broodstock from their ecosystems of origin, research into the different genetic characteristics of different wild stocks and conservation of wild genetic diversity.

The 1992 Convention on Biological Diversity (CBD), signed by 188 countries (the handful that have not signed includes the US) links these diverse policy issues through its three objectives: the conservation of biological diversity; the sustainable use of its components; and the fair and equitable sharing of the benefits derived from the use of genetic resources. The CBD provides guidelines for national policies and laws. Most countries are still a long way from implementing them because of the complexity of creating legislation that is clear, widely supported and enforceable.

Developing policy approaches that accommodate both capture fisheries and aquaculture presents a challenge for policy makers. Governments are paying increasing attention to aquaculture, but policy development has largely been reactive – focusing on public concerns that attract the most publicity, such as environmental impacts and genetic modification. Traditionally, managers of wild fisheries have been preoccupied with the management of fish stocks of greatest importance to commercial fisheries. Sometimes that has meant casting a blind eye to threats to other stocks that may possess important genetic material. And it is only within the past decade that the true extent of genetic variability within species has even been appreciated. Conserving the wild genetic diversity needed to support sustainable capture fisheries and aquaculture and to maintain healthy aquatic ecosystems means focusing on all stocks, not just those with current economic importance.

Access to genetic resources of plants has become an important policy issue in many countries. As food fish aquaculture expands and the demand for wild broodstock increases, clear policies on access need to be in place for aquatic genetic resources as well. For these policies to work, countries will need to support the research needed for better scientific understanding of aquatic ecosystems and will need to develop sound policies for the management of aquatic genetic diversity. International agreements such as the UN Food and Agriculture Organization (FAO) Code of Conduct for Responsible Fisheries and the United Nations Convention on the Law of the Sea (UNCLOS) have provided a useful starting point for approaches to sustainable management of aquatic biodiversity, but national laws with teeth are much in need.

Whose to share?
Ownership and control of aquatic resources

Southern countries with the richest concentrations of biodiversity are usually the primary providers of genetic resources, and northern countries with highly developed technologies are the primary users. This applies particularly to crop enhancement (through genetic modification of plant characteristics) and to the development of pharmaceutical and industrial products through screening of plant and marine samples for biological effects. It's less true of aquaculture, primarily because fish are most successfully bred in conditions that most closely approximate their original habitats – either in the same country or at similar latitudes – and temperate regions have their share of potentially useful aquatic biodiversity.

Before the 1990s, genetic resources were generally considered common property, available to all takers. The negotiation of the CBD led to some hard bargaining. Developing countries noted that the responsibility for conserving biological diversity would fall primarily on their shoulders, both because it is most heavily concentrated in the south and because many northern countries have already made use of or used up their own natural assets (Atlantic cod stocks being a case in point). Southern countries insisted on recognition of national sovereignty over natural resources as a condition of signing the Convention, thus ensuring control over access. (The Law of the Sea, which was also negotiated in the early 1990s, extends a country's sovereignty beyond its coastline to a maximum of 22.2 km and creates a 321.8 km Exclusive Economic Zone with exclusive exploration, exploitation and management rights. Beyond that is the high sea, with open access rights.)

National sovereignty over natural resources provides only a limited measure of control. To commercial users of genetic resources, physical possession of genetic material is usually secondary to the big prize: the patent on the resulting invention (for example, an improved fish strain or process for creating a drug). The World Trade Organization's (WTO) pressure on developing countries to agree to a universal intellectual property law system in return for trade benefits has generated considerable concern among developing countries that it's an attempt to bypass their hard-won national sovereignty over genetic resources (Seiler and Dutfield, 2002). According to some critics, the WTO agreement on Trade-related Aspects of Intellectual Property Rights (TRIPS) is nothing more than an extension of the 'biopiracy' that led to developing countries' demands for control over access to their genetic resources in the first place.

THINKING LOCALLY:
Rights of indigenous and local communities

The first peoples naturally gravitated to areas with the greatest natural abundance; consequently, coastal and inland aquatic biodiversity is most richly concentrated in the traditional territories of indigenous peoples. The 'ecosystem approach' that has recently come into favour in natural resource management planning is a scientific validation of what was once a spiritual belief system for many indigenous peoples. The CBD recognizes the importance of restoring and maintaining traditional ecosystem management practices of indigenous and local communities as an important tool for conserving biological diversity. Obviously, this is easier said than done. Many traditional communities have long since lost control over their lands and resources and, as a consequence, have seen a gradual erosion of their cultures, ecological knowledge and traditional livelihoods. In addition, the traditional fisheries of some coastal fishing communities continue to be depleted by commercial offshore fleets. Today, fishing communities are among the poorest in the world, and poverty is a big barrier to conservation. For a poor fisherman in the Philippines, the choice between using illegal fishing methods and feeding his family is no choice at all.

Through international agreements such as the CBD and UN Draft Declaration on Indigenous Rights, there is greater recognition than ever before of the rights of indigenous and local communities to control over land, natural resources and the use of traditional knowledge. However, translating principles into practice at the national level is a very hard sell indeed. Canada and Australia have been engaged for years in treaty-making with indigenous peoples; and a few other nations, such as the Philippines and Bangladesh, have enacted comprehensive community rights legislation. Most countries, however, have adopted a wait-and-see attitude, while international discussions on the details of implementing the CBD continue. Apart from the inevitable tensions between different levels of government (local, regional, national) over control over natural resources management, the needs of the poor do not always conform with the goals of the powerful.

The Convention takes a tentative step towards the recognition of community rights. Article 8(j) encourages parties to the convention to encourage the sharing of benefits from the use of genetic resources with indigenous and local communities whose knowledge contributes to that use. The logic behind this provision is that users of plant genetic resources (for example, seed companies and pharmaceutical companies) depend on access to traditional knowledge about crop strains or medicinal uses of plants. The same cannot be said of users of aquatic genetic resources. Agriculture dates back several thousand years; the history of aquaculture, with the notable exception of China, can be measured in decades. While local fishermen may have extensive familiarity with the habits of aquatic life, this type of knowledge may be irrelevant to fish farmers or scientists developing new strains of cultured fish. Similarly, pharmaceutical researchers prospecting for marine organisms may be looking for seabed creatures for which local communities have no traditional uses.

For national governments, the logic of linking community rights over access to genetic resources to traditional knowledge is readily apparent: individuals or groups have the right to control the use of their ideas. However, nation states own biological resources (apart from those on private lands) in their physical state, and the CBD calls on parties to the convention to facilitate access to genetic resources. Providing more far reaching rights to communities might simply create regulatory confusion and insurmountable barriers to access, in addition to eroding the strength of national sovereignty for which developing countries fought so hard during the CBD negotiations. Industrial countries are even less inclined to expand community rights over genetic resources. While much depends on variations in political systems, democratic governments are not necessarily any more likely than other forms of government to view expansion of community rights favourably. At the most, communities may be given the opportunity for 'consultation' or 'input' in the decision-making process.

Indigenous groups have divided views about the CBD. Some consider the question of right to consent to access to genetic resources to be secondary to a more fundamental issue: rights to ownership of and control over biological resources in their traditional territories. Why, they ask, should indigenous communities need to negotiate access to something that is theirs already? In 1993, the Draft UN Declaration on the Rights of Indigenous Peoples confirmed their right to:

own, develop, control and use the land and territories, including the total

> *environment of the lands, air, waters, coastal seas, sea ice, flora and fauna*
> *and other resources which they have traditionally owned or otherwise*
> *occupied or used.*

In 2001, the International Indigenous Forum on Biodiversity declared that the 1993 UN Declaration represented the minimum acceptable standard, and that the recognition of the rights of indigenous peoples is necessary to create the trust needed to meet the CBD objective of access and benefit sharing (IIFB, 2001).

Some indigenous groups have called for an outright ban on bioprospecting while human rights issues remain unresolved. And some cynics say that indigenous communities that drive a hard bargain may be merely holding out for an illusory 'pot of gold'. Diversity of motivation and of political agenda is as much a characteristic of indigenous groups as of any sampling of human societies. But motivation is really irrelevant. For access laws to be effective in the long run, some reconciliation between the claims of indigenous rights movements and the reluctance of governments to recognize them will be essential.

ACTING GLOBALLY:
Towards national laws on access to aquatic resources

Each of the 188 signatories of the CBD is expected to implement the Convention through national laws and policies that set the rules for access to genetic resources and lay the groundwork for negotiation of benefits in return. About 50 countries are at various stages of development of these laws and policies. The small handful of post-CBD laws that are already in place (all in southern countries) take a variety of approaches to the management and sharing of biodiversity. For example, while the Philippines and Brazil have enacted laws specific to access and benefit sharing, Costa Rica and India have embedded access and benefit-sharing provisions in comprehensive biodiversity management laws. Access rules typically cover domestic as well as international collections, with more stringent rules for foreign applicants.

For good reason, most countries have been taking a go-slow approach, waiting for further guidance from CBD implementation bodies and from regional associations such as the Association of South East Asian Nations (ASEAN), while carefully observing the experience of the first countries out of the starting gate. Some southern countries have been hesitant about setting rigorous access requirements that may result in a loss of business if collectors of genetic resources (ornamental fish, for example) can get what they want in countries with looser regulations. What the go-slow approach means is that fisheries managers in many countries, states and provinces may not yet have heard of the CBD, though they will undoubtedly feel its effects in due course.

Regulatory obstacles to research are a serious concern for both commercial and academic collectors and one of the most difficult challenges for policy makers. For commercial collectors, the negotiated price of access to genetic resources must be within reason, and the ability of collectors to pay depends very much on the use of the resource, the type of benefit to be negotiated, and the sheer time and effort it takes to negotiate. A pharmaceutical company needs to consider that the odds of developing a marketable drug from a collected sample might be one in 10,000 or lower. Similarly, an aquaculture company collecting wild broodstock may have little idea of the likelihood of achieving a desired commercial result. One reason why the CBD takes such pains to mention non-monetary benefits such as technology transfer is that royalties may be an empty promise, while a significant upfront payment may be intolerably burdensome for a commercial collector who is making numerous collections, sometimes in several countries. In addition, developing countries have been anxious to acquire the technologies that will enable them to further their own research and development expertise in the use of genetic resources.

Academic researchers generally have far less capacity than corporations to make generous deals with communities for access to genetic resources. Yet basic research such as taxonomy is vital to a better understanding of the aquatic world. Drafters of access laws have been struggling to develop effective ways to streamline the approval process and to ease regulatory barriers to academic research, with limited success. For several years after the Philippines passed the world's first access law in 1995, approval of access applications from both commercial and academic researchers came to a virtual halt. Part of the challenge that legislative drafters face is that it may be difficult to draw clear lines between commercial and academic research. Pure academic research can lead to unexpected commercial applications, academic institutions are becoming increasingly dependent on corporate financial support, and many academics cross the line into commercial activities. This is as true for aquatic-oriented businesses such as aquaculture or the development of cancer drugs as it is for plant-based research.

A related challenge is how to define in law the rights of traditional communities to provide or withhold consent to applications for access to genetic resources. What is an indigenous or local community? Who speaks for it? How much information and understanding does a community need to be capable of providing prior informed consent to collections? What are the minimum standards, if any, for reaching agreement with communities? Should the law distinguish between biological resources and genetic resources? Does it matter whether or not the community has traditional knowledge that the collector needs?

The latter issue in particular is problematical for the regulation of access to aquatic genetic resources. Understandably, given that the use of aquatic genetic resources is barely beginning, the development of national access laws appears to have been largely based on the premise that 'genetic resources' means plant genetic resources – and that collectors need traditional knowledge along with the resource. A proposed Peruvian law assumes the provision of traditional knowledge to be a prerequisite for the right to benefit sharing; the Philippines law requires consent with or without traditional knowledge (but has been difficult to implement); and the federal Brazilian law is ambiguous. Defining community rights to consent to the use of genetic resources presents an enormous challenge for developing and developed countries alike; dealing with aquatic genetic resources issues simply adds another wrinkle to an already complicated task.

It has largely fallen on the shoulders of developing countries to lead the way in the formulation of access and benefit-sharing laws. Northern countries, as the users, have less incentive to create a level playing field. The CBD calls on all parties to ensure equitable access and benefit-sharing arrangements. Industrial countries could help to do so by requiring applicants for patents involving genetic modification to demonstrate that genetic resources have been acquired in compliance with CBD principles and the laws of the provider country. In terms of aquatic genetic resources, this would apply particularly to the collection of ornamental fish and of marine organisms for pharmaceuticals research. In addition, certification programmes might provide a useful complement to access and benefit-sharing laws by ensuring that collectors of aquatic genetic resources have met appropriate standards. Certification programmes have proven to be a highly effective means of promoting responsible forest practices, and recently have been adapted to capture fisheries under the auspices of the Marine Stewardship Council.

RESULTS THAT COUNT:
Meaningful benefits for fishing communities

It is in all our interests that agreements for access to aquatic genetic resources promote the sustainable use of aquatic genetic resources and the conservation of aquatic genetic diversity. It may not be enough for governments merely to set minimum standards for the negotiation of fair agreements with fishing communities. While it will be up to communities to determine in each instance what benefits are satisfactory, governments could help ensure productive negotiations (and thereby facilitate access) by, for example, providing negotiation training and developing policy approaches to support a wide range of monetary and non-monetary benefits.

The promise of royalties might be seductive for communities with little understanding of the odds against the development of a marketable product (roughly estimated to be one in 10,000 in pharmaceutical research). Up-front and periodic payments are financial alternatives if collectors are willing to take the gamble that they'll pay off. Local people may also gain some financial benefit if they are employed in the collection of aquatic genetic resources. The CBD and some national laws suggest that financial benefits should be used in ways that promote sound biodiversity management. What might these be? Funding for basic social needs such as health care and schooling, while it may not appear to be directly related to biodiversity management, may be the most important step of all in increasing the capacity of communities to develop conservation-based economies. Healthy, educated communities can better participate in the decisions that affect their lives on both a local and a global level.

The type of technology transfer that is useful at the national level – such as the training of scientists in techniques for drug development or genetic modification – is likely to be irrelevant to indigenous and local communities. However, access to low technologies and training can be extremely useful, especially if they enable the development of sustainable fishing livelihoods and are based on a clear understanding of community characteristics and needs. What kinds of training or technologies could be involved? One example is the training that the South East Asian Fisheries Development Center (SEAFDEC) provided to a Philippines community to start up a successful and low impact mud crab farming operation. SEAFDEC was also instrumental in working with local communities in another part of the Philippines to establish no-fish areas (Agbayani et al, 2000). In another example, Project Seahorse provided the training and technical support needed for another Philippines fishing community to set up a seahorse ranching operation that not only provides sustainable livelihoods, but also enhances wild seahorse populations (Project Seahorse, 2000). In Brazil, Project Piaba has been instrumental in helping fishing communities on the Rio Negro practise a sustainable ornamentals industry that contributes to the protection of the rainforest ecosystem (Chao et al, 2001).

What these solutions have in common is that they involve a hand up rather than a handout – making available technology and training that are appropriate to local conditions and culture, and providing the means for local entrepreneurship to get a toe-hold. A little economic power can go a long way in helping to empower communities generally. It may take a lot of toe-holds to break the cycle of poverty and nurture conservation-based, small-scale fishing economies in countless communities. However, the alternative – a continuing wasting away of aquatic biological diversity by groups with little or no self-interest in conservation – is unacceptable in a world where virtually all nations have expressed agreement with the principle of sustainable economies, sustainable ecosystems and sustainable communities.

The phrase 'act locally' never took on more urgent meaning. The real challenge in the future will be getting the most powerful countries and the most influential multinational corporations on board. In 2002, US Department of State guidelines suggested that American researchers abroad obtain the written consent of indigenous communities prior to collecting genetic resources. The irony of that advice is huge. The most powerful country in the world is one of a very small handful of countries to decline to endorse the CBD, which set the ground-rules to which the state department guidelines refer – and US recalcitrance has contributed mightily to the difficulty developing countries have faced in implementing the CBD.

The success of sustainable livelihoods projects is likely to depend on a clear understanding of the cultural background of a community, ensuring widespread participation in and support for a proposed venture, and designing enterprises that build on traditional community practices and knowledge. A study commissioned by FAO (2001) found that the degree to which fisheries management practices or policies strengthen or weaken small-scale fisheries is directly related to the level of understanding of community fishing cultures. The study found that traditional fishing communities generally share two common characteristics: a detailed and function oriented knowledge of aquatic systems and species important to the community economy, and participation of the entire population, including women, children and the elderly, in fishing, processing, marketing and distribution. Ideally, the design of sustainable livelihoods projects takes into account such community characteristics.

Non-governmental organizations (NGOs) and aquatic sciences institutes might play a useful role as intermediaries in benefit-sharing negotiations with communities, helping to lay the foundation for sustainable fisheries livelihoods. And, although the CBD has provided the impetus for governments to think about community benefits that might contribute to both ecological and economic sustainability, it would be short-sighted to limit such thinking to circumstances in which communities provide access to genetic resources. The cold truth is that, despite all the hopes for quick implementation of the CBD, ten years later there are very few examples of tangible benefits to communities resulting from access agreements for plant or aquatic genetic resources. Is the CBD promise of benefit sharing for traditional communities a fiction? It's perhaps still too early to say, but the signs so far haven't been encouraging.

The conservation and sustainable use of aquatic biodiversity on a global level are crucial objectives, and governments need to take all steps possible to promote the economic, social and cultural well-being of traditional fishing communities, whether or not someone is seeking access to their genetic resources. If that involves maintaining and restoring traditional practices, as envisioned by Article 8(j) of the CBD, so much the better, but sustainable livelihoods do not need to be traditional to be worthy of support. For example, it is estimated that almost all the annual growth in total food fish production between now and 2020 will come from aquaculture, and much of that will occur in developing countries (Delgado et al, 2003). Given that reality, governments should be taking steps to ensure that growth in aquaculture benefits rather than disrupts traditional communities. One example worth studying might be the initiative of the World Fish Center (described in a case study in this book, Chapter 4) to provide training for small-scale pond farmers in African or Asian countries in productive and ecologically sound farming of species such as tilapia.

PUTTING PRINCIPLES INTO PRACTICE

As demands for access to aquatic genetic resources increase, it will be crucial to fill significant policy gaps in the management of aquatic genetic resources and aquatic biodiversity generally. Policy makers need to focus on several key areas: increasing scientific knowledge, integrating traditional knowledge in policy development, improving information gathering and sharing, increasing public and government awareness of aquatic issues, defining and coordinating agency responsibilities and ensuring broad stakeholder participation in policy making. In addition, countries developing access and benefit-sharing policies will need to learn from the experiences of their predecessors, paying particular attention to community rights to prior informed consent, the relevance of traditional knowledge, and the provision of institutional support for fair and effective benefit-sharing agreements between fishing communities and collectors. Finally, all organizations with the power to do so need to develop creative approaches to help traditional fishing communities become self-reliant through technological solutions that are in tune with local resources, means and culture.

Policy makers face an enormous challenge in determining how to facilitate the sustainable use of aquatic genetic resources in a manner that promotes conservation and fair play. Much depends on trial and error, and there is no sure right way or wrong way to achieve the CBD objectives. What matters most is the determination to do so, recognizing that biology trumps politics and nature bats last.

A Note on the Case Studies

There's nothing like a story to flesh out an abstract concept. Case studies can be extremely useful in illustrating problems and possible solutions in a 'real world' context.

Each of the first six chapters in this book concludes with a case study. Each case study highlights a distinct issue, although it may also illustrate themes discussed elsewhere in the book. As part of the research for case studies 1 and 5, we visited the countries in question (Brazil and the Philippines). The material for the remaining case studies was compiled through interviews and literature reviews. The following summary highlights some key points raised by the case studies:

CASE STUDY 1, CHAPTER 1
THE LAW OF UNINTENDED CONSEQUENCES: Conserving the ornamental fish industry in Barcelos, Brazil

The collection of ornamental fish such as cardinal tetras and cichlids is the primary economic activity for small communities along the middle Rio Negro in the Amazon Basin. The trade in ornamental fish contributes at least 60 per cent of the total revenues of Barcelos, which is geographically the largest municipality in the world, containing within its boundaries more than 120,000 km² of largely intact rainforest. Project Piaba, based at the University of the Amazon, has been working with local communities to enhance the economic and environmental sustainability of community ornamental fisheries.

To protect the fishery, Barcelos has banned activities such as logging and mining that pose a potential threat to the habitat of ornamental fish, which migrate far into the rainforest to spawn when river levels rise during the rainy season. Assuming that the municipality is able to continue to stave off pressures for industrial development of the Rio Negro basin, another threat from a far less obvious source could have an equally devastating impact on the local fishery.

Southern Florida is a central hub of activity in the sale, distribution and breeding of ornamental fish. To obtain broodstock for culturing, breeders can simply purchase wild specimens in quantity from the wild trade that originates in areas like the Rio Negro and is shipped out of Brazil by exporters in Manaus. In the past, species such as cardinal tetras have been considered too difficult to breed because of very specific habitat requirements. That all changed in 2000, when Aquatica Tropicals took a Best-in-Show award after successfully breeding cardinal tetras. Generally, cultured fish can be sold for a cheaper price than fish collected from the wild, primarily because of the impact of transportation costs. Project Piaba is concerned that, if the culturing of cardinal tetras becomes widespread, the wild fishery along the Rio Negro will collapse for lack of a market. If that were to happen, local people might have to turn to alternative, less 'environmentally friendly' livelihoods, and the incentive of communities like Barcelos to conserve aquatic ecosystems and keep out development might be considerably reduced.

What policy action, if any, should be taken to support the sustainability of the Rio Negro ornamentals fishery? Should access to wild cardinal tetras used for breeding purposes be regulated? This case study examines some of the policy implications arising from this unusual set of circumstances.

CASE STUDY 2, CHAPTER 2
NO POLICY, NO ACCESS? A salmon farmer's frustrated efforts to collect genetically pure broodstock

Creative Salmon, an aquaculture business farming chinook salmon in British Columbia, decided to enhance its stocks by cross-breeding them with Yukon River chinook. What makes Yukon chinook desirable is the high oil content that is characteristic of fish inhabiting Arctic waters – and an important asset for sale of salmon to Japanese markets.

Because chinook populations mingle in the Yukon River on the way to their separate spawning grounds, Creative Salmon applied to the Canadian Department of Fisheries and Oceans to collect broodstock from smaller tributaries where individual populations would already be separated out from the mixture in the river mouth and lower stages of the river. The company could thus determine later the source of desirable characteristics they hoped to amplify through breeding.

The department refused the request to collect from isolated populations in tributaries because it was concerned not only about setting a precedent for the collection of samples outside areas open for fisheries, but also about the possibility of subsequent collectors approaching First Nations bands for permission to collect gametes (eggs and sperm) in areas with restricted fishing. Instead, the department required Creative Salmon to purchase broodstock from licensed commercial fishers harvesting mixed populations, thereby eliminating the company's chances for genetically pure stock.

In some respects, Canada faces greater challenges than other countries in developing access policies that address the question of indigenous communities' rights to prior informed consent and benefit sharing. The Canadian Constitution and the courts recognize the existence of indigenous rights in traditional territories, but the nature of these rights remains to be defined in a complex process of treaty negotiations (especially in British Columbia) that may take decades to complete. In addition, policy makers with thinly stretched resources have had little opportunity or incentive to develop comprehensive rules for access to aquatic genetic resources at a time when demand still remains relatively low. The same applies to the development of policies governing gene banking.

Indigenous peoples are already sensitive about collections of biological resources and research in their traditional territories. With a few exceptions, collection of aquatic genetic resources in developed countries hasn't yet become a controversial issue in the way it has for plant collections in developing countries, but it can be expected to attract greater attention as the demand increases. Governments need to anticipate such a trend in the course of policy making.

CASE STUDY 3, CHAPTER 3
AN INDIGENOUS COMMUNITY SAYS NO:
Negotiating access to charr broodstock in northern Canada

In another part of northern Canada, the Inuit people along the Arctic coast recently completed an agreement that recognizes both land and resource rights. The Canadian Department of Fisheries and Oceans (DFO) retains a role in the management of sea-going fish, but communities have the right to prior informed consent to collection of fish broodstock.

Icy Waters, the major charr-farming company in the Arctic, proposed a joint venture with Inuit communities and an Ontario university research group to set up a new company, Suvaak Inc, to improve the company's existing broodstock, based on previous DFO collections. Under the proposal, each of seven participating Inuit communities would receive a 5 per cent equity stake in the new company in exchange for sperm from six male Arctic charr from two separate stocks found in waters near the communities. Icy Waters suggested that Inuit communities would also benefit through education and practical experience in fish farming, and access to genetically improved stocks as these were developed. The business proposal provided that each community would own its original fish contribution but that hybrid lines resulting from cross-breeding would be owned by Suvaaq. The proposed project would result in Icy Waters gaining access to a total of 14 genetically distinct charr stocks through local communities.

Several difficult issues emerged during negotiations on the proposal. Local fishermen worried that the sale of genetically improved farmed fish would have a negative effect on markets and prices for wild-caught fish. Icy Waters attempted to allay this fear by suggesting that successful farming could benefit local fisheries by reducing commercial harvesting pressure on wild stocks, ensuring a valuable sport fishery, and increasing consumer awareness of charr. Ownership issues added a further complication. These included not only concerns about Suvaaq ownership of successive generations of charr hybrids, but also the possibility that the university research group might try to obtain a process patent based on genetic mapping of charr. Mapping would accompany the collection of genetic resources and was necessary in order to ascertain whether the genetic differences between the collected populations were significant. Finally, some Inuit expressed concern that the project showed a lack of respect for charr and that the spirit of the charr might take revenge on the Inuit people if the project went ahead, a not unusual sentiment among native people who may accept technologies as a necessary evil yet still feel uncomfortable with the spiritual implications of altering nature. Ultimately, the communities withheld their consent and Icy Waters eventually made other arrangements to obtain a more limited supply of charr broodstock elsewhere.

Icy Waters described the failed negotiations as expensive and time-consuming, complicated by the difficulty of dealing with several different levels of authority, the need to negotiate with several communities over a vast land area, a high level of confusion about the implications of fish farming and a long history of local suspicion of outsiders from southern Canada. The case study illustrates the magnitude of the challenge that collectors may currently face in preparing for and conducting negotiations with indigenous communities – and hence the need for careful planning. At present, every negotiation for access to aquatic genetic resources is an experiment that can help inform the development of future access rules and the development of support for successful negotiations through training in negotiations and cross-cultural communication, etc.

CASE STUDY 4, CHAPTER 4
GENETIC IMPROVEMENT OF FARMED TILAPIA:
Lessons from the GIFT project

The International Center for Living Aquatic Resource Management (ICLARM, now known as the World Fish Center) works with farmers, scientists and policy makers to help the rural poor increase their income, preserve their environment and improve their lives through the sustainable use of aquatic resources.

Tropical finfish currently account for about 90 per cent of global aquaculture production for food. Most species currently farmed are genetically very similar to wild, undomesticated stocks. For aquaculture to be able to meet the expected global increase in demand for fish protein, there is a need for improved strains that are faster-growing, resistant to disease and suited to a variety of pond-farming conditions. The situation is analogous to the early days of agriculture.

Although the majority of Africans rely on fish as their primary source of animal protein, pond farming has generally failed to flourish in Africa. Yet tilapia, a species native to the continent, has proven to be one of the biggest success stories in pond farming in many Asian countries (particularly the Philippines, China and Thailand), where the fish's popularity has become so widespread that it's become known as the 'aquatic chicken'. Tilapias are a major source of protein for the poor in Thailand because they cost half as much as other freshwater species such as catfish and snakehead.

Some of the recent success of farmed tilapia production in Asia is a result of a breeding programme by ICLARM. In the early 1990s, ICLARM developed a new strain of tilapia by cross-breeding several strains of Nile tilapia (*Oreochromis niloticus*). Neither genetically modified nor transgenic, the new strain has been developed using traditional selective breeding methods under the Genetic Improvement of Farmed Tilapia (GIFT) programme. Tilapias were first introduced from Africa to Southeast Asia in the 1970s, and the GIFT strain was developed from collections made in four African countries in the late 1980s and four existing collections in the Philippines.

As the collections were made before the CBD came into effect, obtaining consent from communities where the tilapias were collected wasn't yet an issue. Two decades later, following a further series of ICLARM projects, tilapia farming in rural Africa may finally be about to get a fresh start. In 2000, ICLARM began a project to transfer GIFT's selective breeding technology from the Philippines to sub-Saharan Africa and Egypt. The objectives of the new project were to train African scientists on the use of the selective breeding technology that is the basis for GIFT, initiate national breeding programmes, and develop strategies for the dissemination of the GIFT technology and the genetically improved fish resulting from it. This is a good example of the types of benefits that may be useful, at the national level, to countries providing aquatic genetic resources for use in breeding programmes. With the assistance of the International Network on Genetics in Aquaculture (INGA), national research institutions in 13 developing countries in Asia, Pacifica and Africa have now used the selection methods developed through the GIFT project to initiate national breeding programmes for genetic improvement of their indigenous cultured species (Gupta et al, 2000).

The GIFT project has made a valuable contribution to the availability of low-cost food sources in several developing countries. The project also highlights several issues that are central to making policies for the management of aquatic biodiversity and sharing of genetic resources:

• Selective breeding of farmed fish stocks can play an important role not only in ensuring cheap and abundant food supplies but also in promoting 'environmentally friendly' aquaculture. (There is a world of difference between industrial farming of salmon and rural pond farming in southern countries.)
• Breeders may target wild broodstock for collection in several locations and, indeed, several countries. If projects like GIFT are to be feasible in the future, countries providing genetic resources may find it useful to cooperate to avoid the need for multiple negotiations with multiple communities.
• ICLARM started out with no direct commercial objectives yet years later transferred to a private consortium the right to market and sell an improved strain of tilapia. What started out as a philanthropic exercise eventually took on a commercial aspect. Although there is no doubt that the GIFT project provided significant social benefits, governments in provider countries need to be careful about distinguishing between collections for academic and commercial purposes, recognizing that there may be considerable cross-over.

CASE STUDY 5, CHAPTER 5
COMMUNITY RIGHTS VS RESEARCH CHILL: The Philippine experience with access and benefit-sharing legislation

In 1995, the Philippines became the first country to enact an access and benefit-sharing law, following forceful advocacy by community groups, civil society organizations, and support from a president who wanted to make his mark at a time when biopiracy had become a hot topic in his country. The challenges the Philippines has faced during the initial years of the implementation of Executive Order 247 hold useful lessons for policy makers generally and in particular for those dealing with access to genetic resources in fishing communities.

Executive Order 247 was carefully prepared, with participation by a broad range of stakeholders, and at first glance appears to be a logical and straightforward approach to facilitating access to genetic resources. As so often with the implementation of legislation that represents a major change to the status quo, the devil has been in the details, and the details here are many. At the very least, the difficulties experienced in implementing EO247 suggests that, to be effective, access and benefit-sharing laws need to:

- Provide for an efficient process without unreasonable delays.
- Ensure the availability of adequate government resources to implement and enforce enabling regulations and to process applications expeditiously.
- Ensure that distinctions between academic and commercial research are clear and that academic research applications can proceed without unnecessary obstacles.
- Provide adequate support for the negotiation of prior informed consent at the community level.
- Clearly define the scope of the legislation with regard to the genetic resources to which it applies.

CASE STUDY 6, CHAPTER 6
SHAPING NEGOTIATION TOOLS: A marine bioprospecting agreement in Fiji

Laws requiring the consent of indigenous and local communities to collections of genetic resources mean nothing unless they lead to workable agreements. The effectiveness of future laws and regulations will depend very much on the lessons learned from real-life examples of agreements. In Fiji, the chemistry department of the University of the South Pacific (USP) teamed up with the World Wide Fund for Nature to develop a research project that would advance scientific knowledge while promoting community development and community-based conservation, emphasizing best practices for benefit sharing with communities.

The Fiji constitution recognizes indigenous rights over all resources located in fishing grounds, including the seabed. USP had been doing research for years on the isolation from plants used for medicinal purposes and wanted to extend its work into the marine area. To facilitate this objective, USP approached Smith–Kline Beecham, a pharmaceutical company involved in the collection of marine samples. Although Fiji had no policy on bioprospecting at the time, government departments came to the support of the project by agreeing to adopt a regulatory role that would define the approval process and ensure that the rights of communities were protected.

The resulting agreements with the indigenous community of Verata set detailed procedures for prior informed consent by the community to any research activity and provided for both monetary and non-monetary benefits, including assistance with the development of village-based enterprises and the establishment of a marine conservation area to allow overfished stocks to recover.

Chapter 1

The Gene Rush: Finding New Value in Aquatic Biodiversity

Salmon gene banking in bear country, British Columbia (Photo by Monica MacIsaac)

Out of sight, out of mind. Nowhere does the saying seem more appropriate than in the way we treat underwater life. Our scientific understanding of aquatic biodiversity lags far behind our knowledge of terrestrial life. Naturally, we're quicker to understand the potential for commercial exploitation than we are to decipher and deal with threats to aquatic biodiversity. Food fish aquaculture, which barely existed three decades ago, has since emerged as the fastest growing food industry. Along the ocean floor, the modern equivalent of the gold prospector is the pharmaceutical company researcher, sifting through samples of sponges, ascidians and other bottom-dwelling organisms in the hope of finding cures for cancer and other diseases. As in the plant world, advances in genetics signal that we've barely scratched the surface in our quest for new (and often controversial) uses for aquatic life, whether plugging a flounder gene into a strawberry to increase its resistance to frost or finding a way to use deep sea microorganisms to gobble up oil spills.

We are quickly learning how to expand our uses for the still largely untapped capital of the waters of the planet. But do we really know how to conserve that capital as an investment for the future? If we managed our financial assets the way we manage biological ones, we'd be going down the road to bankruptcy. Generally, global policies for the management of aquatic biodiversity are muddled, reactive and without teeth. Why? Largely because policy makers often lack access to the biological understanding needed for informed decisions and because governments typically cater to the noisiest and most influential 'stakeholders'. There's nothing new about this reality, of course, but no one really likes to admit that it's so.

Understanding the current and potential values of any resource, as well as the threats that jeopardize those values, is the first step towards sound policy development. This chapter describes a diversity of new uses that humans are finding for aquatic biodiversity as well as the not-so-new human threats that continue to undermine the integrity of biological and genetic diversity. The chapter concludes with a case study on the ornamental fish industry in the Rio Negro in Brazil. The study illustrates just how difficult it can be to develop adequate strategies for the conservation and appropriate use of aquatic biodiversity in the face of ever advancing technologies. The Rio Negro story also illustrates the important role that rural communities can play in ensuring the sustainable management of aquatic biodiversity – a theme that we'll continue to develop throughout this book.

Why is genetic diversity so important?

Biological diversity is the sum total of genes, species and ecosystems – what has been described as the great evolving web of life made up of interdependent, fragile strands. Break a thread, and the strength of the whole suffers. Genetic diversity (genetic variability within species) holds the web together and can repair small breaks. Today, we hear a lot about the sustainable use of natural resources – and that means maintaining the biological and genetic diversity that provides the natural capital for human economies.

The diversity of aquatic life

The approximately 1.5 million living species that have been identified to date represent a tenth or less of the total number estimated to exist (Wilson, 1999). Largely because aquatic creatures inhabit a hidden world, far less is known about marine and freshwater species than about terrestrial ones.

Named terrestrial species outnumber those in ocean environments by seven to one, but the deep sea alone may contain 10 million species that have yet to be described (Norse, 1993). Communities of life on the ocean floor are the least understood ecosystems on the planet. Many of the deeper parts of the ocean are largely beyond the frontier of existing knowledge. Scuba divers can't work below about 92 m – about 1/250th of the depth of the deepest parts of the oceans. New forms of ocean life are constantly being discovered. It was only 25 years ago that life was found to exist in hydrothermal vents, approximately 2500 m below the surface, in international waters off Ecuador's Galapagos Islands. That led to identification of many new species of marine organisms, including bacteria adapted to life in near boiling water mixed with toxic chemicals issuing from the vents. Unique forms of tubeworms, crabs and clams that feed on the bacteria may be only the first of a multitude of other species to be discovered in vent ecosystems (Glowka, 1998a).

Freshwater systems are no less rich in the diversity of species that inhabit them. Perhaps 45,000 out of a million freshwater species have been described (McAllister et al, 1997). The abundance of aquatic life in coral reefs is far surpassed in many tropical rivers (Revenga et al, 2000). Freshwater ecosystems account for only about 1/100,000th of the water on the planet, yet contain an estimated 12 per cent of all animal species and 40 per cent of all recognized fish species (Abramovitz, 1995). As with terrestrial biodiversity, the diversity of life varies with geographical location: in both marine and freshwater ecosystems, the number and diversity of tropical species is far greater than in northern waters.

Although there are many more species on land than in water (May, 1988), more than half of all vertebrates are fishes. With the number of known marine and freshwater fish species currently around 25,000 and climbing (Nelson, 1994), there is clearly a high biological diversity at both the species and ecosystem levels. And scientific research is only now beginning to show the extent of genetic variation within aquatic species.

Conserving species and populations: the key to genetic diversity

The bigger the number of species lost, the greater the risk of fragmenting ecosystems irreparably. If one species disappears, another may increase in number to take its place, but if several are eliminated, something like a biological domino effect may occur. The elimination of a snail or trout or salmon species can trigger a cascading effect throughout the food chain that eventually leads other species to diminish or disappear as well. The diversity of biological systems helps ensure that a gap in an ecosystem is gradually filled and that eventually it is restored, if not to its original condition, then to a new and equally stable state.

Each individual in a species contains a vast number of genes – more than 700,000 in some animals (Wilson, 1988) – and this genetic diversity within and among animals enables populations to adapt to local environmental conditions. Each biological species is a closed gene pool – there is no significant exchange of genes between species in the natural world. But within species, genes are constantly exchanged and evolving. Different species of cone snail, for example, have developed different types of venom to suit their needs – depending perhaps on the types of predator and prey they encounter in a variety of ocean ecosystems. These adaptations are passed on, and ultimately further altered, through innumerable generations. A population of neon tetras in a Brazilian river may develop a different coloration than its downstream neighbours, perhaps ensuring better chances of survival in local conditions. Unfortunately for the fish, the rarer the population and its colouring, the more likely it is to be highly prized by discriminating collectors of ornamental fish. Variations in colorations and markings are produced by variations in genetic structures. A local ornamental fish population's desirable characteristic is a genetic resource.

When a species loses too many individuals, it becomes genetically more uniform and less adaptable to changing ecological conditions such as, in the case of an aquatic species, ocean warming or increased turbidity. That essential genetic diversity within a species – the quality that enables it to fill an ecological niche – evolves over hundreds of millions of years. Yet it takes only a blip in history to damage it beyond repair.

Scientific study of the occurrence and functions of genetic resources, though highly sophisticated now and using tools such as DNA fingerprinting, is very new. The science of genetics originated with the Austrian botanist Gregor Mendel's discovery of the laws of inheritance in the 1860s, but the structure and function of the DNA molecule wasn't elucidated until 1953. As genetics becomes more sophisticated, so too will the ability of scientists to identify, utilize and conserve both plant and aquatic genetic resources. In the meantime, with only a small fraction of aquatic species having been studied, their number and diversity are constantly being eroded through overexploitation and human development. Through carelessness or negligence, aquatic genetic diversity is gradually disappearing through an endless progression of small cuts that cumulatively tear a widening rent in the fabric of life.

The conservation of aquatic genetic diversity has yet to receive the attention it deserves. Thirty years ago, for example, fisheries managers in Canada had little evidence that the six Pacific salmon species were made up of many genetically isolated stocks. Today it is common knowledge that as many as 1000 such stocks migrate from the ocean to spawn in west coast streams. Many have become extinct during the last century as the result of logging activities, urban development and other human interventions. Today, fisheries conservation policies have become much more aggressive, thanks to the willingness of policy makers to make conservation decisions that may be very unpopular with commercial fishers. Unfortunately, continuing scientific uncertainty about the status of stocks and the reasons for population swings has fed public scepticism about policy shifts, especially after so many years when commercial importance of a stock overrode all other considerations. But the value of any given stock may become much more apparent in the future if it's the one with the genetic ability to adapt to climate change or to some other natural catastrophe. Unfortunately, the future, unknown values of genetic resources to humanity don't carry much weight in the political process. That, in a nutshell, is the fundamental dilemma facing sustainable development strategies.

Threats to the diversity of aquatic species

Plant biodiversity includes not only wild plants but also hundreds of thousands of varieties of food crops developed over centuries. Aquatic biodiversity, by contrast, is almost exclusively limited to wild stocks, and that biodiversity is threatened. FAO (2000) estimates that approximately 75 per cent of the world's marine fish species are fully exploited, overexploited, depleted or recovering from overfishing, and that catches will decrease if fishing is not reduced. Draggers trawling for bottom fish, using weighted nets that scour the ocean floor, can eliminate virtually all seabed life along the route. Coral reefs, which contain about 25 per cent of all marine fish species (McAllister, 1999), have gradually been destroyed and eroded by the fishers' use of dynamite and cyanide – a practice that is illegal but difficult to control. Damage to reefs by ocean warming, which disrupts entire ecosystems, poses a potentially even more serious threat.

Depletion of life is no less a concern in rivers and lakes. Fish are probably the most threatened of all vertebrate groups (Bruton, 1995, cited in Froese and Torres, 1999), and freshwater species are ten times more likely to be threatened than marine and brackish water ones (Froese and Torres, 1999). One-fifth of all freshwater fish are considered to be extinct or endangered (Heywood, 1995). In North America alone, 123 freshwater animal species have been recorded as becoming extinct since 1900, and it has been estimated that extinction rates for freshwater fauna are five times higher than those for land creatures (Ricciardi and Rasmussen, 1999).

Although overfishing contributes to declines, particularly in marine species, damage to habitat is equally serious. Damming of the Columbia River system in the northwest US wiped out salmon populations to the extent that a recent search by the Nez Perce tribe produced only one Snake River sockeye. In Brazil, the country with the greatest known number of fish species, the routes of migratory populations in many rivers are blocked by dams. Other industrial activities can be just as devastating. In North America, careless logging has frequently damaged salmon spawning streams through a combination of effects, including increased water temperature through removal of streamside vegetation, blocking spawning channels with debris, and concealment of spawning gravel in silt runoff from road construction and logged areas. In some Brazilian rivers, ornamental fish species are threatened by the pollution and increased turbidity caused by gold mining. Even the removal of fruit trees bordering rivers eliminates the primary food source for some large migratory fish species.

Industrial agriculture throughout the world contributes to habitat damage through fertilizer and pesticide runoff. So too, for that matter, does runoff from

Box 1.1 Lost Stocks: The Declining Genetic Variability of Pacific Salmon

For thousands of years, indigenous peoples of the west coast of North America have depended on salmon. Six species of salmon (chinook, coho, sockeye, chum, pink and steelhead) spawn in streams and lakes. Each species comprises hundreds of stocks, and each stock is adapted to a particular spawning environment to which it unerringly returns after an ocean journey that may cover thousands of kilometres and last several years (with the exception of the freshwater steelhead). While all belonging to the same species, different stocks do not interbreed because they are geographically isolated in separate spawning streams. Hence each is genetically unique. A stock's adaptation over thousands of years to a particular water temperature, rapidity of flow, combination of chemical components, etc, is reflected in many ways. The high oil content of Yukon chinook, for example, enables them to survive in frigid Arctic waters. Other chinook stocks, spawning more than 1500 km away in the comparatively warm waters of southern British Columbia, Washington or Oregon, have a far lower oil content because there's no evolutionary need for it.

Hundreds of these salmon stocks have become extinct as a result of human activities. Salmon are a 'keystone species' in a stream ecosystem, meaning that the ecosystem depends on the presence of spawning salmon. Salmon are an essential source of food for bears, eagles and other animals throughout the food chain. Their carcasses, carried into the forest by predators, even provide essential nutrients for the roots of trees (Harvey and Macduffie, 2002). When a stock is wiped out or severely reduced, the ecosystem it supports is also damaged. Extinct stocks can potentially be 'replaced' with hatchery fish from other stocks (or stocks containing banked genes from the native stock), but because hatchery stocks have less genetic variability than wild ones, such 'enhancement' must be done carefully if the replacement stocks are not to be weaker and less adaptable than the originals.

Loss of a genetically unique stock can have far ranging repercussions. The commercial ocean fishery depends on a relatively small number of numerically large salmon stocks. These megastocks provide the numbers for the commercial fishery but do not represent the total genetic variability of each species. If a smaller, non-commercial stock becomes threatened, the variability it represents suddenly becomes inestimably valuable. For example, salmon stocks have evolved by adapting to precise ecological conditions and are susceptible to even minor variations. If climate change results in significant warming of the North Pacific, some stocks may be unable to adapt to temperature increases. If ocean warming happens to change the survival or geographic distribution of commercially important stocks, then the capacity to survive in the changed environment may reside in one of the many small stocks – in other words, in the reservoir of genetic variability.

Variations among wild salmon stocks will become increasingly important to the relatively new aquaculture industry as well as to the commercial fishery as fish farmers continue to look for desirable characteristics to introduce into cultured species. In the future, genetic variability will become as vital to food (and employment) security as it already is for the maintenance of healthy ecosystems.

Over countless generations, indigenous communities have acquired detailed knowledge of each stock's characteristics and habits. This knowledge, transmitted orally from generation to generation, became the foundation for traditional fisheries management practices and can make a valuable contribution to modern fisheries management. In addition, collections for fish farming and hatcheries may rely on the traditional knowledge of indigenous peoples for an understanding of the characteristics of different stocks and when, where and how to collect them. In this instance, as in many others, the economic value of aquatic genetic resources may be directly dependent on the traditional knowledge needed to obtain them. In the case of many salmon stocks, the knowledge may linger on but the stocks have already disappeared.

urban lawns and gardens treated with pesticides and from toxic deposits left on every street by motor vehicles. The impacts of human activities on aquatic biodiversity are widespread. Too often, efforts to create policies to conserve it get short shrift in government. The long-term, intangible benefits of conservation are always a far tougher sell than the shorter-term economic benefits of business as usual.

THE BLUE REVOLUTION: Unlocking the secrets of aquatic genetic resources

The application of biotechnology to aquaculture has sparked a 'blue revolution'. The use of fish hatcheries to supply farms and enhance wild stocks is now commonplace, and we are now well into the second stage of the revolution, namely the use of genetic engineering – including splicing genes from one fish strain or species into another – to produce desired characteristics. If an aquaculture company in New England gets the green light from the US Food and Drug Administration, a 'Super Salmon' injected with a gene from an Arctic pout will become the first transgenic fish available to consumers. And the valuable commercial uses of aquatic genetic resources go beyond aquaculture and are not limited to genetic manipulation. By far the most active players in the field, at least in terms of financial investment, are pharmaceutical companies targeting the development of anti-cancer drugs and other medicines inspired by chemical compounds produced by marine organisms.

In 1999, the combined annual global market for products derived from genetic resources in several key sectors was estimated at between US$500 billion and $800 billion (ten Kate and Laird, 1999). Aquatic genetic resources accounted for a tiny fraction of that amount and, although the blue revolution is well underway and the pace of discovery has been dramatic, geneticists have barely scratched the surface in the search for new and more sophisticated uses for aquatic genetic resources. While discoveries of uses for plant genetic resources have had the benefit of thousands of years of knowledge of crop breeding and of far more advanced taxonomical sciences, genetic principles have been rigorously applied to most farmed fish species only in the last three decades. As a result, most farm-raised aquatic animals and plants remain very close to their wild forms. Genetic improvement programmes are beginning to be applied to more and more aquatic species, but when compared to the levels of domestication in livestock and crops, the aquatic sector is far behind (Bartley, 1997).

Millions of aquatic species yet to be identified, especially those from deep sea ecosystems, may contain valuable properties that could be used for human benefit in decades to come. The range of potential uses is broad. For example, scientists have now discovered that microbial communities discovered in the near boiling waters of deep sea vents only 25 years ago may provide the answer to dealing with oil spills – namely by eating them (Glowka, 1998a). What's next is anyone's guess.

The wider the genetic diversity of wild fish species, the more opportunities for developing farmed stocks adapted for desired characteristics such as rapid growth, resistance to disease, flavour or hardiness. An example of this kind of use of aquatic genetic resources is the cross-breeding of several different populations of wild African tilapia to produce a new strain designed to mature quickly and adapt easily to pond-farming conditions in Southeast Asia (Case Study 4).

Conserving the genetic diversity of wild fish species is as important for its potential social and economic benefits as it is for maintaining biodiversity for its own sake. As Wilson (1999) points out, biodiversity is our most valuable and least appreciated resource. The growing number and severity of threats to biodiversity are not helped by the failure of governments to appreciate the potential future economic and social values of biological and genetic diversity. Wild genetic diversity has inestimable value for conventional harvest fisheries, so basing fisheries management policies only on current commercial values of stocks, and not considering their genetic resources, is a short-sighted approach. For example, several thousand distinct Pacific salmon stocks spawn in the rivers along the west coast of Canada. If ocean warming occurs, stocks that have little commercial significance at present may be far more able to adapt to changing water temperatures than those currently emphasized in management policies.

Getting the most value out of aquatic genetic resources thus means first evaluating and addressing the considerable ethical, environmental and legal issues associated with genetic modification, the management of wild genetic diversity, and the collection and use of genetic resources. Bringing policies for the management of aquatic biodiversity and of the aquaculture industry up to speed is an enormous challenge that will only get bigger as biotechnology continues to advance. The development of these policies needs to go hand in hand with policies governing access to aquatic genetic resources.

The economic and social impacts of today's biotechnology revolution may well be as great as those of the Industrial Revolution three centuries ago. Now, as then, northern countries depend on raw materials from the south. The demand for both plant and aquatic genetic resources focuses largely on the regions of the world with the greatest (and least damaged) biological and genetic diversity. Identified freshwater fish species in Brazil alone, for instance, number in the thousands compared to the hundreds found in North America. The disparity between the south and north in the number of potentially useful species of marine fish and seabed organisms is just as great.

Finally, there is the unique role played by indigenous and local communities. European countries secured the raw materials for the Industrial Revolution through colonization. Determined to assert control over valuable genetic resources, southern countries acquired international legal recognition of national sovereignty over those resources as the price of approving the CBD in 1992. What remains to be seen is how both southern and northern countries will deal with the need for effective policies for access to aquatic genetic resources in indigenous and local communities, whose involvement will be crucial both for conservation of biological diversity and its commercial use.

Box 1.2   What Is the Difference Between Biological and Genetic Resources?

The distinction between biological and genetic resources can be confusing, but it's a crucial one. To understand it, we must consider the meaning of the terms 'genetic material', 'genetic resources' and 'biological resources'. The Convention on Biological Diversity (CBD) defines:

- **Genetic material** as 'any material of plant, animal, microbial or other origin containing functional units of heredity';
- **Genetic resources** as 'genetic material of actual or potential value';
- **Biological resources** as 'genetic resources, organisms or parts thereof, populations, or any other biotic component of ecosystems with actual or potential use or value for humanity'.

Until relatively recently, it made sense to think of genetic resources as plant seeds or animal (including fish) gametes (eggs and sperm) because those were the primary materials available to breeders developing new strains. But now that it's routine to extract DNA from one cell and put it in another, it's clear that every cell contains the functional units of heredity and that genetic resources and biological resources are the same physical entity. Bartley and Pullin (1999) suggest that it is advisable to assume that everything aquatic and alive – and all of its DNA – has actual or potential value because of the significant knowledge gaps in understanding how aquatic ecosystems function to support fisheries, how to choose aquatic species for domestication, how to make rapid progress in domesticating them, and how to harness aquatic biochemicals and biological processes for the benefit of humankind. It follows, they conclude, that aquatic genetic resources are the sum total of all aquatic plants, animals and micro-organisms on the planet, and that aquatic genetic resources and biodiversity (or biological resources) are synonymous.

While such a broad definition may make sense to a biologist, patent lawyers take a different point of view – one that essentially differentiates between the information in (or about) the resource and its physical identity. Differentiating between biological and genetic resources has become a central theme in the current global debate over intellectual property rights agreements about the patenting of life and its derivatives. The International Union for the Conservation of Nature (IUCN, 2001), noting the lack of clarity of the CBD definitions, suggests that 'biological resources' might be best defined as referring to resources of which each specimen is purchased or acquired separately, while 'genetic resources' refer to genetic information – such as, for example, a gene sequence – that can be protected by intellectual property rights or other legal mechanisms.

Such a distinction can lead to head-scratching. Should a salmon used as broodstock for a fish farm ('genetic resource') be treated differently than one that ends up on a restaurant plate ('biological resource')? Should different rules apply to the catching of a flounder not for food but for the purpose of isolating an antifreeze gene, inserting it into a strawberry, and patenting the process? Should genetic resources be defined by their uses, including the genetic information they contain, or by their physical identity? At least for the time being, the answer remains unclear. The evolution of the definition of 'genetic resources' is reminiscent of evolutions in the meaning of sustainable development. The Brundtland report (WCED), which first brought it into common usage, defined it as 'development that meets the needs of the present without compromising the ability of future generations to meet their own needs'. Fifteen years later, a myriad of variations in the definition of the term reflect the differing priorities of the definers, whether they be governments, corporate interests, environmental groups or community advocacy groups.

For the purposes of this book, we define aquatic genetic resources the way the CBD does – genetic *material* (including the aquatic life that contains it) that is or has the potential to be *used* by humanity for the reproduction of life or development of a product. In these practical

Box 1.2 continued

terms, genetic resources mean any cells containing genes – reproductive or otherwise. As we will see later, such a definition has profound implications for the creation of policies that protect the rights of local and indigenous communities.

Ramifications for indigenous and local communities

Efforts to differentiate between biological and genetic resources hold significant ramifications for the rights of indigenous and local communities to control access to life on their territories and to share in benefits from its use. Many indigenous peoples object strongly to defining nature as a 'resource' in the first place because doing so implies nature exists to be exploited rather than respected. During the decade since the CBD came into force, several countries have enacted laws governing access to biological and/or genetic resources. Those that refer to biological resources most commonly require community consent for access; those that refer to genetic resources generally require consent only by communities that provide traditional knowledge that facilitates the use of those resources. This is a distinction whose importance should not be underestimated.

The distinction is most crucial for fishing communities that actually provide aquatic genetic resources to outsiders. The collection of plant genetic resources typically involves tapping into the knowledge of traditional agricultural communities or indigenous communities that use plants for medicinal or other purposes. While traditional fishing communities have developed an extensive body of knowledge about fish species of importance to them and about the management of aquatic ecosystems, their knowledge is far less likely to provide essential information for fish breeders or pharmaceutical companies – the primary actors involved in the collection of aquatic genetic resources. Hence the parallel to plant genetic resources is simply not there.

Access laws, which are generally driven by plant issues, are in the very early stages of implementation, and how they will be applied remains unclear. In the meantime, considerable uncertainty awaits both collectors of aquatic genetic resources and communities providing them. As this book will argue, if confusion persists about the difference between biological and genetic resources, and if laws linking the rights of communities to their provision of traditional knowledge are too rigidly applied, fishing communities may be left out of the equation entirely.

EXPANDING COMMERCIAL USES FOR AQUATIC GENETIC RESOURCES

Food fish aquaculture

Over the past century, the worldwide demand for animal protein was met primarily by cattle ranching and ocean fisheries. With the ecosystems supporting both food sources pushed to the limits of production, growth of wild fisheries has stalled. The slack has been taken up by farmed fish production, which tripled to over 30 million tonnes during the 1990s and is expected to surpass cattle production by 2010. Currently, aquaculture accounts for more than one-third of global fisheries production (FAO, 2000) and is expected to hold a greater share of the market than all other fisheries by the year 2020 (Rifkin, 1998).

The world population is projected to reach 9.3 billion by 2050, primarily as a result of growth in developing countries (SEDA, 2000), many of which rely on fish as their main source of animal protein. Approximately 85 per cent of fish farming takes place in developing countries. While the environmental effects of aquaculture (especially salmon and shrimp farming) remain controversial, significant increases in aquaculture production may be essential to global food security. In 1998, Chinese aquaculture accounted for over two-thirds of world production, or about 27 million tonnes (FAO, 2000). The other developing countries with the most significant output include India (2.03 million tonnes), Bangladesh, Indonesia and Thailand.

Among industrial countries, Japan produces about 812,837 tonnes (including scallops, oysters and yellowtail); the US produces 457,221 tonnes largely made up of catfish; and salmon comprises the majority of Norway's 406,418 tonnes (Brown, 2000).

The importance of genetic diversity in aquaculture

In nature, animals select their reproductive partners from a large pool. When animals are farmed, however, reproduction is usually controlled by the farmer. Farming aquatic organisms is like farming land animals: in the artificial system of reproduction that farming imposes, you need constant injections of genetic diversity to keep offspring from becoming inbred. Genetic diversity is also vital for improving breed performance, a process called broodstock improvement.

Reproduction of domestic farmed animals is controlled either by farmers supervising matings or purchasing genetic resources – sperm or embryos – and using these genetic resources on their own breeders. A cattle farmer, for example, is likely to buy cryopreserved (frozen) semen with the desired genetic characteristics, and use it to inseminate the females selected for breeding; he may also purchase frozen embryos for implantation in his cows. There is a global network supplying such genetic resources.

Farming of aquatic animals also requires a steady supply of genetic variability. The requirement for genetic diversity is probably even greater for farmed aquatic animals than for livestock, because the very high fecundity of aquatic animals makes it far too easy for farmers to obtain all their seed from one or two individuals (a dangerous practice genetically because it dramatically reduces genetic variability, something that is clearly impossible with a cow or pig).

Genetic improvement

One way of increasing aquaculture production is through the use of genetic improvement techniques, including selective breeding, chromosome manipulation, hydridization, production of monosex animals and, more recently, gene transfer. While selective breeding may be the best long-term strategy, a variety of short-term strategies are used for an immediate increase in production. In Venezuela, hybrids of cachama and morocoto account for perhaps 80 per cent of the aquaculture of these species. Manipulation of the sex of tilapia broodstock through hormone-induced sex reversal and subsequent breeding is used to produce predominantly male tilapia with high growth rates.

Deliberate selective breeding is not the only way that different strains evolve. New strains of cultured fish also occur not only because a farmer is trying to improve what he has, but also from bottlenecks that arise when he starts out. Many culture operations begin with only a few pairs of breeders (because fish are very fecund), and after several generations of breeding the stock inevitably becomes genetically distinct from the founder stock. The degree of distinctness, and whether it has any importance for culture, varies tremendously with the species and farming system.

Although only a small percentage of aquaculture production currently comes from genetically improved species (Gjedrem, 1997), support for the promotion of genetic improvement programmes is well entrenched in development circles. The Strategic Plan of the World Fish Center (formerly ICLARM), a member of the Consultative Group on International Agricultural Research (CGIAR) and a major player in the development and dissemination of aquaculture methods in Asia and Africa, illustrates the trend. Focusing on carps and tilapias, the World Fish Center plans to 'develop techniques for improving breeds of fish, the dissemination of those techniques, and the training of staff in their use' (ICLARM 2002). The World Fish Center has long maintained a programme in genetic resource conservation and use, primarily with the intention of ensuring that wild genetic resources are available for breeding so as to improve livelihoods, and that they remain as far as possible uncontaminated by genetic resources from introduced species (often a delicate balance; Pullin, 1993).

This approach to aquaculture development is virtually universal, and some of its pitfalls are well recognized. FAO, for example, acknowledges the drawbacks in its Technical Guidelines for Responsible Fisheries Series (No. 5, Aquaculture Development), citing Article 9.3.4 of the FAO Code of Conduct for Responsible Fisheries: 'States should promote the use of appropriate procedures for the selection of broodstock and the production of eggs, larvae and fry'. FAO notes that 'few fish farmers have the training and experience to do such work efficiently and without significant loss of genetic fitness' and that it is 'advisable to establish specialized facilities for the development of improved stocks and the production of seed' (FAO, 1997).

Collection of broodstock and the role of local communities

Whatever approach is taken to the improvement of cultured stocks, farmers need ready access to genetic resources. Potential sources include:

- Wild stocks in their natural habitat.
- Broodstock collections ('living gene banks') on farms or in research institutes.
- Rural pond farms in developing countries.
- Cryopreserved gene banks (frozen sperm or embryos).

Agriculture and aquaculture are worlds apart when it comes to the collection of genetic resources for improving farmed strains. Crop producers and seed companies rarely need to collect their own seed from the wild. Under the auspices of groups

Box 1.3   Breeding Fish

One of the most important issues in the debate over sharing benefits of plant genetic resources is the investment by small farmers in crop improvement. The argument goes as follows: farmers put time, energy and money into developing local breeds or varieties; if the results of their efforts attract the attention of a seed company, they are due a share in the benefits from its further development and distribution.

The question is, do 'small' aquaculturists in local communities fit this pattern? The answer is critical to the development of access and benefit-sharing policies, because it will tell us how important traditional knowledge is in the use of aquatic genetic resources.

To answer this question we need first to consider how fish are bred, and how the process differs from plant breeding (fish are used as an example; similar logic applies to cultured shellfish, although the reproductive methods are different). Crops, of course, are produced from seeds, which are easily collected from a portion of the year's harvest. Hybridizations between different strains of crop are also usually easy. Fish, on the other hand, reproduce in water and in response to a number of environmental cues that are still poorly understood for many species. In fact, many cultured fish species will not reproduce or even reach sexual maturity in farm conditions.

The culture of such species has thus been a stop and start process involving:

* Reliance on wild-caught fry ('seed');
* Rapid expansion to the point where natural fry sources are inadequate;
* Investment in research to develop techniques for artificial spawning and fry production;
* Extension work to either transfer these techniques to farmers or build supply lines for fry produced in central hatcheries.

In most cases the spawning techniques have involved hormone injection or, more simply, manipulation of environmental conditions to trigger gonadal development (Harvey and Hoar, 1979; Harvey and Carolsfeld, 1993). Either way, the methods are a lot more complicated than planting the best maize seeds from the previous year.

Much of the technology development has been and continues to be done by universities and government fisheries agencies, with funding from national and international aid agencies. The technology is then transferred to farmers. For example, the snakehead, a common freshwater fish in Malaysia, became increasing popular in the early 1990s when it became known for its 'healing' properties – which may have some basis in a high content of arachidonic acid, a precursor for chemicals that promote wound healing. Higher demands led to a market for snakehead fry, and simple hatchery methods were developed at the Universiti Sains Malaysia and transferred to farmers (Yaakob and Ali, 1992). Given the right training, farmers can also become small-scale fish breeders, for example in Cambodia, where small-scale 'household' hatcheries are being set up with assistance from the Mekong River Commission (Touch and Griffiths, 2001).

Global spread of genetic resources through fish culture

The emphasis on hatchery production and stocking of fish fry in natural and manmade bodies of water has produced a genetic co-mingling at least as pervasive as that in agriculture, and as hard to sort out. It also means that roles shift (from farmer to fry producer, for example) and that it is hard to identify a genetic chain of custody. Despite the relatively recent start to aquaculture, the global translocation of popular cultured species of aquatic animals has been impressive, and analogous to the geographic spread of crops. The Japanese oyster and Manila clam, for example, were both deliberate introductions to North America and are now mainstays of the North American bivalve industry. Pacific salmon

> **Box 1.3** continued
>
> indigenous to North America are grown in Chile and New Zealand, while Atlantic salmon from Europe are farmed in both North and South America. Tilapia, an African fish, is ubiquitous, and through aquaculture transfers and subsequent escapes has become a serious environmental pest in many countries. Even the migratory South American species such as pacu and tambaqui, whose controlled reproduction is a recent achievement, have been deliberately transferred to Asia, where they are cultured in China and Taiwan.
>
> All these transfers happened before the CBD came into being. The pejerrey, for example, an estuarine Argentine species, was introduced to Japanese lakes in 1966 and has become well established in the Japanese market (it is used in sashimi and tempura dishes). The fish is now produced in Japan and is believed to be a genetically distinct stock. Chinese carp (there are three main cultured species) have the longest history of geographic transfer: within a decade of developing methods for controlled reproduction in the early 1960s, the fish were being grown throughout Europe, the US and in the United Arab Republic (Bardach et al, 1972).
>
> The end result of all this moving around of fish is a situation where genetic patrimony is hazy. For this reason, and because the breeding efforts of small fish farmers are either not recorded or, more likely, relatively minor in comparison to the investments by state research agencies and private companies, it is probably unwise to automatically transfer the logic of benefit-sharing policies directly from the plant world. For crops, benefit sharing rides on the back of traditional knowledge, a factor that is probably small in aquaculture (although quite important for collection of broodstock or experimental animals for bioprospecting surveys).

such as the CGIAR, gene banks in many countries collect, store and distribute seeds from a myriad of plant strains produced by generations of farmers, as well as from wild varieties. Just one bank, at the International Rice Research Institute in the Philippines, stores more than 90,000 samples of cultivated rice and wild species (IRRI, 2004).

Aquaculture, by contrast, is starting from scratch. Outside of species such as the common carp, cultured in China for several thousand years, there's little history of farming to draw upon and no network of knowledge built up by previous generations of farmers. Moreover, understanding the characteristics of wild fish strains and how they can be used to improve farmed stocks is very much a work in progress. The work of building collections (both broodstock collections and cryopreserved gene banks) has barely started. Currently they are few and far between with nothing like the organization and coordination that exists in the plant world (the development of fish gene banks is discussed in detail in the following chapter).

For selective breeding purposes and to build up collections, research institutes and aquaculture operations collect broodstock from the wild. Case studies later in the book describe three such initiatives. One was the fruitless effort of a Canadian salmon farmer to obtain government permission to collect genetically pure wild broodstock to cross-breed with existing farmed stock (Case Study 2). Another Canadian company was equally unsuccessful in negotiating access to Arctic charr broodstock in Inuit communities on the Arctic Ocean (Case Study 3). Case Study 4 describes the World Fish Center's collection of Nile tilapia from four African countries, resulting in the development of a strain of tilapia that is now widely farmed in Southeast Asia.

Box 1.4   Collecting Aquatic Genetic Resources: A Primer for Policy Makers

There are two common kinds of aquatic genetic resource collection. The first is gene banking, which includes collections of cryopreserved sperm or 'living gene banks' of adults maintained in captivity. The second involves prospecting for marine invertebrates. Both activities are substantially different from plant gene banking. What do they actually look like in the field?

Gene banking

Both kinds of gene banking – for sperm and for adult breeders – involve fishing. Because the point of gene banking is to collect wild genetic material, collectors must be capable of going onto rivers, lakes or the ocean with the means of finding and catching live, wild fish. Anyone who has ever gone fishing knows what is involved, with the added complication that the animals captured have to be alive. Moreover, sperm donors generally have to be captured ripe, at their reproductive peak, or else it is impossible to obtain samples. This requirement causes more complications, because fish are only ripe at certain times of year, they tend to frequent certain locations when they are ready to spawn, and they may travel in spawning groups that cannot be disturbed by the removal of a few fish.

A typical fish gene banking collection trip, whether for endangered catfish in South America or for salmon in North America, involves first of all a planning phase when collectors secure the necessary permits, usually from the national fisheries or environmental agency. They then consult spawning records for timing, location and abundance of fish, with input from local experts, who may be fisheries agency biologists, local commercial sport fishing guides, local fishermen or aboriginal people. Wherever the information comes from, the success of the expedition depends on it, and the cost of a failed expedition can be high.

Once the most likely whereabouts of the fish have been determined, gear must be assembled for catching the fish, for sampling and handling gametes, or for transporting live fish if the purpose is a broodstock collection. Hence the gear includes typical fishing tools such as boats, motors, nets and waterproof clothing for rivers, as well as cryogenic tanks if sperm is to be frozen.

Catching fish in a river is usually a matter of placing nets in their path, or encircling them, either from shore or by using a boat to pull a net around them. Where waters are deep or turbid, as is often the case, good guides are essential. If broodstock are sought, they need to be netted and handled carefully, and transported to the holding facility (the living gene bank) with minimal mortality from handling stress. Transportation is usually by truck, and has to be limited to less than a day to ensure good survival.

If sperm is to be frozen, male fish must be manually sorted for ripeness, and the sperm of the selected donors obtained by squeezing the abdomen of the fish. Both procedures involve skill and local knowledge. The freezing process is simple, and involves mixing the sperm with a cryoprotectant mixture that helps the cells survive freezing, loading the protected sperm into plastic straws, and placing the straws in a cryogenic container. Removal of sperm does not harm the donor fish, which are often returned to complete their natural spawning in the wild. Collectors usually aim to sample at least 50 males from each stock, so local knowledge is important in guaranteeing sample size.

Live broodstock that have been collected to form a living gene bank are usually kept in tanks, ponds or pens, with controls in place to ensure that they and their progeny don't escape, either to neighbouring enclosures or to the outside world (they may be from a different watershed and need to be kept from mixing genetically with the local fish). Frozen sperm is transferred from the field containers (which are relatively small and portable, about the size of a keg of beer) to secure, long-term storage. Storage facilities can range from small tanks of liquid nitrogen on site in a research lab or farm, to rented space in large liquid

Box 1.4 continued

nitrogen tanks in a cattle insemination centre. The software for keeping track of cryopreserved fish samples is nowhere near as developed as plant gene banking software, but most
collections are relatively small (fewer than 2500 samples) and can be managed using
spreadsheets.

Prospecting for invertebrates

Collecting aquatic invertebrates with reputed biological activity is analogous to collecting
wild plants, but the methods obviously differ. Both activities share a heavy dependence on
local knowledge, although in cases where a species or ecosystem has been academically
studied there may be no need to consult local people.

   Where aquatic collection differs most from terrestrial ones is in the range of environments
that have to be searched. Animals that are exposed at low tide can be harvested on foot, but
many live at depth or in the water column and can only be extracted by towing nets or by
diving. Diving is slow and laborious and requires scuba gear, support vessels and people
trained to recognize the animals in question. Nets require a boat big enough to tow them and
allow onboard sorting of the catch, as well as facilities for preserving, processing or pack-
aging for shipping. Weather is often a factor.

   As with catching fish for gene banking, the invisibility of aquatic creatures beyond the low
tide line means that reliable local guides are indispensable.

At the time of the collections described in the case studies, neither Canada nor
the African countries had policies on access to genetic resources in indigenous and
local communities. They still don't. The authority of the Inuit communities to
provide or withhold consent was the result of a recently approved land claims
agreement. Subsequent chapters will discuss the importance of access policies and
any progress towards their implementation.

   Finally, and perhaps most important, in none of these three examples did the
collectors depend on local knowledge of the fish stocks they wanted to breed. This
is not to say that traditional knowledge of fish stocks is never relevant to collectors.
However, it is less of a factor than in the plant world, where the value of genetic
resources to collectors depends almost universally on local knowledge – whether
it's the expertise of traditional breeders or community knowledge of medicinal
uses of plants. As discussed later, this difference is critical because local knowledge
of genetic resources has been the primary rationale for the development of national
laws defining community rights to benefits from their use.

Lessons from the green revolution

It is too early to say whether the blue revolution created by advances in aquatic
genetic science will – or should – have an impact equivalent to that of the green revolution, which transformed agriculture by using genetic improvement to produce
new varieties of crops. While the green revolution greatly increased agricultural
productivity, particularly as a result of enhanced growth rates, it also raised concerns
about crop diversity and community economies. These included decreases in crop

varieties available to farmers, the inability of farmers to save seeds from sterile crops for subsequent use, and changes in income distribution among farmers.

There is growing, but by no means universal, recognition that genetic improvement in aquaculture must go hand in hand with genetic conservation. This means ensuring the survival of local breeds that may appear inferior to imported strains, based on short-term measures of growth rate, but in the long term may be more robust (eg resistant to local diseases or climate extremes) and hence provide better returns to local farmers. It also includes ensuring the survival of wild genetic resources. If the blue revolution is to increase overall food productivity and maintain healthy local economies, it will be essential to apply the lessons learned from agriculture.

Addressing environmental risks and controversies

The CBD calls on member countries to adopt the precautionary principle in biodiversity management. The difficulty of doing this is nowhere more evident than in identifying and addressing the risks of industrial aquaculture. Public concerns are growing. While the pond farming of species such as the tilapia in developing countries may actually produce some environmental benefits by recycling waste and producing fertilizer, the risks of genetic and other environmental effects are considerable, just as they are for other species such as salmon, shrimp, and yellowtail. The biodiversity effects of mariculture have recently been reviewed, and symposia and consultations now regularly confront the environmental risks of a variety of aquaculture technologies.

The impacts vary according to the type of operation and species farmed. In southern countries, shrimp farming has come under attack for its impact on local economies and cultures. Shiva (1999) argues that 'luxury consumption' of shrimp by northern communities comes at great cost to the communities that produce them, with ecological impacts such as salinization and removal of mangrove forests leading to a destruction of livelihoods of the poor in coastal regions of the developing world.

The list of potential environmental impacts of net pen farming of salmon is also extensive and has led to repeated calls for its abolition by environmental groups. There is still no scientific consensus on the extent and likelihood of a broad variety of environmental impacts, especially for migratory species such as salmon. In 2002, the salmon farming industry in British Columbia argued successfully for the lifting of a seven-year moratorium on the licensing of new salmon sea pen farms, even though some scientists believe that the likelihood of negative environmental impacts is in fact greater than when the government established the moratorium. Genetic issues related to farmed salmon are becoming better understood each year, and new threats, such as the role of farmed fish in spreading diseases and parasites, are producing conflict and increased research spending (Gardner and Peterson, 2003).

It is now clear that the impact of food fish aquaculture cannot be measured simply in terms of increased productivity. Moreover, it's pointless to defend aquaculture by saying it holds the answer to the world's food problems when the main

---

Box 1.5   Genetic Modification: Better Fish or Foul Play?

The application of contemporary biological knowledge to issues like food and nutrition and human health has to occur. It has to occur for the same reasons that things have occurred for the past ten millennia. People want to live better, and they will use the tools they have to do it. Biology is the best tool we have (Robert Shapiro, chairman and CEO, Monsanto Company (quoted in Specter, 2000)).

Genetic resources are the raw material for genetic modification. While conventional breeding practices serve mainly to amplify desirable characteristics that already exist in a species or variety, genetic manipulation enables breeders to incorporate single traits selectively and quickly, without the normal limitation that breeding can only be between members of the same species. Traditional methods of plant and animal breeding, hybridization, and chromosome set manipulation all constitute genetic modification, but international agreements and national legislation define genetically modified organisms much more narrowly as transgenic organisms – those that have had genes from another species or genus inserted into their cells (FAO, 2000). However, the World Fish Center uses a broader definition that includes the products of captive and selective breeding, hybridization between species, development of monosex populations, and several other techniques (Penman, 1999).

The products of genetic modification are everywhere. More than 60 per cent of supermarket foods are estimated to contain genetically altered products, and the number is steadily rising to the point that what used to be the exception is rapidly becoming the rule. Hundreds of foods contain products from varieties of all the major crops, genetically engineered for characteristics such as enhanced growth rate, pest and disease resistance, or adaptability to cooler climates. Domestic livestock reflect the results of genetic research in ways ranging from the simple use of cryopreserved semen to propagate a herd of beef cattle to the experimental creation of clones of especially productive animals.

In principle and to some extent already in practice, the kinds of genetic advances that permeate the farming of terrestrial plants and animals are all possible for aquatic organisms. Fish gene banks have existed since the early 1980s, and several species of genetically engineered farmed fish have been developed (although, as this book is written, they have yet to receive marketing approval).

Manipulating the gene: A primer

The basic unit of living matter is the cell. The diversity of life ranges from single-celled organisms such as amoebae and bacteria to humans, with approximately 3 trillion cells. Inside each cell, chromosomes (two sets of 23, in the case of humans) store genetic information on long strands of deoxyribonucleic acid (DNA). The information for how any cell is structured and functions is encoded on segments of DNA called genes.

Each gene contains codes with instructions for the production of a specific protein – a chain of amino acids, each with a different function. Proteins can be transport molecules, antibodies, messengers, enzymes, hormones (such as growth hormone) or structural proteins. Genes contain 'promoters' and information blocks that read, accept or reject messages for gene activation for the creation of proteins. A gene in a rose petal will respond to a message to produce red pigment, but a palm leaf gene will block the same message. The genetic code of an organism describes the essential characteristics that will be inherited by each individual – the distinctive coloration of a neon tetra, the cold tolerance of a winter flounder, the toxicity of a cone snail. The entirety of the genetic information stored in an organism is called its genome.

Biotechnology can be broadly defined as any technique that uses living organisms or their parts to make and modify products, improve plants and animals, or develop microorganisms for specific purposes (Hobbelink, 1991). The earliest forms of biotechnology –

Box 1.5 continued

selective breeding of plants and animals and using microorganisms to make products such as beer, wine, bread and cheese – have been in existence for several thousand years, but techniques for manipulating the essential foundation of living structures have appeared only in the past three decades. These techniques include tissue culture, cell fusion, embryo transfer and recombinant DNA technology that enable scientists to create whole organisms from single cells, fuse different cell types to create hybrids with the qualities of both parent cells, implant animals with embryos of other animals, and isolate genes from one organism and insert them into another.

Genetic engineering involves the disarranging and recombining of gene fragments, often of unrelated species. By cutting a fragment of a genetic sequence and pasting it into cells of an unrelated species, scientists can insert a gene of one organism into an unrelated one. As a result, a plant may be fooled into accepting messages that turn its leaves a different colour, or promoters may be introduced into fish genes so they will respond in a desired manner when transferred into the cell of a strawberry – eg producing a hormone for cold tolerance. Genetic engineering in effect provides a shortcut around conventional selective breeding by directly altering the essential characteristics of a species – although with the disadvantage that by excising only short segments of DNA, scientists may well be overlooking other essential sections of the genome.

While it has become well established in agriculture, genetic engineering is largely at the experimental stage in aquaculture. Most commonly, aquaculturists improve stocks or species by using the sperm of one strain or variety to fertilize the eggs of another. For example, a salmon farmer who wants to produce fish with high oil content may cross-breed a colder water salmon stock with another stock that is adapted to the warmer environment where the offspring are intended to be grown. Genetic engineering offers a speedier road to the same destination.

The coming of super fish – transgenic research in aquaculture

Production of farmed fish can be considerably enhanced through the culturing of stocks with traits amenable to production in captivity. Such traits include growth rate, disease resistance, and temperature tolerance. A desirable trait achieved through conventional cross-breeding (inseminating the eggs of one stock with the sperm of another) is slow to emerge and often unpredictable. Using molecular biology to identify and isolate such genes and then transfer them to broodstock can considerably accelerate the process. In addition, new traits not present in a genome can be transferred to it from an unrelated species, enabling the production of new phenotypes (Hew and Fletcher, 1997).

Aquaculture currently relies almost exclusively on conventional breeding techniques, namely those that mate parents from the same species. However, species such as salmon, tilapia, and channel catfish are being actively investigated as candidates for the development of transgenic varieties that utilize genes from different species. A prominent example is the development of the so-called Super Salmon, which may achieve several times the rate of growth of unimproved stocks. Researchers initially produced the strain through the transfer of growth promoting genetic material from an ocean pout into Atlantic and Pacific salmon species. In other experiments, anti-freeze protein genes from coldwater fish such as the winter flounder have been incorporated into the genome of the Atlantic salmon, which lacks the anti-freeze gene and cannot survive the subzero temperatures that may occur in sea cage farming in the northwest Atlantic (Hew and Fletcher, 1997). In both examples, a genetic resource from one aquatic species was used to change the genetic make-up of another.

Although no transgenic fish are yet being sold, they may be on the market in the next few years if health and environmental issues are addressed (FAO, 2000). A/F Protein, the company developing the Super Salmon on the east coast of Canada, reportedly has orders

Box 1.5 continued

for 15 million genetically modified salmon eggs. Aqua Bounty Farms, a subsidiary, has applied to the US Food and Drug Administration for permission to market the transgenic fish. If the application is approved, the Super Salmon will be the first transgenic animal approved in the US for human consumption (Moore, 2000). Assuming this occurs, the penetration of markets could proceed quickly, as it has for agricultural products: in 1993, no genetically engineered crops were sold commercially; a mere five years later, an estimated 28 million hectares globally were planted with transgenic crops (Crucible Group, 2000).

The fish in the strawberry: Gene transfers between phyla

Genetic manipulation has progressed to the point where gene transfers occur not only within species or between related species (for example, one species of fish to another), but also between much more distantly related organisms. For example, subsequent steps in enhancing cold tolerance in salmon could include the use of insect proteins to develop a potent anti-freeze gene for fish (Fletcher et al, 1999). Testing is underway in the US to introduce insect genes into striped bass to enhance disease resistance (FAO, 2000). Researchers have implanted fish anti-freeze genes into strawberries (Specter, 2000) and tobacco (Reid et al, 1993) to promote frost hardiness, and have inserted salmon calcitonin producing genes into rabbits to control calcium depletion in bones (FAO, 2000). In addition to enhancing aquaculture production, anti-freeze proteins may also improve the quality of frozen foods, and could prove useful in medical applications. For example, they can extend the shelf life of blood platelets prior to transfusion and, used in conjunction with cryosurgery, can destroy malignant tumours (Fletcher et al, 1999).

It is estimated that biological knowledge doubles every five years. In the field of genetics, however, the quantity of information doubles every 24 months. Biotechnological discoveries are constantly fuelling new techniques for using aquatic genetic resources. Rifkin (1998) suggests that the commercial possibilities are limited only by the human imagination and the changing demands of the marketplace – a claim many scientists would take issue with but that nonetheless reflects the potential social impact of biotechnology. The key point for this book is that every new commercial application, and the research that demonstrates it to be viable, requires the collection of genetic material, sometimes from many locations in several countries. As the pace of discovery continues to increase, regulatory clarity regarding access will become essential.

Ethical and environmental concerns about genetic engineering

Kneen (1999) says that 'the fact that we do not really know what the long-term consequences of genetic engineering will be, and are not prepared to move slowly and to find out, means that a grand experiment is taking place, and the outcome is anyone's guess'. Many proponents of genetic transfers maintain that there is little or no risk and that the social benefits, especially global food security, are paramount. The general public, as well as much of the scientific community, remain to be convinced. While genetic manipulation for medical purposes has largely found public acceptance, altering the molecular foundations of the food supply hasn't. Even people who accept the notion of genetic manipulation within species may draw the line at inter species transfers. For some, it's simply an ethical matter – humans shouldn't tamper with nature by 'playing God' with living creatures.

One of the biggest unresolved issues is the potential environmental impact of raising genetically modified animals. If a farmed Super Salmon grows to three times the size of a wild chinook, will escapees from farms compete or breed with wild stocks? Whether escaped, genetically engineered fish have a selective advantage over wild stocks is hotly

> **Box 1.5** continued
>
> debated, but it's nevertheless a concern to the public. Even if such concerns are largely hypothetical and many scientists would disagree with them, the fact remains that they represent the mood of the public and must be taken seriously. And because policy in this area tends to reflect the public mood, they must be considered when developing guidelines for the collection and use of aquatic genetic resources.
>
> In 2002, several African governments joined to keep food aid containing genetically modified organisms from entering their countries, fearing contamination of crop diversity and possible risks for human health (GRAIN, 2002b). What will happen if and when transgenic fish hit the market? Will some countries ban the use of transgenic fish in aquaculture for fear of contamination of wild stocks, prohibit the collection of wild broodstock for such a use, or even bar the importation of transgenic food fish for consumption? So far, policy makers have largely steered clear of fish transgenics because so many thorny issues surround the practice, but the time will come sooner rather than later when it needs to be dealt with. If that time is when a genetically engineered cold-tolerant tilapia begins to invade North American lakes, then it will be far too late.

beneficiaries are countries with no food shortages. More than anything else, the heated controversies over the impacts of industrial aquaculture point to the need for better scientific information and solutions, improved biodiversity management policies, and an end to 'decide, announce, defend' approaches by governments intent on promoting new industries. Ultimately, although aquaculture is likely to create the largest demand for aquatic genetic resources among commercial users, the rate of its growth will depend on whether public benefits (in addition to private profit) exceed public costs.

Public controversies about the environmental and social impacts of aquaculture are particularly relevant to this book because they may affect community decisions on applications for access to broodstock for fish farming. On the Canadian west coast, some indigenous peoples work on or want to set up their own salmon farms; others not only oppose new operations but call for the removal of existing ones, for both environmental and political reasons. It is very likely that the willingness of indigenous and local communities to consent to access to aquatic genetic resources, in countries that have established their right to do so, will depend on the aquaculture industry's ability to mitigate or prevent environmental impacts.

Ornamental fish breeding

The trade in ornamental fishes is big business. The global trade value for exports of all fish and fish products was estimated at over US$51 billion in 1997 (Watson, 2000). By contrast, the value of the trade in ornamentals is hard to gauge but has been estimated at US$15 billion (Bartley 2000). It has increased annually by an average of 14 per cent since 1985 (FAO, 1999) and is reported to involve about 4000 species, with an approximate 50–50 split between freshwater and marine. Europe, North America and Japan are the primary markets, with the US accounting for an estimated 60 per cent of the demand (Baquero, 1999).

Distinctions between the freshwater and marine trades

Although the highest value freshwater ornamental species are almost exclusively collected from the wild and may be sold in very small quantities (50 to 100 a year for some species), about 90 per cent of freshwater ornamentals are cultured (Bartley, 2000). Hong Kong, Singapore, the US (Florida) and Czechoslovakia are primary centres of farming activity. Employment in the culturing of ornamental fish is also significant in several other countries. In Sri Lanka, for instance, about 25,000 people depend on the industry (Rajapakse, 1998).

By contrast, only about 25 of 8000 marine ornamental species can be easily cultured. Captive breeding currently accounts for only about 3 per cent of the total supply and is growing very slowly because of biological and technical constraints (Marine Aquarium Council, 2001). The seahorse, for example, is notoriously difficult to raise in captivity because of its dependence on live food. Nevertheless, there is a strong push to breed and domesticate this and other high value species (Bartley, 2000), creating a need for collections of wild broodstock.

During recent years, as new technologies and an improved understanding of reef ecology provide the means to create functioning mini reefs in home aquariums, there has been increasing demand for collections from coral reefs in the South Pacific. Although over 90 per cent of the ornamental fish kept in the US are freshwater species, the demand for marine ornamentals is steadily growing. Approximately 85 per cent of marine aquarium fish exported to the US and Europe are captured from reefs in the Philippines and Indonesia, which contain the greatest diversity of desired species such as wrasse, butterfly fish, anemone fish, damsel fish, angel fish and surgeon fish. Clams, sea anemones, sea stars, sea cucumbers, sea urchins and a few other invertebrates are also a growing part of the trade from the south (Baquero, 1999).

Collection of wild ornamentals for the aquarium trade

In many developing countries, collecting freshwater and marine ornamental fish provides an important source of income in areas with few employment alternatives. For many indigenous and local communities, the collection of ornamentals is the primary economy activity. Aquarists pay high prices for specimens of rare or exotic freshwater ornamentals such as juvenile sting rays or miniature catfish. Equally important in the capture trade are low-cost species sold in large quantities. The annual export of ornamentals from Amazonas state in Brazil, for example, averages about 20 million specimens (Chao et al, 2001), and the town of Barcelos on the Rio Negro derives the majority of its income from the sale of cardinal tetras and cichlids.

The collection of ornamental fish typically depends on villagers familiar with their habits. In Malaysia, for example, killi fish are gathered by women and children who rely on traditional knowledge to find them in leaf litter at the bottom of streams. Many ornamental fish are nocturnal and can only be captured by local people thoroughly familiar with their habits. Typically, local fishers are paid a small amount by middlemen who provide a list of species and numbers needed and sell the catch to exporters.

Collections for breeding

Breeding of the most popular freshwater species (guppies, mollies and neon tetras) has such a long history, and has produced so many varieties, that there is virtually no demand for wild specimens for genetic enhancement of cultured stocks.[1] However, in other sectors the demand for wild fish is increasing as improved technologies enable the culturing of a wider range of freshwater and some marine ornamental species. To a breeder of an ornamental fish, genes that produce distinctive colorations and markings offer the same type of value that cold resistance or growth genes do for food fish breeders.

How does a breeder obtain the broodstock needed to produce these characteristics in a cultured population? Depending on the circumstances, there are three options:

1 As in food fish aquaculture, make an expedition to the fish's natural habitat and collect specimens from the wild. This may involve making a deal with local fishers to do the work. It may also involve taking advantage of their knowledge of where to find fish and how to catch them. In these circumstances, collections for breeding ornamentals are comparable to collections for food fish aquaculture.
2 If the species has already been bred over many generations (as in the case of neon tetras), selectively breed from existing collections to produce desirable colorations or markings in their offspring.
3 If there is already a significant live trade in the fish from its country of origin, buy specimens from an importer and use them as broodstock. This option is significant for communities involved in collecting fish for sale because, where such a live trade exists, it may be impossible to determine whether fish collected in a river in South America or an African lake will end up in a hobbyist's aquarium or be bred commercially.

Impacts of aquaculture of ornamentals on community fisheries and ecological values

The culturing of ornamental fish stirs up none of the controversy that surrounds the farming of salmon and shrimp. Indeed, some environmentalists might assume it could have a beneficial effect by reducing fishing pressure on vulnerable or endangered species. While that may be true in some cases, competition by aquaculture with the wild trade can be devastating for local fisheries and, ultimately, for fish habitat. Many indigenous and local communities are completely or substantially dependent on the ornamental fish trade.

The neon tetra fishery in South American indigenous and local communities was wiped out many years ago by the trade in farmed fish, now based primarily in Hong Kong. Case Study 1, at the end of this chapter, illustrates that a similar fate could await the cardinal tetra fishery on the middle Rio Negro in Brazil. The bottom line is that people have to make a living, and if they can't make it from fishing, they'll do whatever they need to put food on the table, including logging and mining. The end of the cardinal tetra fishery could be the death knell for local efforts to protect the fish's rainforest habitat. The case study describes the efforts of Project Piaba to promote sustainable livelihoods for local fishers, protect fish habitat, and anticipate the impacts of competition from aquaculture in other countries. It also illustrates the complications inherent in designing access policies that take into account different uses of aquatic genetic resources, different types of collections, and the cultures of fishing communities.

Pharmaceutical and industrial uses of marine organisms

The value of aquatic genetic resources is by no means confined to reproductive cells. In strictly monetary terms, the chemical compounds produced by many marine organisms are far more likely to be a source of 'blue gold', in this case for the pharmaceutical companies engaged in their collection. As in the case of food fish aquaculture, the future commercial value of these aquatic genetic resources will certainly depend on the success of research and development programmes. However, it will also depend on the regulatory requirements for access to and use of aquatic genetic resources.

In all the examples that follow, and in discussing bioactive compounds from the sea in general, one must be careful to distinguish between the levels at which these biological resources can be tapped. At the simplest level, they can be collected, sometimes in prodigious quantities, and extracted for the drug. At another level, biotechnologists may be able to work out ways to synthesize a compound or an even more effective analogue, which reduces the need for further collection. Finally, actually isolating the gene or genes that produce the drug opens the door to inserting that gene in another organism, either a micro-organism that can be grown in large quantities and used as factories for the drug, or even directly into a human patient. All of these approaches, while using different technologies, depend on genetic resources.

Marine organisms are especially interesting because they are a rich source of bioactive compounds, many from novel chemical classes not found on land. Currently, about half the world's best-selling drugs contain chemical structures derived from compounds found in nature (Glowka et al, 1998). Unlike plants, marine organisms possess primitive versions of human genetic systems and therefore hold particular promise for new drugs. All the major pharmaceutical firms – Merck, Lilly, Pfizer, Hoffman–LaRoche and Bristol–Myers Squibb – have marine biology divisions. Interest in marine bioprospecting may lead to a further rush of activity among large and small companies when the first ocean-derived pharmaceuticals come onto the market in the next few years (Plotkin, 2000). Exploration for marine genetic resources is typically an international undertaking in which companies and government institutions in industrialized countries prospect in the marine waters of other nations, often tropical ones, that contain biodiversity rich marine ecosystems such as coral reefs.

Several compounds isolated from marine sources are currently in various phases of clinical trials. These include four anti-cancer agents (from an Indian Ocean mollusc, a Caribbean tunicate, a sea whip, and the US west coast bryozoan *Bugula neritina*), as well as an immuno-suppressant from a Bahamian sponge (ten Kate and Laird, 1999). While no compound from a marine source has yet advanced to commercial use, a variety of drugs now on the market do owe their existence to aquatic life. For example, the most commonly prescribed antibiotics in US hospitals were derived from aquatic molds. The hormone calcitonin, extracted from salmon, has been found effective in preventing osteoporosis. And protamine sulfate, derived from salmon sperm, provides an antidote to the anticoagulant heparin (Plotkin, 2000).

Anti-cancer drugs: The Holy Grail of the pharmaceutical industry

The 100+ known varieties of cancer share a common characteristic: the uncontrolled growth of cells that take on abnormal shapes and cease their normal functions. The most effective anti-cancer drugs work either by selectively poisoning cancer cells or by preventing them from reproducing. Some of the most promising progress in recent years has been based on research into the defence mechanisms of marine animals and plants, especially those from southern oceans. Many parts of the ocean floor are populated by organisms that look vulnerable because they move slowly or not at all, and have no protective shells or any apparent ability to resist a predator. What they often do have, however, are toxins so potent and complex that there's no need for any other defence.

Eleutherobin, a chemical derived from a soft coral originally collected off the northwest coast of Australia, works by preventing cancerous cells from reproducing, and could be more effective than taxol (a derivative of the bark of the yew tree) in treating breast and ovarian cancer. Although eleutherobin sounds like a wonder drug, there's one major catch that may stymie development of a product – even if all the soft coral capable of producing eleutherobin were collected, there still would not be enough to meet the demand for clinical testing, let alone the world market. Once the coral's anti-cancer properties were detected in laboratory tests, it took three years to synthesize eleutherobin, the compound responsible, and synthesis is expensive. The rewards, however, are great.

Initial testing of a sea squirt found in the Philippines has shown it to be effective in killing colon cancer cells in the test tube, but considerable quantities may be needed for further testing. Cyanobacteria (formerly known as blue-green algae), some of the most ancient of all living organisms, produce compounds that may fight other diseases as well. Research has shown that the cryptophycins produced by cyanobacteria not only have anti-cancer potential but may also be effective against viral diseases such as herpes and HIV. Like eleutherobin, cryptophycins can be synthesized, but only at a prohibitive cost.

The sponge is one of the most prolific sources of existing and potential pharmaceutical products. For more than 30 years, one of the most effective treatments for leukemia has been a drug based on chemicals produced by a sponge found in the Florida Keys. The same sponge has also been found to be effective in killing certain viruses. This led to the development of the first drug that can be taken internally as an effective treatment for herpes and shingles. Global sales of ara-A and ara-C now exceed US$100 million annually. Other species of sponge, in addition to producing a variety of potential anti-cancer compounds, have led to the development of anti-inflammatory and anti-malarial drugs (Plotkin, 2000).

Box 1.6   Cone Snails: Potent Painkillers in Pretty Shells

The decorative shell of the cone snail, long prized by collectors, provides no clue to its reputation as one of the most toxic creatures on the planet. The cone snail has an ingenious means of catching faster moving prey on the coral reefs it inhabits – it simply launches a miniature harpoon (a disposable tooth) that can kill a large fish almost instantly. Cone snail venom contains a variety of toxic compounds, each of which has a different effect on the nervous system. One of these compounds interrupts pain signals from the body to the brain by blocking the transmission of proteins through nerve cells. One drug produced from cone snail venom, ziconotide, is considered to be hundreds of times more potent than morphine and has the added benefit of not being addictive. It has been estimated that ziconotide, if and when marketed, may produce sales of up to a billion dollars a year. As there are about 500 species of cone snail, each of which may produce 200 different poisons, there may be enormous potential for development of other equally beneficial and profitable products, assuming that the necessary research can be done (Plotkin, 2000).

Obtaining the snails' venom ducts for screening used to be a simple matter: a researcher would simply go to the beach and buy cone snails from fishermen, who would discard the flesh anyway before selling the shells to tourists.[2] Then, in the early 1990s, came a national campaign to combat biopiracy of genetic resources by foreign interests. The end result was the Philippines' bioprospecting law, Executive Order 247, which established regulations for the collection of all biological resources and created requirements for prior informed consent by communities. For years afterwards, uncertainty in the scientific community about how to obtain approval for access delayed research into the properties of marine organisms, including cone snails. This phenomenon, since dubbed 'research chill', will be referred to several times in later chapters.

Box 1.7   Underwater Chemical Warfare and the Rise of Genetic Databases

Most people know that some jellyfish can sting, and that eating improperly prepared *fugu* (puffer fish) can kill you. They are probably aware that stepping on a stingray or crown of thorns starfish can land you a fatal injection of venom. These examples reflect the widespread ability of aquatic animals to produce chemicals that have dramatic biological effects on other organisms. Plants do the same thing – many important bioactive compounds produced by plants are defence mechanisms – but the aquatic world is where chemical warfare really thrives.

At all levels of the aquatic food chain, chemical defences are highly developed and represent some of the most fascinating strategies and molecules known to science. For example, tetrodotoxin – the *fugu* fish poison capable of inducing paralysis in tiny doses and probably the most studied natural poison – is actually produced not by the fish itself but by a marine bacterium it eats (and to which it remains immune).

The marine environment is especially conducive to the emergence of toxic natural compounds that give animals or plants a competitive edge. The search for bioactive compounds in rainforest plants and animals may be much better entrenched in the public imagination, but the fact is that the aquatic world is undoubtedly just as productive – just harder to explore. Nevertheless, there are already a staggering amount of data collected not only on the occurrence of toxic or medicinal compounds in aquatic plants and animals, but also, to an extent that might surprise many people familiar only with terrestrial bioprospecting, on the chemical make-up of the compounds and even their genetic codes.

By way of illustration, consider the three principal banks of genetic information: GenBank (USA), the European Molecular Biology Laboratory Nucleotide Sequence Database (Europe) and the DNA Database of Japan. Most scientific journals now insist that DNA and amino acid sequences that appear in articles be submitted to a sequence database before publication.

Box 1.7 continued

Each group collects a portion of the total sequence data reported by scientists worldwide, and all new and updated database entries are exchanged between the groups on a daily basis.

One can reach the GenBank database through FishBase, and advocates of benefit sharing will be sobered to learn that this database alone contains entries on over 2000 fish species (that is, it ignores molluscs, algae, bacteria, echinoderms, reptiles and aquatic plants that produce bioactive molecules). The entries provide nucleotide sequences – genetic blueprints – for chemicals isolated from each species, and in most cases those chemicals have pharmacological effects. For the stonefish *Synanceia verrucosa*, the most venomous fish in the world, the genetic sequence for verrucotoxin is provided. The venom, like tetrodotoxin and most other biological agents, has a multitude of pharmacological effects, some of which have academic interest, and others of which may have practical application including the development of pharmaceutical drugs.

For bioactive agents like verrucotoxin that also happen to be proteins, the path towards production of the compound by genetic engineering is relatively straightforward. It involves incorporation of a manmade copy of the gene into a suitable 'producer' (a bacterium, for example) that can be grown in large quantities. The bacterium produces the chemical in the same way as insulin is now manufactured.

What this means is that the pace of scientific discovery, specifically our understanding of the genetic basis of basic cellular functions, is advancing extremely rapidly and is generating vast libraries of genetic data. These data may have practical application totally out of proportion to the investment in time and effort needed to collect the 'donor' – a single animal is often enough – on which they are based. Local communities may intuitively see the connection between an aquarist or fish farmer collecting males and females for breeding, but if a gene sequence for a bioactive compound can be obtained from a single specimen, patented, and used to produce the compound in a bioreactor, how realistic is it to insist on royalties from a company a dozen steps removed from the original collection?

Bacteria with bite: Mining microbial life

Enzymes from bacteria inhabiting waters near the boiling point in seabed hydrothermal vents are being tested for their ability to consume toxic wastes and oil spills. Freshwater hot springs are another potential source of bacteria whose adaptability to extreme ecological conditions may be useful in industry.

The Taq polymerase enzyme for the polymerase chain reaction, now in routine use by researchers, originated from heat-resistant bacteria found at a geyser in Wyoming's Yellowstone National Park. In 1997, the Diversa Corporation made an agreement with the US National Park Service to begin bioprospecting at Yellowstone. The Edmonds Institute, a small environmental group in Washington state, successfully challenged the agreement in court and won an order for an environmental review, yet to be conducted. Diversa has been gradually building an extensive microbial genomic library through the collection of samples from many countries, and intends to use the libraries to develop products for the pharmaceutical, agricultural, chemical processing and industrial markets (Diversa Corporation, 2000). In 2002, the company applied to Environment Canada for approval to study organisms at paper or pulp processing facilities on private lands and expressed an interest, in expanding its activities to public lands. Diversa made its proposal public at the World Indigenous Peoples conference in British Columbia, where some indigenous delegates denounced it as 'biocolonialism'

(Dalton, 2002). Even bacteria have become controversial in the debate over access to genetic resources.

Time and cost of drug development

Isolation of chemical compounds of value to the pharmaceutical or cosmetics industries can prove extraordinarily lucrative. Global sales of pharmaceuticals have been estimated at US$300 billion a year, of which the component derived from genetic resources accounts for between $75 billion and $150 billion (ten Kate and Laird, 1999). A compound derived from a sea sponge to treat herpes was estimated a few years ago to be worth US$50 million to $100 million annually. Current estimates of the potential value of anti-cancer agents found in marine organisms range to well over US$1 billion a year. The full potential of marine organisms to produce valuable compounds is unknown, because so few have been tested and because the ocean floor is largely unexplored. If regulators and policy makers think protecting local rights to plant genetic resources is a challenge, they have only to consider the complexities of marine life, its trans-boundary habits and its untapped potential to realize that aquatic genetic resources represent an awesome challenge waiting in the wings.

While profits from drug sales can be extraordinarily high, so are the costs of research and development. Testing for compounds that may prove useful is a little like aiming for a dartboard in a dark room. Success is rare. Perhaps one in 10,000 chemicals produces a promising lead, and fewer than one-quarter of the chemicals reaching clinical trials are likely to be approved as a new drug (McChesney, 1992). Moreover, a commercially marketable drug takes several years of development, including the process of screening candidate compounds, isolating active compounds, testing for possible toxicity, and undertaking clinical trials.

Although bioprospecting has generally been increasing, some companies involved in it suggest that if natural product research becomes too expensive, it will be abandoned for other more profitable approaches like synthetic and combinatorial chemistry, genomics and bioinformatics. The amounts of raw material needed to yield usable quantities of anti-cancer compounds can be enormous. For example, a tonne of Caribbean sea squirts produces only a gram of the anti-cancer compound ecteinascidin (Plotkin, 2000). However, the use of combinatorial chemistry can reduce the need for collection by enabling researchers to rapidly generate a huge number of chemical compounds for screening and to ease the identification and production by chemical synthesis of the active compound. Continuing advances in biotechnology could mean that future demand for access to aquatic genetic resources drops off (ten Kate and Laird, 1999), a scenario of which regulators need to be aware.

Collection of samples

Collectors of marine organisms may need only a scientific permit (as in Canada) or the equivalent to harvest samples for screening. While local divers may be paid to help with collections, more often than not there is little or no community involvement in the collection process, and no requirement for community consent. Areas where collections take place are generally outside traditional community boundaries, although the recognized rights of some indigenous communities (as in Fiji) may extend to offshore waters and the seabed. Indigenous groups involved in negotiations for land and resource rights (as in western Canada) may claim similar rights. Dependence on local knowledge of marine organisms is less likely to be a factor than in collection of fish genetic resources, simply because communities may have no traditional uses for, or may even be unaware of the existence of, marine organisms far beyond the shore. However, as illustrated in Box 1.8, traditional medicinal uses of some aquatic animals and plants are not uncommon.

Requirements for collection permits are likely to become more stringent with the development of national access and biodiversity conservation laws. However, as many species of marine organisms are not endemic to particular countries, collectors can avoid regulatory requirements by moving their operations to more 'friendly' countries. This is one reason why countries such as those in the ASEAN have adopted a regional approach to the implementation of access laws.

Given the cost and time involved in collection, and the abundance of marine organisms in many countries, payments for access to genetic resources have typically been low to date. It was estimated in 1991 that the total revenue likely to be received by developing countries seeking royalties for unimproved genetic material of any kind, terrestrial or aquatic, could be less than US$100 million annually (Barton, 1991, cited by Reid et al, 1993). In the pharmaceutical industry, royalties paid for samples with unknown clinical activity have amounted only to 1 to 5 per cent of net sales. Nevertheless, while the relative amount involved may be low, the scale of revenues generated in the pharmaceutical industry means that even a small share of net profits can produce extremely large revenues for a developing country once a product has been developed and marketed (Reid et al, 1993).

In the 1990s, Shaman Pharmaceuticals, operating in the botanicals field, announced a 'reciprocity' programme that would return benefits to indigenous communities from which samples had been collected. The company expressed a commitment to provide various types of benefits regardless of whether a marketable product was developed or whether indigenous knowledge was essential for product development (Bierer et al, 1996). Other companies have found Shaman's innovation too risky to adopt. Typically, very few returns from drug development trickle down to indigenous and local communities where collections are made.

Box 1.8   Medicinal Uses of Aquatic Plants and Animals

Although we have said that local knowledge does not have the same importance for aquatic genetic resources as it does for terrestrial, medicinal properties of aquatic plants and animals certainly exist. Many aquatic plants are harvested for medicinal purposes, just as others have always been used as food. Examples of the latter are cattails, which have edible shoots and roots, and arrowheads, whose large edible tubers were eaten by Native Americans. Medicinal aquatic plants include watercress (*Rorippa nasturtium-aquaticum*), also widely used as a salad green, and water lily roots that are commonly eaten in many parts of the world as well as used for medicine. Marshmallow roots, flowers and leaves have medicinal uses including as a cough suppressant, immune system booster and wound healer, while pennywort (*Hydrocotyle* spp) has been used to alleviate symptoms of arthritis.

Seaweed was a popular food and an important trading item among Northwest Coast peoples in western Canada. Dried red laver (*Porphyra abbottae*), containing all essential vitamins and minerals, was commonly made into cakes, sometimes flavoured with the juice of chewed rock chitons (a shellfish). Cultivation of nori, a close relative of red laver, is a US$10 billion industry in Japan, and industrial production of the plant is beginning in North America as well. Coastal tribes commonly traded dried seaweed to interior tribes such as the Carrier and Gitksan, who used it as a medicine for goitre, an affliction caused by iodine deficiency. Other medicinal applications of seaweed included the use of the gelatinous material in rockweed receptacles to treat burns and sores, to strengthen limbs, and to remove foreign objects or soothe stinging in the eye. The Nuu-chah-nulth people used bull kelp to make a skin salve (Turner 2000, 2002).

On the aquatic animal side, medicinal leeches are undergoing a revival in popularity, after being collected to near-extinction in Europe during the last century. As a result of severe loss of habitat, the medicinal leech is now listed on Appendix III of the Bern Convention, Appendix II of CITES and Annex V of the Habitats Directive. It is also listed as Vulnerable by the IUCN and as Rare in the GB Red List. Leeches have proved uniquely useful in cleaning and oxygenating the sites of plastic and reconstructive surgery, and the best known species, *Hirudo medicinalis* is now bred in captivity in Europe and the US. The southern African species *Aliolimnatis buntonensis* is another candidate for surgical use, but has yet to be bred in captivity (Appleton, 2001). Wild populations of medicinal leeches would seem to be a valuable genetic resource.

Practitioners of traditional Chinese medicine rely on a variety of aquatic plants and animals, some of which are used for multiple healing purposes. Cuttlefish bone, for example, is used to staunch bleeding, stop nocturnal emissions, treat diarrhoea, and cure skin ulcers. Pipefish are used to cure impotence and treat swellings. Clamshell, kelp and sargassum seaweed are combined to clear phlegm and stop coughing. Both marine and river turtles are used in the treatment of fever. Seahorses remain in high demand for the treatment of arthritis, impotence and urinary tract infections, and they have many other uses. Ground oyster shell is used for its calming effect, and abalone shell is used in the treatment of headache, dizziness and tremors (Bensky and Gamble, 1993).

Whether one subscribes to theories of medicinal value or not, the fact is that many aquatic organisms are already used for medicinal purposes, either by local communities (as in the example of the arrowhead plant) or, as in the case of seahorses, on an industrial scale that raises serious conservation concerns. The difficulty of addressing these concerns is often increased by the fact that many local communities rely on the collection of creatures such as the seahorse for a substantial part of their income, even if they have no local use for the animal.

INDIGENOUS VIEWS ON VALUING NATURE

Many indigenous communities that have traditionally subsisted on aquatic resources have developed and maintain a relationship with them that is foreign to Western concepts. Fish have made such a vital contribution to the well-being of indigenous peoples living on lakes, rivers, and ocean coastlines that they have come to form an integral part of community cultures and belief systems over hundreds or thousands of years. Some cultures rejected the Western notion of human dominance over other living beings. In the northwest coast of North America, for example, indigenous peoples such as the Nuu-chah-nulth revered the salmon. They would carefully return salmon bones to the river, both in gratitude for the gift from the spirit of the salmon and as a symbol of rebirth and renewal. The image of the salmon was central to the development of a sophisticated body of art, songs and dances that celebrated the salmon spirit.

Not surprisingly, some indigenous communities consider it inappropriate to describe fish as biological or genetic 'resources', as such a definition connotes ownership and is alien to their beliefs. The argument by geneticists that there's nothing sacred about 'pure' species contradicts fundamental principles guiding indigenous cultures. Indigenous peoples may oppose genetic modification of aquatic genetic life simply on the premise that it demonstrates a lack of respect for creatures with a spiritual life of their own – or lack of respect for the Creator of those creatures. The opposition voiced by some Canadian indigenous peoples to the establishment of salmon farms may be based in part on such beliefs. Many indigenous people accept the idea of salmon hatcheries only grudgingly, as an evil necessary for the rebuilding of stocks, and strongly oppose the idea of collecting genetic resources for later use.

CASE STUDY 1. THE LAW OF UNINTENDED CONSEQUENCES:
Conserving the ornamental fish industry in Barcelos, Brazil

Environmental groups that protest against industrial food fish farming because of its environmental impacts may throw their support behind the culture of ornamental fish, assuming that it can help save wild fish populations. As this case study illustrates, the opposite may be true – but not for the reasons one might expect.

One of the difficulties with setting policy for managing aquatic genetic resources is the wide variety of local cultural and ecological circumstances that need to be taken into account. In the 1990s, following the passage of the Convention on International Trade in Endangered Species of Wild Flora and Fauna (CITES), some airlines prohibited the transportation of live ornamental fish.[3] Some environmental groups have also pushed for the culturing of ornamental fish to relieve pressure on wild stocks. At the 22nd Professional Fish Show held by the Florida Tropical Fish Farms Association (FTFFA), Aquatica Tropicals took the Best in Show award for the cardinal tetra.

These seemingly unrelated events shared one thing in common – the potential to damage a thriving Amazon Basin subsistence fishery, the survival of which may be crucial to the protection of riverine ecosystems from industrial development. The airlines eventually rescinded their ban on the transportation of live ornamentals. FTFFA members, meanwhile, have high hopes that successful culture of the cardinal tetra will lead to a commercial industry that, operating without high handling and transportation costs, could compete so well that the wild cardinal tetra fishery might follow the example of the neon tetra fishery and become merely a historical footnote.

Links between the ornamental trade, the local economy, and ecosystem conservation

The diversity of fish in Amazonia is such that more than 3000 species have already been identified. The middle Rio Negro – the primary fishing grounds for live ornamental fish in the Amazon Basin – exports approximately 20 million live fish annually, generating about US$3 million for the local economy (Chao et al, 2001). The cardinal tetra accounts for over 80 per cent of ornamental fish exports from Brazil (Chao, 1998). The trade in ornamentals (primarily cardinal tetra and discus) contributes at least 60 per cent of total revenues in Barcelos, a community 400 km upriver from Manaus with a population of 16,000. An estimated 1000 local fishermen make their living from the fishery, with entire families, including women and children, typically being involved in collection, sorting, handling and transportation (Prang, 2001).

The collection of cardinal tetras has a short history compared to most traditional fisheries. It was only in the mid-1950s that the aquarist Herbert Axelrod discovered the existence of the cardinal tetra after hearing stories from local fishermen about a species similar to the neon tetra but larger and more brightly coloured (Axelrod, 2001). The cardinal tetra became an instant hit in the world of aquarium hobbyists and within a few years the trade had grown to millions of specimens, providing a new and steady source of income for villagers along the river near Barcelos, which had languished since the end of the rubber trade earlier in the century.

Cardinal tetras are highly prolific, but the health of their populations largely depends on pristine river and forest conditions. The fish are vulnerable to turbidity and pollution in the Rio Negro, the waters of which are highly acidic and ionic – one of the main reasons why cardinal tetras are so difficult to breed in aquaria. During the rainy season, when the river rises more than 9m, the tetras migrate from shallow streams into vast areas of the flooded forest to breed. In most countries, protection of fish habitat is secondary to the needs of industries with greater economic value. The reverse is true in the Rio Negro basin. Barcelos, which covers an area of 122,490 km² of largely intact jungle (and is geographically the largest municipality in the world), has passed bylaws prohibiting both industrial logging and gold mining in order to protect the ornamental fishery.

As development pressures throughout the Amazon Basin continue to increase, Barcelos has the potential to act as a buffer zone – provided that the municipal and higher levels of government are able to cooperate and that the ornamental fish industry continues to provide satisfactory livelihoods for local people. It is ironic that one of the most serious threats to the continuation of the fishery has come from efforts to protect Amazon ecosystems by curbing the trade in live animals. Blanket conservation policies can have unintended and counterproductive consequences if they're made without an adequate understanding of variations in local uses of species and in economic and cultural circumstances.

The threat of aquaculture to the wild fishery

If the Barcelos fishery is hurt by competition from a new aquaculture industry in another country, that too will be an unintended consequence of not understanding or acknowledging local conditions. The Florida aquaculture industry would simply be following the law of supply and demand. If hobbyists want cultured tetras because they're cheaper and less fragile and there's a willing seller, why should governments intervene? Already, over 90 per cent of freshwater ornamental sales are farmed fish. Popular home aquarium species such as guppies, mollies and neon tetras have been bred for decades. Advances in breeding technologies are simply making it possible to culture species once thought impossible to farm – the cardinal tetra being one of the most recent examples. Barcelos is by no means unique in its concern about the impact of the continuing expansion of ornamental aquaculture on the capture industry. In Sri Lanka, for instance, the ornamental fishery represents 8 per cent of the volume of exported fish but accounts for 70 per cent of its value, and supports so many people that few fishers are willing to support aquaculture (Bartley, 2000; Watson, 2000, cited in Tlusty, 2002).

Policies on aquaculture generally focus on environmental impacts where farming operations occur. However, the situation is more complicated than this. Tlusty (2002) suggests that, while aquacultural production of species has many benefits for the aquarium trade, captive cultivation should be avoided when the wild harvest maintains habitat and when a cultural and economic benefit would disappear if collections come to an end. Assuming the government of Brazil took seriously the threat of foreign aquaculture to the Barcelos fishery and, ultimately, the rainforest ecosystem, how should it act? Control over access to cardinal tetras for breeding is one option, but may be virtually impossible in the circumstances under which the trade in live ornamentals operates.

In fact, it's unlikely that the CBD's efforts to ensure that provider communities and countries have a say in and receive benefits from new uses of genetic resources are likely to work very well for communities like Barcelos. Emerging access and benefit-sharing laws, including that of Brazil, focus almost exclusively on bioprospecting. Collection for ornamental breeding works very differently. Breeders have no need to make forays deep into the jungle to find promising specimens. For the most part, they can simply gather broodstock by purchasing wild-caught fish that are already shipped abroad for sale to aquaria. In the case of the cardinal tetra, there's no need to tap into traditional local knowledge at all – that was done 50 years ago when Dr Axelrod first 'discovered' the tetra.

Some critics of the effectiveness of the CBD have suggested that importing countries need to take further steps to discourage biopiracy in developing countries and their communities. For instance, patent offices might require applicants to identify the location from which material (or traditional knowledge) used to develop a new strain was collected. While such a requirement could conceivably be useful for the protection of communities providing sea squirts or sponges, it's hardly likely to be relevant for ornamental breeders who have bought their fish from importers and have no knowledge of the precise origin of their aquarium stock.

Chain of custody certification has been suggested as another way to encourage both conservation and fair play in dealings with aquatic genetic resources. In a recent poll, US hobbyists indicated that they would be prepared to pay as much as 50 per cent more for quality fish from a 'green' fishery than for substandard fish from a poorly managed fishery (Dowd, 2001). Certification of wild fish collected along the Rio Negro could help promote the Barcelos fishery, and the work of Project Piaba (discussed below) should help facilitate certification approvals. The Marine Aquarium Council already has a certification programme in place and is planning to extend it to cover the use of aquatic genetic resources.

The relevance of Brazilian access law to the Barcelos fishery

Assuming that collectors do wish to travel to Barcelos to search for and collect populations of cardinal tetras that might lead to a new cultured strain, what protection does the new access and benefit-sharing law (Provisional Act No. 2186–16, August 2001) provide to communities?

Prior to the creation of this controversial law, foreign collectors of ornamental fish needed approval from the Instituto Brasileiro do Meio Ambiente e dos Recursos Naturais Renováveis (IBAMA), the national environmental management agency. Such collections, often made by individuals, have not always proceeded without incident. For example, in 1999, IBAMA officials apprehended a German aquarist who was collecting cichlids in the Rio Negro region to study their feeding habits.[4] Generally, even if agencies are tipped off by local people, the remoteness of most parts of the Amazon makes enforcement of regulations very difficult. The effect of Provisional Act 2186–16, which covers scientific research, technological development, and bioprospecting, is to limit the issuance of collection permits to national public or private institutions. Individuals can no longer obtain them. Consequently, an aquarist would first have to make an agreement with an accredited Brazilian institution, which in turn would be required to obtain the consent of the indigenous or local community where collections will occur. A local community is defined in the law as 'a human group … differentiated by its cultural conditions, which is, traditionally, organized along successive generations and with its own customs, and conserves its social and economic institutions'.[5] It's not clear whether such a definition would apply to a municipality such as Barcelos or to one of the many scattered family villages within its boundaries.

Either way, the consent of a community (other than on indigenous lands) is required only if the collection involves the use of traditional knowledge related to genetic heritage. The original collector of cardinal tetras, Herbert Axelrod, made his find through chance information provided by local people. Once he had established a demand for the species, the fishery began, less than 40 years ago. Assuming a villager provides information to an aquarist today about a previously unknown (to aquarists) subpopulation of cardinal tetras, would that constitute traditional knowledge for the purposes of the act? Is it enough that a villager simply knows about the coloration or markings of a population for which a community has no traditional use? If an aquarist only wishes to collect specimens from populations already fished for the ornamental trade, is it enough that villagers only know how and where to collect them, in order to be eligible for the right to consent? Generally, other national laws are no more clear than Brazil's about the nature and scope of provisions on traditional knowledge, and the fact that they have been drafted primarily for plant bioprospecting offers considerable room for confusion about their application to aquatic genetic resources.

Assuming the knowledge of local fishermen confers the right to informed consent, then what? The Brazilian act provides that any traditional knowledge related to genetic heritage may be deemed to be held by the community even if only one member of the community holds this knowledge (Article 9). The community then has the right to receive benefits from the economic use of their traditional knowledge by third parties (eg a fish farm outside Brazil). Presumably, those benefits would be negotiated by the aquarist and a Brazilian national institution, as the act does not appear to contemplate direct negotiations of benefits with a community, which only has the right to decide on the use of its traditional knowledge (Article 8). A share of royalties is the most likely benefit to be negotiated. The big Catch 22 is that any Rio Negro community that consents to the use of ornamental broodstock for aquaculture outside its own area is likely to be quickly blacklisted, creating serious divisions among local groups.

In short, what the Barcelos fishery most needs is assistance with maintaining a sustainable and reasonably profitable capture fishery, and the only benefit that matters is keeping the aquaculture industry at bay. Are aquatic genetic resources blue gold? Perhaps in the minds of the national government and national institutions, but certainly not to Barcelos – or to similar communities in other countries that rely on capture fisheries for wild ornamentals. This is precisely the reason why makers of access and benefit-sharing laws need to have a clear understanding of the implications of legislative provisions for aquatic as well as plant genetic resources and of variations in local circumstances that have a direct bearing on conservation objectives.

Maintaining a sustainable fishery: The work of Project Piaba

The real profits in the Amazon ornamental industry are made by the exporters in Manaus and importers in Florida and elsewhere. The earnings of a Barcelos fisherman roughly approximate the minimum wage in Brazil. However, as Prang (2001) points out, the ornamental fishery provides greater returns than other extractive activities in the Amazon and provides one of the few opportunities to earn enough for basic necessities and consumer goods. The ornamentals trade makes it possible for peasant fishers to remain in the interior rather than emigrating to urban centres like Manaus. Without the trade, local people would likely be driven to find alternative work in logging and gold mining, and the municipality would have less incentive to try to keep environmentally destructive industries out.

While higher returns to local fishers would be desirable, their most important need is assurance that a sustainable fishery can continue indefinitely. To this end, Project Piaba, based at the University of the Amazon and primarily funded through the Herbert Axelrod Foundation, has undertaken a variety of activities aimed at maintaining the live ornamental fishery at commercially feasible and ecologically sustainable levels. Its objectives are to:

- Collect baseline data on the ecosystem, socio-economy and diversity of fishes in order to analyse the impact of the ornamental fish trade on social and natural environments.
- Diagnose diseases and reduce mortality of captive fish, introduce fish care techniques to improve the survival and quality of fishes and turtles, and eventually establish protocols for export quarantine.
- Provide environmental education and socio-cultural history to local children, fishermen, distributors and public, and promote career development in aquarium science and conservation.
- Create community-based fishery management strategies for managed harvest levels, stock enhancement of fishes and turtles and the development of aquaculture of native species where appropriate.
- Assist in the revision of policies by regulatory agencies in order to protect vulnerable species and enhance the economic viability of the region.
- Encourage local entrepreneurship, ecotourism, the production of local crafts and the commercialization of other sustainable natural resources.

Project Piaba objectives are based on the premise that sustainable fisheries require a scientific basis for management together with support for community management strategies. So little is known about the Rio Negro ecosystem that extensive baseline data are required before developing integrated management strategies. During its first ten years (1989–1999), in addition to conducting baseline surveys of fish diversity and socio-cultural implications of the ornamental fishery, Project Piaba established a public aquarium and environmental education programmes in Barcelos and worked with local people to define issues that need to be addressed if community-based management strategies are to be effective (Chao et al, 2001). The Project has also provided training in handling and transportation techniques to reduce mortalities and increase the quality of the fish catch.

The Barcelos fishery illustrates the complexity of developing complementary policies for the management of and access to aquatic genetic resources, and the importance of taking into account local economies and ecologies. In the Barcelos case, these include the following:

- Policies for the collection of aquatic genetic resources need to take into account both direct and indirect environmental and social impacts of different uses in different locations.
- Policies for access to aquatic genetic resources need to go hand in hand with aquatic resources management policies that recognize a complementary relationship between science-based and community-based management. They also need to ensure coordination between municipal and higher levels of government in implementing policies that promote sustainable uses.
- Access laws and regulations need to clearly identify communities having rights to prior informed consent. Laws that restrict that right to communities providing traditional knowledge need to clearly define the nature of traditional knowledge to which the laws apply.
- Benefits to communities may be most usefully directed to maintaining sustainable livelihoods that in turn contribute to conservation of aquatic ecosystems.

Chapter 2

Managing Aquatic Genetic Resources: Tools and Policy Gaps

Returning a dourado to the Taquari River after DNA sampling, Coxim, Brazil (Photo by David Greer)

When it comes to effective policies for the management and conservation of biological and genetic diversity, fisheries are the poor cousins to agriculture. Why the comparison? There are three reasons:

Firstly, agriculture has relied on genetic resources for decades, using gene banks and other formal and informal collections. This process is only now beginning to happen in aquaculture.

Secondly, countries have long cooperated to make sure that samples of plant genetic resources (from both farmed and wild strains) are collected and stored in trust for the future benefit of humanity. Countries could and should be doing the same for aquatic genetic resources, but no national or international governmental initiative has yet occurred to make it happen.

Finally, once the genetic modification of crops started to become commonplace and the conservation of plant genetic resources came to be seen as important, governments had to start making laws and policies to deal with all the problematical issues that surfaced.

The thorniest issue of all was the question of ownership and control of genetic resources. When countries began to discuss how to deal with such issues, as they did during the negotiation of the CBD in 1992, it seemed to make sense to talk about genetic resources generally, not just crop genetic resources. The problem, as we'll discuss in this and following chapters, is that crops are so different from fish that policies that may make sense in an agricultural context may be irrelevant or even counterproductive when applied to the fish world.

Assuming that's the case, how does one go about developing policies that are specific to aquatic genetic resources? Firstly, one needs to ensure that there's already a good foundation of policies for the management of aquatic biological (as opposed to genetic) resources. Secondly, policy makers will need to be well informed about current and potential issues that policies on aquatic genetic resources will need to address. As this chapter will explain, considerable progress needs to be made in both these areas.

CONSERVING AQUATIC GENETIC DIVERSITY – Still a new idea for fisheries management

The genetic diversity of the aquatic world is slipping away while governments for the most part remain either oblivious to the extent of its decline or reluctant to act forcefully to conserve it. It comes down to basic political realities. Until very recently, we lived in an era when the bounty of river and sea was considered virtually inexhaustible – which might have been true enough until industrial fish-harvesting technologies and a wide variety of habitat destroying activity on land had taken their toll. Even today, whenever a fish population temporarily rebounds, usually for reasons beyond human understanding, some fisheries managers use the event as a reason to dismiss concerns about threatened aquatic ecosystems as misguided doom and gloom. We've seen it with climate change, we've seen it with the Atlantic cod fishery: regardless of what the preponderance of scientific evidence might say, governments are reluctant to take meaningful and coordinated action as long as there are louder voices pressing them to stay the course.

In the late 1980s, the UN's Brundtland commission issued a wake-up call by drawing attention to the interdependence of economic, environmental and community long-term well-being. 'Sustainable development' has been a common phrase ever since. The problem remains that, without strong government commitments and a clear understanding of what it takes to achieve sustainable development, what was once a call to arms risks being reduced to an empty catchphrase.

With aquatic ecosystems, it's all too tempting to adopt an 'out of sight, out of mind' approach and hope for the best. Who knows? Maybe things aren't as bad as they seem. But that's a faint hope at a time when it appears the world will increasingly depend on fish for its food needs. Is aquaculture the answer? Then we need to make sure that we conserve genetically diverse wild stocks so that we still have the opportunity to breed the best farmed ones.

It's essentially the same story in the search for powerful medicines or novel industrial applications that are based on the knowledge we get from studying deep sea organisms and other forms of aquatic life. Increasingly, we see the potential value of aquatic genetic resources for all kinds of social purposes, but they're disappearing before we've had a chance to understand how they might be used – and in some cases before we've even discovered that a species exists in the first place.

Changing attitudes towards conservation: A steep learning curve

The genetics of fish have been studied for decades, and even before the advent of fast and sensitive tools such as DNA fingerprinting it was clear that single species could be subdivided into separate, genetically distinct populations. But the importance of this fact was generally lost on fisheries managers – the people who make the decisions on where, how and how much fishermen can fish. And since there was no fish farming until comparatively recently, the practical value of aquatic genetic resources, as opposed to their evolutionary significance, simply wasn't recognized.

Fisheries managers are gradually beginning to pay attention to genetic diversity. What is difficult for people familiar with genetic resources issues in agriculture to appreciate is the struggle this newfound awareness represents, and the 'newness' of the concept of aquatic genetic resources to policy makers. As illustrated by Box 2.1, it can take a very long time for this awareness to translate into policy change, especially at a time of declining government resources and increasing competition for a share of dwindling fisheries resources.

Box 2.1 Protecting the Genetic Diversity of Pacific Salmon

Before the mid-1980s, commercial salmon fisheries in British Columbia and the large recreational fisheries for trout were managed with little if any attention to genetic diversity. Little was known about the actual genetic separation of different stocks of the same species of salmon or trout, and most of the basis for even assuming there were separate stocks was anecdotal. Fishermen claimed they could recognize different stocks, and there was genetic evidence that pointed to separation, but the fish were generally harvested as though each species was homogeneous.

When Canada's DFO opened a sockeye salmon fishery on the Fraser River, the fact that there were numerically small sockeye stocks that went up small tributaries, and huge stocks that went up others, was not generally taken into account. Sockeye were sockeye, and if an opening had a disproportionate impact on certain stocks nobody was worrying about it, officially or unofficially. For trout, which are traditionally 'enhanced' through hatcheries to serve the sports fishery, transplantation of a single hatchery stock into innumerable small lakes was the norm. Trout were trout. And that was the situation not just for salmonids in Canada, but for fish everywhere – at a time when plant gene banking was already extensive.

In 1992, when a non-profit organization tried to interest fisheries authorities in saving salmon genetic resources, the response was generally negative. While the occasional government biologist saw the need to preserve genetic diversity and worried about the effects on small stocks of the mixed stock fishery, their managers were protective, and the image that upset them most was the gene bank. Gene banks were 'technical fixes', which deflected attention away from the 'real' problem of habitat loss and, in the words of a one time provincial Director of Fisheries, they were a way to turn a quick profit on fish genetic resources.[1] The implicit objection, and possibly the most powerful, was that collecting genetic resources for conservation was another way of saying that fisheries managers weren't doing their jobs, and in a decade of turmoil where fisheries were being shut down and closures were almost daily media events, managers were understandably sensitive. When several British Columbia First Nations later became interested in salmon gene banking, the government of British Columbia formally declined to support it.

But the decline in the British Columbia salmon fisheries was undeniable, and after relentless criticism from conservation NGOs, fisheries agencies in British Columbia began to change their policies on genetic diversity. The first development was a reversal of decades long reliance on salmon hatcheries that provided large numbers of genetically similar fish for stocking streams. Hatcheries came to be seen as another 'technical fix', and in the mid-1990s the federal fisheries minister stated publicly that genetic diversity was important and needed to be conserved. Fishing openings that could adversely affect small, genetically unique stocks were closed in a courageous attempt to reduce the 'editing out' of genetic diversity that mixed stock fisheries entailed. DFO began developing a new Wild Salmon Policy that specifically elevated genetic diversity to a cardinal principle. In 1998, the department contracted the training of its own technicians in gene banking and began collecting selected stocks from several salmon species. In 2002, the department took over the gene banking programme entirely, essentially importing a technology it had abandoned research on 15 years ago.

The point is not that DFO is doing its own gene banking but rather the painful process by which fisheries managers became sensitized to the importance of genetic diversity. In 15 years, one government department went from funding its own research on genetic conservation to reinventing it at many times the original cost. Multiply this experience by the thousands of fisheries departments in the world, and add in the youth of fish farming as an activity that relies on genetic diversity, and you have some idea of the gulf between plant and aquatic genetic resources. Aquatic genetic resources have always been there, but their significance has been hidden because they were the basis for the last great wild harvest indulged in by humankind – fisheries. It was only when fisheries began to falter, and aquaculture began to make demands for starting material, that aquatic genetic resources seemed to matter.

What to conserve?

Because so little is known about fish species and stocks that may become important to aquaculture, industry and conservation in the future, it is important to conserve not only currently economically valuable aquatic genetic resources but also those that may be useful in the future. In southern countries, fisheries have generally proceeded in the complete absence of information on the very existence of individual genetic stocks. In other words, there has been a tendency to focus on abundance of fish stocks that are economically valuable now rather than the genetic diversity needed to ensure future value.

The mobility of fish and the financial and technical constraints to gene banking are two factors that differentiate fish genetic resources conservation from crop and forestry genetic resource conservation (Hodgkin and Ouedraogo, 1996). Yet there is another consideration. Sustainable management of aquatic biodiversity depends on conserving the many diverse aquatic organisms that make up food webs and contribute to maintaining environmental quality (Pullin and Casal, 1996). While an ecosystem approach to conservation would help sustain ecosystem health while protecting individual species, creating genetic resource policy that reflects such complex ecosystem needs has never been done before. In the past, governments have been reluctant to adopt an ecosystem approach to fish conservation, primarily because of cost, conflicting economic interests, and scientific uncertainty. This attitude is changing, but the practical ability to 'manage for biodiversity' is still limited, probably because it is so daunting. If every aquatic organism depends on every other one, which one do you conserve?

Taking communities into account in conservation policy

The three interdependent components of sustainable development are a sustainable economy, sustainable ecosystems, and sustainable communities. It's well understood that government and industry have a responsibility to conserve ecosystems that, if protected, will provide the natural capital for future generations. Healthy economies and healthy ecosystems in turn contribute to maintaining healthy communities. The part that's often overlooked in the equation is the important role that traditional communities, as opposed to government or industry, can play in conserving ecosystems – provided they have the right, the means and the motivation to do so.

The importance of community stability to the conservation of aquatic resources may seem obvious, but it has not always been front and centre in policy making. In the market-based economy, the chips fall where they may. Traditional community livelihoods can disappear for any of a number of reasons, including the inability to compete with large-scale commercial fisheries (or aquaculture) and the destruction of fish habitat as a result of logging, mining, or urban development. Many long established indigenous and local communities have developed a careful balance between maintaining stable local economies and sustaining the ecosystems needed to support them. When local economies are disrupted, traditional ecosystem management systems are disrupted as well. Local people need livelihoods that are both conservation based and economically sustainable. Case Study 1 graphically illustrates how dependent ecosystem conservation can be on the protection of local fisheries livelihoods in areas like Brazil's Rio Negro.

The countries that have ratified the CBD (almost all the countries in the world) are committed, under Article 8(j), to maintaining and promoting traditional community practices relevant to the conservation and sustainable use of biological diversity. Governments can use a variety of tools to do so. These may include actively promoting co-management of aquatic ecosystems and resources, developing programmes to support the expansion of sustainable fisheries livelihoods, and directly involving communities in making policy. In addition, as suggested by Article 8(j), they can ensure that indigenous and local communities share in the benefits resulting from the use of aquatic genetic resources. Carefully considered benefits, whether monetary or non-monetary, can strengthen the economies of fishing communities in a way that takes ecosystem sustainability into account as well. We will discuss how this might be achieved in later chapters.

BANKING BLUE GENES:
Collections of aquatic genetic resources

Aquatic genetic diversity can be conserved in three ways:

- By protecting the habitat of aquatic creatures from urban development, dam building, forestry, pollution, etc.
- By regulating fishing.
- By collecting and storing genetic material (eg fish sperm or whole fish) in gene banks that can both guard against extinction and preserve material until science is ready or able to use it (eg to enhance farmed stocks).

Ideally, all three of these approaches complement one another. Ironically, the third approach – by far the simplest and least expensive – has proven to be the most difficult to implement.

Where once farmers in local communities stored seeds from one year's harvest to use in the next, today an elaborate system of international gene banks stores genetic material from around the world, in trust for the benefit of all humankind. For example, the International Rice Genebank, established in 1977, now holds in cold storage more than 90,000 samples of cultivated rice and wild species, donated by more than 100 countries. The IRRI states on its website (www irri.org/GRC/irg/biodiv-genebank.htm) that the seeds are held in trust and are made available to the world's scientists in the public and private sectors.

As we'll discuss later, the rules for access to genetic resources collections held by plant gene banks are one of the most troublesome issues for policy makers (Who really owns the seeds? The gene bank? The country that provided them? The communities from which they originally came? The farmers whose ancestors developed new strains either accidentally or by design?). The point is that someone had the foresight to make sure that plant genetic resources around the world are conserved for humanity's best interest, however that might be determined, and governments around the world have come on board to encourage and support the collections. Regardless of the politics, the theory of conserving what might be lost forever and using it for future human (consumer and commercial) benefit is sound. The same theory is equally applicable to aquatic genetic resources.

Current collections of aquatic genetic resources are usually maintained in gene banks for aquaculture or conservation. Gene banks have already been introduced in Chapter 1, and both end uses of gene banking rely on similar technologies and pose similar questions of policy. In the discussion that follows, the emphasis is on gene banks for aquaculture, but many of the issues regarding collection and access are the same for gene banks aimed at research or 'restoration' of endangered stocks.

Why bank fish genes?

A gene bank is a collection of genetic resources. Collections may take many forms. They may be living plants or animals conserved in situ (in place) or ex situ (at a location remote from their natural habitat). Alternatively, they may contain only reproductive material such as seeds, which can be stored for years before needing periodic regeneration, or cryopreserved sperm, which can be stored indefinitely. Either way, gene banks maintain the raw material for food security and the means to breed better crops, farm better fish, or repopulate depleted stocks.

Agricultural gene banks have proven invaluable where an agricultural crop has been devastated by disease, for example, the case of rice in Indonesia in the mid-1970s. A gene for resistance to the disease was found in one sample of a variety of rice collected in 1963 in India. Without its presence in a gene bank, it is unlikely that a gene for resistance would ever have been found. There are over 460 plant gene banks throughout the world, including approximately a dozen major ones established under the auspices of the CGIAR. These gene banks all communicate with one another and exchange material.

Fish gene banks could fill many of the same functions as plant gene banks, as well as new ones, such as providing wild genetic material for efforts to rebuild depleted stocks. Collections of aquatic genetic resources can be 'broodstock collections' ('living gene bank') or 'cryopreserved gene banks' of frozen sperm or embryos. Broodstock collections take up space and are more expensive than cryopreserved banks to replenish and maintain. Most cryopreserved banks are for fish sperm, although methods for freezing bivalve (oyster and clam) gametes and embryos have recently made possible gene banks for these groups. There is still no technology for gene banking of crustaceans (shrimp, etc).

The history of fish gene banks is short (approximately two decades) and although there are a number of large state-run collections (for example, those in Norway, India, Russia, and Finland), the bulk of the cryopreserved material is held in small private or university-based banks whose numbers are nowhere near those for plants. There is no coordination between these banks. Nevertheless, the range of species held is broad, and techniques for new species are being developed all the time. Those that do exist serve a variety of functions, including as repositories of wild genetic material as a source for breeding, private banks of genetically improved broodstock, and banks of sperm collected by government agencies and aboriginal groups as a means of assisting recovery efforts for wild stocks. Banks of sperm from freshwater fish predominate, which reflects the preponderance of cultured freshwater species rather than any greater ease of freezing gametes from such species (marine species are in fact technically easier to cryopreserve).

Commercial use of frozen fish germplasm has already begun. For example, west coast salmon farms in Canada have recently begun to draw on private gene banks in their broodstock programmes (see Case Study 2), and genetically improved tilapia strains bred from wild broodstock collected in Africa are represented in a bank in the Philippines (Case Study 4). Fish breeders or conservationists without access to these banks must rely on existing wild stocks to obtain the raw material needed to rebuild depleted stocks and engage in selective breeding of farmed stocks, and access will only come with the development of regional and national policies on exchanging material held in fish gene banks.

The collection of genetic resources for fish is coloured by a sense of urgency that reflects the extreme pressures on aquatic ecosystems. By the time aquaculturists and hatchery managers make significant progress in developing genetically improved broodstocks, there may be much less wild genetic material left to work with. Overfishing and habitat destruction have both taken an immense toll, and climate change may well contribute to further losses of aquatic genetic diversity. Gene banking helps ensure that genetic variability of threatened fish stocks will not be lost while efforts to restore and preserve habitat continue. For species with economic value in aquaculture, gene banking safeguards biodiversity for later use in selective breeding.

Policy implications: Getting local permission to collect aquatic genetic resources

Future developments in cryopreservation technology will undoubtedly expand the number of aquatic gene banks, and this will have implications for ease of use and type of user. Before about 1995, for example, cryopreservation of fish sperm required costly equipment and laboratory facilities. With the introduction of inexpensive field kits, however, companies, fisheries agencies and aboriginal groups are now able to create their own gene banks, relying on outside assistance only for training and inventory management.

As the number of banks grows, so does the number of potential conflicts, especially as collections begin to concentrate on species and populations that are declining. The most likely conflicts will be where access is sought to genetic resources of commercially important species in areas where local and indigenous communities have some management rights. Paradoxically, this conflict may be worsened by the move towards greater local participation in resource management, as local communities deal with more requests for genetic material from locally managed stocks. Development agencies and governments cannot encourage communities to manage their own resources, including genetic resources, without also providing the policy tools for maintaining some degree of local control. In this sense, a request to extract genetic resources is no different from a fishing incursion by a neighbour or competing stakeholder: both require guidelines and policies.

The collection, storage and transport of plant and animal genetic resources has been the subject of intense international debate for decades, and there is a growing body of standards specifically for plants and animals. While the CBD is meant to encompass all genetic resources, in reality it is the outcome of the debate on plant and terrestrial animal resources. For aquatic animals, there are no standards beyond what some local agencies and jurisdictions have set for themselves. The Canadian DFO, for example, does salmon gene banking (for conservation reasons) within the framework of existing rules on transplantation of gametes and disease control, but there are no specific guidelines or policies for access and benefit sharing. Canadian First Nations, several of which collect salmon genetic resources (also for conservation and possibly including some of the same stocks that DFO collects), may opt to operate according to their own internal guidelines. The situation is like all ad hoc arrangements: convenient, and more or less smoothly functioning until too many people get involved. As we have seen above, increased involvement is inevitable. If policies are not developed to cope with it, conflict will also be inevitable.

Increases in regulatory complexity for collection of aquatic genetic resources will mean increased cost to collectors. As a relatively new commercial activity, fish farming is likely to go through many cycles as species enter culture and become established. For many species, a boom follows establishment of the first farms, then is succeeded by a decline in prices (as supply increases) and the eventual weeding out of players. Hence it is difficult to predict how commercial operations will view any increase in costs associated with new policies for collection and exchange of genetic resources. Regulations that apply to the industry are still being developed for other areas (pollution, certification, other environmental effects), so it's reasonable to assume that farms will take new policies on genetic resources in their stride.

Meanwhile, fish farmers wait for access policies to be developed. Case Study 2 at the end of this chapter describes the dilemma of a salmon farmer, frustrated and thwarted in his attempts to collect 'pure' broodstock from a spawning stream because the government had yet to turn its mind to policy development.

Steps towards an international system for aquatic genetic resources

The present plant gene banking system has grown out of many decades of collection of plant genetic resources and their use in developing new crops. It has followed the metamorphosis of genetic resources from the 'heritage of humankind' to the subject of the largest international convention ever signed, from an era when disinterested collectors were welcome in local communities to a time where national governments are shutting down access. It primarily serves the needs of crop breeders working with highly evolved breeds grown on a large scale in monoculture in simplified ecosystems.

As we have seen, aquatic genetic resources are important not only in large-scale, intensive aquaculture (the closest parallel to modern agriculture), but also in small-scale farming systems that are more connected with natural ecosystems, as well as in the production of wild stocks that continue to be provided by ecosystems that are essentially unaltered. The collection and use of aquatic genetic resources for these kinds of endeavours is just beginning. In some ways this is a good thing for policy makers, because with the CBD in place in so many countries the ground-rules are far clearer than they ever were for plants. The problem for aquatic genetic resource collections is thus less one of knowing the rules and profiting from the experience in the plant world, and more a matter of organization and coordination. One similarity is, however, very clear: as in agriculture, aquaculture seed supplies are becoming concentrated in fewer and fewer hands as fish farmers look to outside sources for fish seed (Welcomme, 1999). In some cases they may in fact have no choice, and local varieties with desirable culture characteristics may actually be supplanted by species or varieties being promoted by seed companies. Nevertheless, many fish farms still depend on collection of wild broodstock, and research on genetic modification of farmed fish relies heavily on the analysis and selection of traits from a wide diversity of wild stocks.

One of the main problems with having a number of disconnected collections that have been assembled for various reasons (aquaculture, conservation/ enhancement, pharmaceutical, pure research) is that there is no common ground or purpose. A private company maintaining a bank of catfish sperm for their aquaculture operations is unlikely to travel in the same circles, read the same journals or attend the same meetings as a research scientist with a gene bank of zebra fish sperm or a government biologist collecting wild salmon genetic material for conservation. All of them may be unfamiliar with the CBD. If one considers that gene banking of aquatic organisms has been going on, in small, scattered programmes like these since the mid-1970s, two things are clear: Firstly, a lot of aquatic genetic resources are being collected, managed and used for many purposes. Secondly, the standardization so evident in plant gene banking (collection techniques, preservation techniques, consent and publication of holdings) is completely absent.

There are, however, clear signs that this situation will change. Since the late 1970s, FAO has convened periodic consultations and conferences on aquatic genetic resources, aided in the 1990s by World Fisheries Trust and ICLARM (now World Fish Center). This series of consultations led in the late 1990s to recognition that there already exists a large amount of information on aquatic genetic resources. Drawing on the experience of FAO in creating the Domestic Animal Diversity Information System (DADIS), World Fisheries Trust and FAO began to promote a similar consolidation and standardization of aquatic animal diversity information. The programme, provisionally called Fisheries Information Network on Genetic Resources (FINGER), began with an expert consultation in Rome in November 2001, and has now progressed to a pilot study to collect existing information on key species.

Although FINGER goes well beyond the collections of aquatic genetic resources held in gene banks (it includes, for example, gene sequences from aquatic organisms, as well as museum collections) it is probably a necessary step in the creation of a gene banking system anything like the one that exists for plants. It will certainly have some basic differences from the plant system, but it will definitely be a powerful tool for policy creation, because the system will establish standardized communications between isolated collections, as well as rules for access to information on the collections.

Although building the system will take time, it will eventually afford a unified picture of the state and extent of aquatic genetic resource collections. If a unified gene banking system for aquatic organisms ever does emerge, it will reflect the diversity of uses and motives revealed by FINGER.

ACCESS TO AQUATIC GENETIC RESOURCES COLLECTIONS

Countries' interdependence on genetic resources

Even the most biologically self-sufficient countries look to other parts of the world for genetic resources for crop development. Wheat originated in the Near East, but the genes that led to semi-dwarf wheats came from Japan via the US and Mexico. Disease-resistant genes found in Central America may support crop yields as far away as India (Crucible Group, 1994). The deliberate movement of aquatic species out of their countries of origin is much more recent, and less extensive, than that of plants, primarily because of the relative difficulty of transporting fish over long distances (although movement of alien species 'by accident' is another matter). With the exception of a few widely cultured species, the diversity of a food fish species is likely to be confined to a country or a group of neighbouring countries.

The exceptions to this rule are, however, significant. Tilapias, for example, are an African fish now cultured all over the world (see Case Study 4), and the Atlantic salmon is now cultured widely in North and South America, thousands of kilometres away from its original habitat. In both cases, culture of the transplanted domesticated species has caused controversy related to genetic effects on native species, and has even reduced the options for culturing them. When a subsistence farmer wants to supplement his income with small-scale fish culture, farming a local species may not be an option, especially when (as in Brazil, for example) the state is actively promoting tilapias.

Interdependence among countries for crop genetic resources has been a primary stimulus for international collaboration in their exchange and use. Examples are the formation of the CGIAR germplasm collections, and efforts to develop a multilateral system for access to genetic resources and the sharing of benefits. There is much less evidence of such collaboration in the fish world, although this may change as further progress is made in fish breeding efforts and exchange (Raymond, 1999). The existence of regional aquaculture networks such as the Network of Aquaculture Centres in Asia is evidence of such a trend, as is FAO's work towards establishing the FINGER information system for aquatic animal genetic resources.

Kinds of demand for access

As we have seen, collections of aquatic genetic resources are developing in an ad hoc way. Pharmaceutical and aquaculture companies, research institutes and government agencies have been the primary initiators. In addition, some indigenous communities have recently begun cryopreserving fish sperm. Communication about the nature, purpose, location and indeed the very existence of collections is poor. As communication improves, demands for access to collections (now so commonplace for plant genetic resources) will begin to occur. What will these demands be like, and what should be the policies to deal with them?

Examples of access demands might include a government agency requesting genetic resources collected by a conservation society, an aquaculture company requesting genetic resources held by an indigenous community, or a university researcher wishing to experiment with genetic resources collected by government, industry or a local community. All such requests will raise a number of issues, not all of them related to ownership. For example, are the genetic resources (which may exist in the frozen state) any different from the fish that provided them? Does the requesting party need to go through the identical permission steps followed by the original collector? If the genetic material is to be transported outside the original watershed, who grants permission?

Clearly if there are no policies in place regarding the original collections, the situation will only get more complicated once requests are made for access to them. This is illustrated, for example, by CGIAR's (2001) development of guidelines for the acquisition and transfer of aquatic germplasm. The guidelines are designed to comply with Article 15 of the CBD, which provides that access to genetic resources shall be on mutually agreed terms and subject to the prior informed consent of the contracting party (country) providing the resources. The guidelines require CGIAR Centres to obtain 'proper, formal permission from the relevant authorized government body prior to collecting or acquiring any germplasm' by way of a letter of agreement, germplasm acquisition agreement, or other legal document, contract or agreement. While the guidelines may satisfy the requirements of Article 15, there is no guarantee that nations of origin have developed policies that govern access to collections within the country or to aquatic genetic resources generally. In most countries such policies are non-existent or haphazard at best, yet their development will be essential to achieving the CBD's objectives.

The following examples illustrate some of the difficulties created by current policy gaps.

Canada: Cultus Lake sockeye

One characteristic of genetic resource collection, especially those in gene banks from which samples can literally be taken 'off the shelf', is their unpredictable utility. A current example is provided by the case of Cultus Lake sockeye salmon.

Cultus Lake sockeye are a much diminished population of British Columbia salmon that spawn in a small lake attached to a tributary of the Fraser River.

Representative males of the stock were gene banked in 1995 by the Canadian DFO, as part of a study demonstrating the utility of cryopreservation technology. The samples remained in storage for six years, paid for by the departmental research laboratory originally involved in their collection. Recently, two events raised the profile of the collection. First, the Cultus Lake stock became critically depressed, to the extent that it was proposed for listing under the new Species At Risk Act, and a separate division of the same fisheries department began to contemplate using the collection to restore the stock, and indeed to add to the collection.

Second, a new parasite began to decimate many of the salmon stocks in the area, including the Cultus stock, and the material frozen in 1995 had a sudden interest for researchers wanting to compare gametes from present day stock with stocks in 'pre-parasite' days. The upshot is that a stock cryopreserved almost at random is now the subject of discussion between two government departments, which will have to share a limited collection. A neighbouring First Nation, whose sockeye stocks have been hard hit by the same parasite, is now interested in taking part in any expanded gene banking operation in the coming years.

Brazil: DNA fingerprinting and cryopreservation of fish sperm

Another example is from Brazil, where the recent acquisition of Canadian technologies for fish gene banking and DNA fingerprinting has created local capacity not only for collection, storage and exchange of genetic resources (in the form of frozen sperm) but also for amassing information on the genetic structure of fish populations. Both the banked gametes and the DNA sequence information have potential application in conservation, management and aquaculture. The government of Brazil has been careful to insist on a clause in the technology transfer agreement that stipulates that no genetic material shall leave the country, and there are regulations in place within the country that theoretically control the access to aquatic genetic resources both by Brazilian nationals and by foreigners. Outsiders must, for example, secure the cooperation of a Brazilian institution before collecting any biological material, and IBAMA grants a special scientific collecting licence to Brazilian scientists to collect specimens for research.

Neither arrangement says anything about the acquisition or transfer of genetic resources between sectors within the country. However, collections of migratory fish genetic resources are slowly being built up in Brazil by universities, the private sector and government. Transfer between sectors is entirely feasible. An example might be the use of cryopreserved wild genetic resources for aquaculture trials by a university extension department, resulting in development of an improved brood-stock that could then be provided to farms throughout the country. Yet there are no formal national policies to control such transfers. The government of Brazil is clearly sensitive about genetic resources leaving the country, but how they are moved around within the country and between sectors seems not to be regulated.

Both of the technologies in this example – cryopreservation and DNA finger-printing – are rapidly expanding into new countries and organizations, and both are capable of quickly generating highly mobile collections of genetic resources or genetic resource information. DNA fingerprinting is especially powerful and, once the technology is in place, demands very little in the way of sample collection. A tiny clip of fin or even a single scale is enough to provide valuable genetic information about the population being studied, and that information has value not only for management of stocks but also potentially for breeding. The proposed FINGER referred to earlier would provide a 'home' for such information, and by its very creation stimulate the development of policies on its sharing.

Access to indigenous collections

The ability to cryopreserve fish sperm in the field means that collections can be started by anyone. If an indigenous group is involved, the need for policy becomes acute. For example, several collections of salmon genetic material, including those of the Carrier-Sekani and Shuswap First Nations in Canada, are maintained independently of any government agency. Collectors notify the DFO of their intention and receive 'permission' to take sperm from salmon, but one need only consider the implications of the ongoing treaty process between First Nations and government to imagine a number of scenarios for which there is presently no policy framework whatsoever:

• Does a First Nation really need the permission from the government?
• If a company requests a sample of genetic material from a First Nation's gene bank, who adjudicates the request, and against what criteria?
• If the company wants to start its own collection in a First Nation's 'territory', to whom should they apply for permission?
• Once gametes are 'on the shelf', should they continue to be treated as though they are simply part of a fish that was freshly collected for research purposes?

Questions like this need to be confronted when developing policy. In the case described above, the only existing permitting mechanisms deal exclusively with living fish or their gametes, and are intended to prevent disease transmission or the transfer of fish from one watershed to another. Gene banking is not even contemplated.

Access to locally developed breeds

Small-scale fish farmers often invest years of selective breeding effort in developing broodstocks that thrive in local conditions. The original broodstock need not necessarily be an indigenous species. In Vietnam, for example, a farmed strain of the indigenous common carp may be an important reservoir of genetic diversity with characteristics that are important for poor families. This particular strain, grown in rice fields, is valuable because it does not leave terraced fields when they are periodically flooded. An 'improved' strain of carp, with better growth performance, is now being promoted for rice field culture, yet this new strain requires significant physical improvements in the pond environment. The biodiversity value of the existing strain is now being recognized, and represents a considerable investment on the part of farmers over many years (Edwards et al, 2000).

The situation is analogous to a farmer cultivating a crop variety that represents several generations of improvement. The result, in both cases, is genetic material with added value. In the plant world, the concept of farmers' rights arose to protect this investment of effort, but there is no similar concept for aquatic farming.

MANAGING AQUATIC GENETIC RESOURCES:
Filling the policy vacuum

In 1992, the CBD emphasized the need for effective national policies for the conservation and use of biodiversity and genetic resources. More than ten years later, a few developing countries have put new laws into place, but most countries have made little progress towards effective policies for aquatic genetic resources. Such policies are needed not only to ensure better management but also to pave the way for policies for access to aquatic genetic resources. The absence of clear or enforceable policies regarding fisheries management, aquaculture development and gene banking, for example, could complicate developing guidelines for evaluating access applications. Clear policies, supported by adequate information, can also facilitate the negotiation of access agreements by determining how the provisions of an agreement can promote conservation, as well as the usefulness of aquatic genetic resources to donor countries and communities.

Efforts to create aquatic versions of plant-related policies are doomed to failure. While legal regimes governing the conservation and use of different types of biodiversity may share some common characteristics, it is also important to develop policies that reflect the biological and social realities of the harvest of aquatic life. Because so few of these are known, aquatic genetic resource policy is generally conspicuous by its absence.

Conservation of aquatic genetic resources works at several levels, including sustaining individual fisheries and ecosystems that depend on diversity. In recent years the depletion of fish stocks has sparked an intense interest in fish genetic resource conservation (Harvey et al, 1998). Conservation mechanisms can include fishing quotas or prohibitions, habitat protection and restoration, gene banking, and promoting sustainable community fisheries. The primary emphasis to date has been on fishing limitations and habitat protection.

Yet the degradation of fish stocks and expansion of conservation programmes comes at a time when the aquaculture industry's need for wild genetic material is increasing rapidly. Moreover, the wild relatives of most farmed aquatic species greatly exceed, both in abundance and genetic diversity, the farmed populations (Bartley and Pullin, 1999), a situation that is the reverse of that for domestic animal diversity. Hence there is still a reservoir of wild genetic diversity for sustainable use. Unfortunately, there are few national or state policies for its conservation.

Development of policies governing fish gene banking is a good example of the complexity of the problem, as it must consider the technology not only as an insurance policy against extinctions but also as a source of genetic material for breeding programmes. These are two very different applications that are usually promoted by different stakeholders. Policy must also take into account how the technology can affect spread of disease among watersheds, facilitate introductions and transfers of stocks and species outside their natural ranges, and raise ownership and control issues that arise not only out of collection of genetic resources but also out of their potential use years or even decades later (Harvey, 1999).

The bottom line: Poor information equals poor policy

Policies for the conservation and sustainable use of aquatic genetic resources are still poorly developed in most countries. Those that exist have tended to be developed in reaction to crises, through closure of vanishing fisheries such as cod in Atlantic Canada. Until recently, policy making for fisheries and aquaculture has rarely considered genetic resources, concentrating instead on harvest levels of individual species and protection of fish health. Mismanagement of aquatic genetic resources has continued in spite of growing public awareness of environmental issues (Bartley and Pullin, 1999).

Several related factors contribute to the current policy vacuum. In addition to limitations on knowledge of aquatic compared to other types of biological resources, the inaccessibility of the aquatic realm and the difficulty of policing what cannot be seen act as deterrents. Lack of understanding of the genetic structure of fish populations has been an obvious impediment: if genetic diversity is not yet described, how can it be the subject of policy? And until recently, the myth that aquatic production is inexhaustible has prevailed, and fish have been viewed as common property available to all takers, within a wide range of access regimes. Policies on using aquatic genetic resources also have to take into account public concerns about the use of genetically modified organisms and environmental impacts of industrial aquaculture, and need to acknowledge uncertainty about the functioning of genes and genotypes in aquatic systems both in nature and on farms (Bartley and Pullin, 1999).

Barely scratching the surface: Limitations to scientific knowledge

Most aquatic genetic resources have yet to be characterized (Correa, 1999). Many are still undiscovered, while the genetic fine structure of those species that *are* known has only begun to be studied. Unlike terrestrial life, aquatic life inhabits a hidden and relatively inaccessible environment. Despite repeated calls for 'ecosystem-based management' of fisheries, knowledge of aquatic ecosystems is far less complete than that of terrestrial ones.

Although the majority of known species are terrestrial (May, 1988), some marine biologists have suggested that 80 per cent of all species that will eventually be discovered will be aquatic (Plotkin, 2000). For example, only about 45,000 out of a potential million freshwater species have been described (McAllister et al, 1997). The potential for new discoveries of aquatic organisms that can be farmed or extracted for useful chemicals is huge, and maximizing the potential for aquaculture development alone will depend on a much better understanding of wild fish stocks and their properties.

Identification of new marine species largely follows academic interests, although any interesting finds are likely to prompt at least a preliminary look from the pharmaceutical industry. Scientific research itself requires access to genetic resources quite apart from any later collection for 'economic' purposes, yet encouragement of research is vital to understanding the value and threats to aquatic genetic resources. Strategies for their use and conservation cannot be developed without this knowledge.

The FAO of the United Nations maintains fishery production statistics that represent one of the best data sets on aquatic resources and are relied upon for management decisions. However, such statistics are based on harvest and do not include a complete assessment of stocks (Bartley and Pullin, 1999).

Moreover, they are heavily compromised by the ability of individual nations to report them and hence give a very imperfect picture of the biodiversity of oceans and especially of inland waters.

Limitations of traditional knowledge

Traditional knowledge of plants contributes enormously to the development of improved crop strains in the agriculture industry and of drugs in the pharmaceutical industry. The knowledge held by traditional fishing communities can complement and help focus research activities and is an important asset in determining the properties of aquatic genetic resources. Familiarity with fish migration routes, spawning cycles and the habitat preferences of different species, for example, has been passed from generation to generation and today can contribute to efforts to identify desirable characteristics for breeding farmed stocks and conserving wild ones. Especially in southern countries, communities may also have knowledge of marine organisms and their toxic or medicinal properties that may be useful in the development of drugs and other products.

But plant and aquatic genetic resources differ greatly in both the nature and extent of traditional knowledge, a key point that affects the development of access policy and to which we will return at length in Chapter 4. Much of the knowledge that has proven most useful in the genetic modification of plants relates to domesticated crops and has been accumulated by farmers over hundreds or thousands of years. Some rural communities have a lengthy (but much shorter) history of pond aquaculture, primarily in developing countries, but no experience farming species currently favoured in industrial aquaculture. What traditional fishing communities can offer is extensive knowledge of aquatic ecosystems and their management. What they lack, as Chapter 4 will illustrate, is the type of knowledge of genetic resources that collectors are likely to need – an important deficiency that could well bar community efforts to negotiate benefits as long as countries specifically link benefit-sharing rights to traditional knowledge.

Research needs

Scientific understanding of aquatic species and ecosystems is a necessary foundation for conservation of aquatic genetic resources. Research on aquatic genetic resources is not only far less advanced than for plants but also faces additional complications associated with the complexity of aquatic ecosystem interactions and the relative inaccessibility of aquatic ecosystems. Within the last decade, the fisheries management literature has become dominated by calls for 'ecosystem-based management'; however, the same literature acknowledges that the scientific understanding of aquatic food chains is nowhere near where it needs to be for this change in management to occur. At present, the only true ecosystem-based management that can occur in fisheries is to set aside protected areas or no-take zones, a kind of ecosystem management by default.

Both developed and developing countries have paid relatively little attention to research and development of aquatic genetic resources. In the US, for example, only 1–2 per cent of the total federal investment on biotechnology has been devoted to marine biotechnology and aquaculture (Correa, 1999). In Canada, it is only in the last decade that governments have invested heavily to identify genetic differences between salmon populations, and it was not until 1999 that the federal government, which has management authority for salmon, formally declared conservation of genetic diversity an important management goal. In Africa, fish are fairly well known at the species level, but within species genetic diversity (the genetic resources of species) has hardly been studied. Even for African tilapias, the genetic resources of which have been studied to some extent, the information available on genetic resources covers less than 40 per cent of the about 70 species known (Abban, 1999) – and this is the aquatic animal whose culture is spreading fastest around the world. Developing countries need all the support they can get to strengthen their aquatic biodiversity information systems and scientific capacity.

Although the importance of research on aquatic genetic resources is now appreciated more than ever (as can be seen from the rapid increase in publications on fish genetic structure), spending cuts in many countries have taken a significant bite out of research. The result has been a shift towards corporate sponsored research, which tends to be focused on practical, profitable applications. Partnerships, for example, between a university and a corporation, can obviously bring their own problems if they mean that work is skewed towards industry needs. It may mean putting the cart before the horse because the cart carries the cash. Logically, basic science should precede and lead to applied science, but applied science is more likely to receive corporate funding. The relatively undeveloped state of research on aquatic genetic resources, combined with the urgent need for information, means that it is particularly susceptible to this bias.

Much of the basic research on genetic resources that has already been done in the plant world, before access requirements became an international issue, remains to be accomplished in the fish world. This research includes the all important characterization of genetic make-up at the subspecies (population or strain) level, where gains from selective breeding are likely to arise. We have already referred to the explosion in this kind of research, primarily using the tools of microsatellite

DNA analysis, for salmonid fishes. Microsatellite research requires the collection of tissue samples from individual fish (usually a small 'clipping' of fin) and while the procedure is non-invasive it results in the carrying away of genetic material. Until southern fisheries research laboratories acquire the technology for DNA fingerprinting, a process that is still in its early stages, genetic material will need to be taken from its country of origin for study. If scientific researchers are subject to the same access rules as corporate bioprospectors, DNA studies or indeed any kind of biodiversity research project may be subject to cumbersome and expensive access negotiations. These may further discourage research, especially given the limited ability of research institutions to provide compensation. Yet without the basic knowledge of aquatic biodiversity that research provides, governments will find it difficult to evaluate access applications objectively (Grajal, 1999).

It's a conundrum that will prove difficult to resolve. In the meantime, biologists and taxonomists in many national biodiversity research institutions are finding it increasingly difficult to collect genetic material even within their own countries, and to do their work in the field to generate basic scientific knowledge (Ruiz, 1998). The lag in aquatics-related knowledge means that access to aquatic genetic resources for basic research may be even more crucial than in plant research, and impediments are likely to delay advances in uses of aquatic genetics resources, especially in aquaculture.

Public concerns about genetic modification

One reason policy makers are sometimes reluctant to deal with genetic resources is that genetic modification is such a hot issue for the general public. Public concerns about ethical, environmental and health issues related to the use of aquatic genetic resources differ in nature and extent from those about use of plant genetic resources. Concerns about environmental impacts of industrial aquaculture include, for instance, the impact of fish farm escapees on the integrity of wild stocks, the possibility of spread of disease, and the impacts of farming on local ecosystems.

'Genetic modification' has only recently entered the public vocabulary, but it hasn't taken long to become controversial, and public and media concerns are frequently exacerbated by confusion about its meaning and implications. The media focus on polarized views has simply clouded the picture. Genetic modification of crops by companies such as Monsanto may receive more attention than work done on fish, in part because so many food products contain genetically modified ingredients (notably soy derivatives). However, concerns about uses of aquatic genetic resources are in some respects more intense because a higher form of life is involved. Many people even refuse to eat farmed fish. For these people, genetically modified 'super fish' are even less acceptable. Even the idea of a fish gene being implanted in a strawberry to improve frost resistance is abhorrent to some, even though the end result may be a berry identical in taste and appearance to any other.

In addition to worrying about the possible health risks of eating antibiotic-treated fish, and especially fish from genetically engineered varieties, some consumers may feel it's inappropriate to tamper with the genetic structure of living creatures. A representative of the US Food and Drug Administration, charged with evaluating Aqua Bounty's request for permission to market the genetically modified 'Super Salmon', noted that 'ethical concerns among the public over the appropriate use of animals are issues not evident with transgenic plants, and may affect public acceptance of transgenic animals as food sources' (Environmental News Network, 22 October 2001). While this may exaggerate the extent to which public perceptions of fish and plant products differ, the distinction does appear to influence marketing approvals and will most certainly affect policy. One has only to consider the spate of official government pronouncements that follow any announcement of advances in human cloning to appreciate the position of policy makers.

Efforts by concerned citizens (and policy makers) to make informed judgements on genetic modification issues are frequently confounded by misinformation. For example, the article quoted above also stated that 'genetically engineered salmon are designed to grow between 10 and 30 times faster than natural salmon' – a tenfold exaggeration of Aqua Bounty's description of the growth rate of the 'Super Salmon'. Distortion of information to support strong positions is a common failing of advocacy groups on both sides of genetic modification issues and simply magnifies public confusion.

In the same way that public interest in wildlife conservation focuses on the 'cute and cuddly', concerns about genetic modification of fish tend to target species like salmon that capture the public imagination either because they are prized for their taste or because they are romanticized for their appearance and dramatic life cycles. By comparison, the genetic modification of mundane species such as tilapia appears to generate little public attention, perhaps in part because the fish is rarely sold unprocessed in northern countries. If more people were aware they were eating tilapia in their fish burgers, this situation might change.

For all these reasons, informed public understanding of the role of aquatic genetic resources in sustainable development and food security, and of the complexities of environmental and health issues, is vital to sound policy development. In the plant world, the international collaboration referred to above has helped promote public awareness. For example, the International Plant Genetic Resources Institute (IPGRI) has tried to increase awareness of the benefits of agricultural biodiversity among policy makers in developing countries, using an approach that targets the media, NGOs and governmental officials (Raymond, 1999). Given the greater complexity of issues surrounding the use and conservation of aquatic genetic resources, there is a need to enhance both public and policy makers' understanding of these issues. In many respects, public understanding is as vital as scientific knowledge in creating conservation and use policies that are needed to support the development of access policies.

Box 2.2 The Value of Science

Policy makers, like any decision makers, want 'facts', They blend these facts with social and moral considerations and come up with what seems to be a fair compromise – a policy. In the case of aquatic genetic resource policies, both scientific and traditional knowledge are important. We have already seen that traditional knowledge has potential value when it can lead people to genetic resources, but how important is science?

First, what *is* science? Science is a tool for describing the natural world in unambiguous terms. Science works to reduce uncertainties, although it never eliminates them completely. Scientists are taught the scientific method, which involves asking answerable questions. The results of scientific enquiry are continually being refined and, along with traditional knowledge, provide two legs of the three-legged stool on which human societies sit (the third leg is moral and spiritual beliefs).

Science is important to policy making in several ways. Firstly, it is fundamental in unequivocally **describing** genetic variability. Taxonomy identifies genera and species; behavioural biology describes where they may be found; and genetics helps us draw the blueprints of their DNA. Science also tells us about the **status** of aquatic genetic resources through catch statistics, tagging studies and censuses. Thirdly, and perhaps most important, ecosystem studies tell us how each component of genetic variability **interacts** with every other level of the food chain – a very important insight that can help us predict the effects of removing that variability from the system.

Policy makers need all of the above kinds of scientific information. The status of genetic resources alone is enough to illustrate the importance of science – if people have no idea of how many members of a species or population actually exist, and their prospects for continuing to exist, how can they devise policies for sharing access? In another example, one of the most commonly heard calls following the signing of the CBD was for more taxonomy, because it is impossible to create policies on genetic resources that have not been described. The Global Taxonomy Initiative of the CBD was recently created in response to the 'taxonomic impediment' to the sound management of biodiversity, and is evidence that this call has been heeded.

What happens when policies on aquatic resources are made in the absence of adequate information? A good example is in the management of freshwater aquaculture in countries where invasive, exotic species are being promoted. In Brazil, for example, tilapia farming is promoted by the Ministry of Agriculture, while the management of wild fish stocks is more closely allied to the Ministry of Environment. If neither is aware of the degree of invasion of tilapias into natural waters – something that is measured by science – how can fair policies be created? If sterile tilapias are created – also a product of science – how does this development alter policy?

Another example is from temperate aquaculture, namely the farming of salmon. There is now widespread concern that escaped farmed salmon will breed with wild stocks and cause a fundamental change in their genetic make-up. To create fair policies on farming – which we have already seen involves the collection of genetic resources – people need to know the incidence and risks of this kind of hybridization and its probable outcomes. These answers can only be provided by scientific enquiry.

GLOBAL INITIATIVES FOR IMPROVED MANAGEMENT OF AQUATIC BIODIVERSITY

To judge by the number of international agreements related to the conservation and use of aquatic biodiversity, everyone's agreed that the situation is pretty desperate and it's time for concerted action. The problem with international agreements is that (a) they're not always binding on member countries, (b) countries whose participation is most crucial all too frequently opt out, and (c) at the national level, it may take a long time to grapple with domestic complications and conflicts when it comes to implementing high-minded principles. In the case of aquatic genetic resources, the problem is that many governments have been far too preoccupied with difficult plant genetic resources issues to pay much attention to fish.

International agreements related to aquatic biological diversity

While most international agreements on aquatic biodiversity focus on fishing, they frequently mention principles that have direct relevance to the management and sharing of aquatic genetic resources and can be a good starting point for policy development.

Some of these agreements will be useful simply for background reference to aquatic biodiversity issues. Examples of this kind of agreement include the United Nations General Assembly Resolution on large-scale pelagic drift net fishing, the United Nations Convention on the Law of the Sea (UNCLOS), the United Nations Agreement on Straddling Stocks and Highly Migratory Species and the Kyoto Declaration adopted at the Conference on the Sustainable Contribution of Fisheries to Food Security. The Ramsar Convention on Wetlands (1971) provides the framework for international cooperation on the use of wetlands and their resources – a vast designation that embraces virtually all inland waters including very large, periodically inundated areas that provide subsistence fishing for many local communities.

Other agreements are more directly relevant. The FAO Code of Conduct for Responsible Fisheries is a good example. This comprehensive document, with its accompanying Technical Guidelines, contains the principles of sustainable fisheries and is valid not only for nations but for communities as well. The code promotes the sustainable use of aquatic biodiversity and includes (in Article 7, Fisheries Management) sections on aquaculture and small-scale, subsistence and artisanal fisheries.

Another good example is the Jakarta Mandate on Marine and Coastal Biological Diversity, adopted by signatories of the CBD in 1995. The Jakarta Mandate not only raised the profile of aquatic biodiversity (a very important development for policies on access and benefit sharing), but also triggered a Plan of Work whose activities include local and indigenous communities. A similar process is currently under way within the CBD, namely the development of a Plan of Work on Inland Waters. Once this plan of work is created and implemented the

CBD will house not only the general principles on access and benefit sharing but also the specific actions on marine and freshwater biological diversity.

Finally, the Marine Stewardship Council (MSC), a global programme that promotes sustainable use of aquatic biodiversity through product certification ('eco labelling') illustrates a practical application of the principles of sustainable use of aquatic biodiversity. The MSC certifies individual fisheries using criteria contained in the FAO Code of Conduct described above. Active since the mid-1990s, the MSC originally concentrated on fisheries in developed countries. In response to criticism that the certification process actually worked against small-scale fisheries, the MSC recently began a programme of community certification and is actively building networks that include community fisheries. This development underlines the importance of local communities in fisheries management and, coming from a pragmatic programme like the MSC, should encourage policy makers interested in protecting the rights of those communities not simply to go fishing, but to have a say in access to aquatic genetic resources in their territory.

Aquatic biodiversity issues: The countries' views

Signatories to the CBD have agreed to develop National Biodiversity Strategies and Action Plans that describe the status and trends of biodiversity in their countries, important issues, and activities directed towards resolving problems. Not all countries have produced the strategies, and the quality is highly variable. Nevertheless, the National Biodiversity Strategy and Action Plans (NBSAPs) offer a unique window into the national perception of biodiversity issues.

World Fisheries Trust (WFT) recently examined the NBSAPs of 52 countries in terms of their coverage of aquatic biodiversity issues. The analysis was done as part of a report on fisheries and biodiversity that provided national biodiversity planners with a compendium of key issues and the materials they need to better incorporate fisheries issues in biodiversity planning (World Fisheries Trust, 2002a). Although WFT's study concentrated on nations with 'outstanding aquatic biological diversity', and included some of the major fishing nations as well as developing countries, the findings are instructive for policy makers interested in access and benefit-sharing issues and the roles of local and indigenous communities in conserving and using aquatic genetic resources.

If the content of National Reports to the CBD Secretariat is any indication of national priorities, then it must be said that the WFT study on NBSAPs did not uncover evidence of national concern over access to aquatic genetic resources. Articles 15 and 8j (access and traditional knowledge, respectively) are generally not explicitly represented, a situation that reflects the almost complete lack of national policies on aquatic genetic resources. National biodiversity planners are much more likely to worry about aquatic biodiversity in terms of assessment and monitoring or pollution reduction than from the standpoint of the sharing of genetic resources.

However, the importance of aquatic biodiversity for local communities is reinforced in other ways. Of 17 issues in aquatic biodiversity identified by WFT, two of the top three (in terms of frequency of citation by countries) were 'governance' and 'responsible fishing', each of which was cited by 70 per cent of the countries examined. Calls for better governance were near universal, and generally represent a desire to find new ways of including local communities in fisheries management. 'Alien species', 'native species' and 'aquaculture' were less frequently cited on their own, but together totalled 80 per cent of the countries – a clear indication that the raw material of aquatic genetic diversity is also a subject for concern among planners.

These observations reinforce the main point being made throughout the present book, namely that aquatic biodiversity is threatened, and local communities are demanding a greater choice in its management – but they also make it clear that, for most national policy makers, control over 'aquatic genetic diversity', is simply not being considered as something to which local communities have rights. There are exceptions – for example Burundi's attempt to involve local communities in preserving biodiversity, or Cameroon's difficulty in integrating indigenous land claims into biodiversity planning – but by and large the issues of equity and access are not perceived as important. This situation does not appear to reflect any geographic or political bias because it pertains to both developed and developing countries. It may not satisfy the Inuit people who are unwilling to allow genetic prospecting of their Arctic charr stocks (Case Study 3), but it is the political reality such communities must confront.

This reality may be explained by any of a number of factors, including a lack of appreciation of the positive role indigenous and local communities could play in the management of aquatic genetic diversity given the means to do so; a lack of willingness to delegate authority to 'lower levels' of government, and an absence of coordination among government agencies. However, assuming that a greater demand for access to aquatic genetic resources materializes in the future, developing effective access and benefit-sharing policies should be a vital part of each country's aquatic biodiversity strategy.

CASE STUDY 2. NO POLICY, NO ACCESS? A salmon farmer's frustrated efforts to collect genetically pure broodstock

A Vancouver Island fish farmer's efforts to collect salmon broodstock in Canada illustrate the need for policy makers to quickly develop policies governing the collection of aquatic genetic resources. As this case study illustrates, existing policies for fisheries management are simply not adequate to deal with such collections, and may result in evaluations of applications based on irrelevant criteria. Policy makers need also to ensure that access policies are broad enough to deal with a wide range of issues.

Five species of salmon – chinook, chum, sockeye, coho and steelhead – return from the ocean to spawn in the rivers of the Yukon Territory. For some chinook, the journey lasts four months and covers more than 3000 km from the Bering Sea to the creeks in the southern part of the territory where the fish originally hatched. Yukon chinook support commercial and sports fisheries as well as indigenous food fisheries. The fish is especially prized in Japanese markets for its high oil content.

As in the Northwest Territory and Nunavut, authority to issue germplasm or broodstock collection permits rests with the Canadian DFO. Like the Inuit, the Yukon First Nations (indigenous peoples) have negotiated a land claims agreement with the Canadian government. Under the terms of the agreement, the main instrument for salmon management is the Yukon Salmon Committee, which comprises both First Nation and non-First Nation members and makes recommendations to DFO on fisheries management and policy. Applications to collect broodstock are made through the Committee, and the Yukon DFO office issues a collection permit provided the Committee approves the application and DFO has no objections. The committee can refer applications to individual First Nations bands, but does not yet have clear protocols for doing so.[2]

Creative Salmon Ltd, an aquaculture business farming both chinook and Atlantic salmon in British Columbia, several hundred kilometres south of the Yukon Territory, decided in the late 1980s to improve its operations by culturing Yukon River chinook. Domesticating this strain would take several years and require annual collections of eggs and sperm from the wild. It would also be complicated in more southerly waters because of the strain's exacting requirements for day length and temperature.

Because chinook populations mingle in the Yukon River on the way to their separate spawning grounds, Creative Salmon applied to DFO to collect broodstock from smaller tributaries where individual populations would already be separated from the mixture in the river mouth and lower stages of the river. The company could thus determine later the source of desirable characteristics it hoped to amplify through breeding. It argued that the gene banking they planned to carry out could also act as an insurance policy against the risk of extinction (a use to which it is currently put by DFO for other salmonid stocks at risk in British Columbia), and offered to leave half of the collected semen in the Yukon for local conservation purposes. Creative Salmon concluded it would need 50 pairs of parent fish to establish a diverse gene pool (the usual number recommended for establishing a new broodstock), but would settle for five pairs.[3] The company began by collecting living adult fish and using their gametes (eggs and sperm) to produce fry.

DFO refused the request to collect from isolated populations in tributaries because it was concerned not only about setting a precedent for the collection of samples outside areas open for fisheries, but also about the possibility of subsequent collectors approaching First Nations bands for permission to collect gametes in areas with restricted fishing.[4] Instead, the department required Creative Salmon to purchase broodstock from licensed commercial fishers harvesting mixed populations, thereby eliminating the company's chances for genetically pure stock.

Having obtained permission to collect gametes, although not from distinct populations, Creative Salmon now faced the problem of arranging for incubation of the fertilized eggs it would produce. The company was forced to keep the eggs in the Yukon because quarantine regulations do not permit them to be moved until they are certified to be free of disease, a process which takes about three weeks, after which time the eggs would unfortunately be too fragile to move.

Creative Salmon thus made an arrangement to pay a local hatchery, operated by a private utility company, to care for the developing eggs – in effect to become a living gene bank.

In the late 1990s, Creative Salmon decided that wild Yukon chinook genetic material could now be incorporated in its breeding programmes by collecting sperm and cryopreserving it, then using the frozen sperm to continue genetic improvement of its resident broodstocks. The collection of eggs was therefore phased out and replaced by a cryopreservation programme that allows the company to continue its efforts to domesticate Yukon chinook. However, despite the company's having invested in the collection of sperm samples over several years, Yukon chinook are not yet being produced for commercial sale and Creative Salmon has recovered none of its development costs.

At present there appears to be considerable confusion at all levels (including government, fishing communities and First Nations) about the nature, role and implications of gene banking in conservation and in the improvement of farmed stocks. Some First Nations fishing communities have probably never heard of gene banking; at the other extreme, some First Nations such as the Shuswap in British Columbia have adopted short-term gene banking programmess, expressing frustration with the absence of government policy and action. Others, such as the Carrier-Sekani Tribal Council, have quietly pursued long-term gene banking programmes in the interest of conservation and with the cooperation of DFO. In the case of Yukon chinook, according to the chair of the Yukon Salmon Committee (a member of the Teslin First Nation), Creative Salmon's efforts could benefit Yukon First Nations involved in commercial fisheries by advertising the qualities of Yukon chinook. The Committee may consider referring future collection applications to band councils in territories where collections occur.[5]

In some respects, Canada faces greater challenges than other countries in developing access policies that address the question of indigenous communities' rights to prior informed consent and benefit sharing. The Canadian Constitution and the courts recognize the existence of indigenous rights in traditional territories, but the nature of these rights remains to be defined in a complex process of treaty negotiations (especially in British Columbia) that may take decades to complete. Some indigenous peoples, such as the Yukon First Nation, have already completed the negotiation of land claims that confer a combination of ownership and management rights. Other indigenous peoples aren't involved in the treaty process either because they have chosen to negotiate their rights through the courts or because they signed treaties before Canada became a nation.

In the case of completed land claims negotiations in areas such as the Yukon, Canada retains decision-making rights regarding the management of anadromous fish such as salmon that spend part of their life cycles in the ocean – outside traditional indigenous territories. Generally, land claims agreements do not specifically address the issue of consent to collection of aquatic genetic resources, and DFO policy doesn't require consent. The most interesting aspect of the present case study may in fact be that First Nations were not directly involved in the granting of permission to collect – not because they were being deliberately excluded from the process, but simply because the removal of genetic resources for the purpose of gene banking is not specifically addressed by any existing policy or legislation. But collection of adults in the mixed fishery, as Creative Salmon eventually ended up doing, is DFO's responsibility, so that agency ended up, de facto, ruling on a gene banking request that may have more to do with stocks that spawn in First Nations' traditional territory.

Canada, like many other countries, is still a long way from defining specific policies on access and benefit sharing. Indigenous peoples are already sensitive about collections of biological resources and research in their traditional territories. With a few exceptions, collection of aquatic genetic resources hasn't yet become a controversial issue the way it has for plant collections in developing countries, but it can be expected to attract greater attention as the demand increases. Governments involved in the implementation of the CBD need to anticipate such a trend and not lag in the development of appropriate policy.

Chapter 3

Whose to Share? Ownership and Control of Aquatic Resources

Farmed catfish, Brazil (Photo by Joachim Carolsfield)

Chapter 2 discussed the need for better policies for conservation and use of aquatic genetic resources. One of the biggest challenges to policy making is the question of ownership of and control over aquatic genetic resources. Who has the right to permit or deny access to genetic resources (whether salmon or seaweed or sponges) and under what circumstances? It's a complicated enough question in the world of plants and, as we shall see in this chapter, it's far more complicated when it comes to fish – and not just because fish have a penchant for migrating large distances. Unlike plant genetic resources, many of which already exist in collections, aquatic genetic resources are still mainly gathered from in situ sources – ie from their natural habitat in the wild.

During the past 20 years we've seen the international community replace the traditional notion of genetic resources as common property with recognition of national sovereignty over genetic resources. We've seen increasing tensions between North and South over the patenting of inventions using genetic resources. After concerted efforts by indigenous groups, we're seeing some countries beginning to recognize indigenous rights over lands and biological resources to a far greater extent than has happened in previous decades. More generally, we're seeing increasing support for the devolution of decision-making powers over resource use to communities, growing out of a recognition that the best hopes for sustainable development may lie in making use of local knowledge, skills and motivation.

Translating theory to fact is another matter. There is no shortage of international conventions recognizing community and indigenous rights over genetic resources and over their traditional knowledge of how to use them. As we shall see later, dozens of countries are currently in the process of working out how to meet their international commitments to expand community rights over genetic resources – and countless research institutions worry that their access to vital scientific and commercial information may be jeopardized if new regulations are too strict. Uncertainty about how to respond to concerns about 'research chill' is one reason why countries have been so slow to put access and benefit-sharing laws and policies into practice. A second reason is uncertainty about whether to include only genetic resources within the ambit of such laws or whether to require community consent for access to all biological resources regardless of how they'll be used.

The value of genetic resources depends as much on ideas as it does on control of the resources themselves. Genetic resources are merely the raw material for invention – useless without the knowhow to produce a new fish or plant strain or develop a drug. The commercial value of genetic resources has sparked an expansion in the law of intellectual property rights (IPRs) that has been every bit as controversial as the expansion of laws restricting access. Should inventors be allowed to patent life forms? If so, what constitutes invention? Should countries providing genetic resources have the right of free access to inventions derived from them? And how can provider countries make sure that intellectual property laws aren't used by collectors to bypass national access laws?

Many indigenous and local communities have equally strong concerns about control over access to genetic resources and the use of ideas, but with a different slant. With few exceptions, communities have little say in who gets to use aquatic life or how they may do so. Indigenous movements in particular have been pushing hard for greater recognition of ownership and control rights and have some backing from international human rights agreements to support their cause.

In recent years the obvious value of traditional knowledge to users of genetic resources has added fuel to the fire. Traditional medicinal uses of plants have inspired the development of many pharmaceutical products. Seed companies have benefited from the knowledge of generations of farmers in other parts of the world. Who owns traditional knowledge and who has the right to consent to its use?

OWNERSHIP OF AQUATIC GENETIC RESOURCES:
Agreements and claims

Unlike agricultural crops, aquatic life largely inhabits publicly owned territory. Authority to manage fish genetic resources (which are still almost universally thought of as 'fisheries') may be divided between different levels of government, as in Canada, where the federal government manages ocean resources as well as fish that migrate inland to spawn, while provincial governments are in charge of inland fish. In some cases, management authority may also be devolved to indigenous groups such as the Nunavut people of northern Canada, whose land agreement with the federal government gives them the right to control access to biological and genetic resources. Depending on national constitutions, laws and administrative practices, there may be a chain of management authority that includes national governments, state/provincial governments, local governments, unorganized indigenous and local communities, and local cooperatives such as those that hold exclusive fishing rights in the Philippines.

The concept of fish being caught for food is straightforward enough, but when fish take on the grander identity of 'aquatic genetic resources', everything changes. Under that guise, they're being used as broodstock for aquaculture operations, or perhaps their DNA is being transplanted into a different species. In those circumstances, it might be said, a fish is no longer a fish but a collection of 'genetic material' – or, as the CBD puts it, 'material … containing functional units of heredity' (eg sperm, eggs or DNA). When fish are used as aquatic genetic resources, ownership takes on a whole different level of importance – both because that fish may be worth much more as a genetic resource than as a barbecued fillet and because the knowledge of how to use the fish as a genetic resource has its own separate worth – more on this later in the chapter. The bottom line is that the multiplicity of fisheries management regimes in different countries can't do the job of determining who has the right to collect – or permit the collection of – an aquatic genetic resource. It doesn't help matters that it may not always be easy to tell whether a fish is being used simply as a fish (eg a cardinal tetra for display in an aquarium) or as a genetic resource (a tetra for breeding), as our earlier discussion of the ornamental fish trade in the Rio Negro (Case Study 1) made clear.

For most of the 20th century, aquatic genetic resources were considered common property, available for everyone's use regardless of the location of the resource or the nationality of the user. Two international agreements in the early 1990s radically changed the rules for ownership and control of aquatic life. These were the UNCLOS and the CBD.

Ocean resources: The Law of the Sea

The Law of the Sea came into force in 1994 and has been signed by more than 130 countries. An international agreement that sets conditions and limits on the use the oceans, including the seabed, UNCLOS establishes the rights and obligations of coastal states in contiguous waters, sets conditions for the conduct of marine research, and obliges countries to provide access to surplus catch.

Sovereignty

UNCLOS both defines and limits coastal countries' sovereignty over the seas and their biodiversity. Coastal states can claim full sovereignty over their territorial sea to a maximum of 12 nautical miles (22.2 km) (Article 3). Beyond the territorial sea, UNCLOS creates a 200 mile Exclusive Economic Zone (EEZ) in which coastal countries can claim exclusive rights for exploration, exploitation, conservation, and management of all natural resources (living or non-living) on the seabed and in its subsoil, and overlying waters (Article 56). Some countries have not yet ratified UNCLOS, and many have not yet claimed their EEZ. Beyond the EEZs are the high seas, to which all countries have open access rights. The CBD, in Article 22, confirms the rights and obligations established under UNCLOS and requires all parties to implement the convention consistently with those rights and obligations.

Research

UNCLOS grants each coastal state the exclusive right to regulate, authorize, and conduct scientific research in its territorial sea (Article 245). However, each state is required to consent, in normal circumstances, to scientific research projects in EEZs or on the continental shelf (which includes the territorial sea) by other states or international organizations 'to increase scientific knowledge of the marine environment for the benefit of all humankind' (Article 246). In turn, foreign researchers must provide information on their research activities, accept the participation of the coastal state research programmes, and allow the coastal state access to all data and samples derived from the marine scientific research project (Article 249). These provisions, designed to facilitate access and benefit sharing at the national level, apply to waters adjacent to coastal communities, as the territorial sea begins at the low water line.

Surplus catch

Each state must determine its capacity to harvest living resources within its EEZ. If it is unable to meet the allowable catch it has established, it must provide other states access to the surplus (Article 62). While this provision is clearly intended to apply to food fisheries, it could theoretically apply as well to other life such as seabed invertebrates.

Inland waters: National sovereignty

Biological diversity flourishes most richly in tropical regions while the countries with the technology to make the most advanced use of genetic resources are generally the northern, most developed countries. Consequently, the benefits from the commercial use of genetic resources have largely been enjoyed by companies in the North. Yet, following the new found global concern about disappearing biodiversity, the responsibility for conservation inevitably falls on the poorer southern countries. The rush for genetic resources by transnational corporations has been unfavorably compared to Europe's colonization of southern countries, two centuries earlier, to gain access to the raw materials needed for the Industrial Revolution (eg Shiva, 1997).

During the negotiations leading to the CBD, some southern countries insisted on recognition of national sovereignty over genetic resources as a condition of agreeing to the CBD. In theory, recognition of national sovereignty meant the ability to control access and negotiate a fair share of the benefits arising from the use of genetic resources.

The CBD is the most comprehensive international instrument for the management of biodiversity. Its three objectives are the conservation of biological diversity, the sustainable use of its components, and the fair and equitable sharing of the benefits arising out of the utilization of genetic resources. The extent of global commitment to the CBD is reflected by the fact that, by June 2004, it had been ratified by 188 countries – almost all of the nation states in the world (with the notable exception of the US). While the Convention doesn't have the force of law, ratification signifies a commitment to enact national laws to bring its provisions into effect.

In addition to recognizing national sovereignty, the CBD creates rights and responsibilities for member countries regarding access to genetic resources. It calls on all Parties to 'create conditions to facilitate access to genetic resources for environmentally sound uses' by other Parties. It requires provider countries' informed consent to access to genetic resources and calls on collecting parties to share with provider countries 'in a fair and equitable way' the results of research and development and the benefits arising from commercial and other uses.

Recognition of national sovereignty under the CBD means that aquatic genetic resources in the wild are owned by the country in which they are located. National sovereignty over public lands extends as well to inland waters (with rare exceptions, such as in some Scandinavian countries) and to the aquatic life they contain. Although the CBD recognizes sovereign rights over genetic resources, it must be borne in mind that tenure and ownership systems are neither uniform across all countries nor clearly defined in any given country. Ownership rights may range from traditional common tenure to state enforced private rights to land and natural resources, including biodiversity (Columbia University, 1999). The fact that aquatic genetic resources are more likely than plant genetic resources to be publicly owned has significant implications for the management of access. One of these is that the resources commonly exist within the territories of traditional communities that may have rights to control their use.

The implications of national sovereignty for conservation and aquaculture

National sovereignty over genetic resources is clearly a done deal, but whether it will advance the cause of conservation is debatable. Certainly that wasn't the motivation of the developing countries that insisted on recognition of national sovereignty in return for signing the CBD. They were more concerned with having a substantial say in the burgeoning international trade in genetic resources – not that they could be faulted for resentment over past exploitation by northern countries and corporations. Nevertheless, for the CBD's conservation objective to succeed, both developing and developed countries will need to come to the realization that it's in their own best interests to prevent the further erosion of genetic diversity.

It was not without good reason that the FAO International Undertaking formally adopted the concept of genetic resources as the common heritage of humankind. The reasoning of that agreement was that the principle of free exchange was essential for the most beneficial exploration and use of genetic diversity for plant breeding and other scientific purposes. As Jain (1994) points out, as the world's population continues to grow rapidly, it will become increasingly important to identify new genetic variability for higher crop yields. This will require a great deal of international cooperation in research, including the ready exchange of plant genetic resources and new technologies.

If that's true for plant genetic resources, it will also be so for aquatic genetic resources during the next two decades. Developing countries went from consuming 45 per cent of the world's fish to 70 per cent today. It is expected that by 2020 that figure will increase to close to 80 per cent (IFPRI, 2003). Given the declines in wild fish populations, it appears likely that capture fisheries will be unable to meet the demand and that the gap will need to be filled by a growth in farmed production. Existing aquaculture operations have barely tapped the possibilities offered by genetic diversity among food fish species.

As discussed in the previous chapter, the efficiency with which the aquaculture industry is able to meet global food needs will depend to a large degree on effective international cooperation in sharing genetic material and knowledge. As national access laws are still in the formative stages and are being written with an almost exclusive focus on plants, it's too early to say how big an impact national sovereignty (and, for that matter, emerging community rights of consent) will have on international sharing of fish genetic resources. It would be both ironic and unfortunate if the door to best quality fish genetic resources was to be shut at a time when aquaculture is poised to overcome its environmental shortcomings and begin to make a major contribution to global food security.

Ownership in traditional communities

National systems for ownership of genetic resources are often very much at odds with traditional community practices. Most traditional communities in developing countries have continued to apply their own tenure system for biological resources, while the state enforces private and public property rights on goods and resources, and intellectual property laws on industry and commerce. Some traditional tenure systems regarding genetic resources are grounded on collective ownership or heritage, and sometimes, particularly in the case of medicinal plants, on religious and mystical considerations (Khalil, 1995).

In many cases where governments have asserted sovereign rights over genetic resources, the land remains under traditional community tenure. The end result is that the state reaps the benefits from agreements for the use of resources, while the burden of conservation might be said to rest with the communities. The danger is that, once communities have lost control over local resources as well as the ability to practise traditional livelihoods, they may lose as well both the knowledge and the motivation to take care of local ecosystems. The choice between doing whatever it takes to feed one's children and conserving an endangered fish population is no choice at all.

Although the CBD's provisions apply to agreements at the national level, they also take into account the role of traditional communities in conserving and using biodiversity. Article 8(j) requires Parties to the CBD to 'respect, preserve and maintain knowledge, innovations and practices of indigenous and local communities embodying traditional lifestyles relevant to the conservation and sustainable use of biological diversity' and to encourage the equitable sharing of benefits arising from the use of such knowledge, innovations and practices. Article 8(j) confers no rights to communities but is based on the premise that sharing in benefits from the use of genetic resources will help contribute to their conservation and sustainable use.

How to implement Article 8(j) has been one of the greatest challenges for CBD Parties. Discussions at the Conferences of the Parties have generally assumed (a) that the use of genetic resources generally depends on traditional knowledge and (b) that those using genetic resources are usually based in countries other than the provider country. As we'll explain in the following chapter, the first, critical point is far less true for aquatic than for plant genetic resources. Indigenous peoples, local communities and their advocates have high hopes that Article 8(j) will mean greater recognition of community rights over traditional resources, but this may not be the result for fishing communities if these rights are tied to an intimate knowledge of genetic resources.

Recognition of indigenous peoples' rights

In the traditional cultures of indigenous peoples in widely separated parts of the world, the concept of 'ownership' has little meaning. First Nations participants at a workshop we hosted during the preparation of this book emphasized that they consider it inappropriate to refer to fish as 'resources' – genetic or otherwise. Indigenous peoples' attitudes about equality or 'oneness' of all living creatures, while they may be an essential part of spiritual beliefs, are likely to be rooted in a common sense recognition that surviving in a natural ecosystem requires maintaining the cycles of species, and that ownership is superfluous where there is abundance to be shared.

But times change. Today, claims of ownership make a frequent appearance in the rhetoric of the indigenous rights movement – but mainly as matter of political necessity in campaigns to win legal recognition of the right to use lands and biodiversity in traditional areas of occupation. 'Ownership' and 'title' are words well understood by courts that may have more difficulty relating spiritual beliefs to Western property law.

Ownership of land and control over aquatic life has become a contentious issue in coastal and riparian indigenous communities because of the broad extent of and fragility of fish habitat, the traditional importance of fish for sustenance, and frequent uncertainty about rights of access to fisheries. Recent attention to fish as genetic resources has added a new twist that isn't an issue for plant genetic resources: in the case of migratory fish, several indigenous communities may claim traditional ownership and the right to be consulted by a collector regardless of where broodstock is collected if a fish passes through their territory at some stage in its life cycle.

Most countries have made little progress towards resolving indigenous rights issues. This will undoubtedly impede efforts to facilitate access to genetic resources in indigenous communities. One notable exception is the Philippines, which under the 1997 Indigenous Peoples Rights Act extends a prior informed consent requirement to virtually all potential uses of natural resources in recognized indigenous territories. Another is Canada, where court decisions recognizing indigenous rights have led government negotiations of treaties with some indigenous peoples. Case Study 3 at the end of this chapter, although it describes an unsuccessful negotiation with indigenous communities for access to broodstock, illustrates one useful model for access negotiations with communities with co-management or ownership rights.

Although there is no unanimity among indigenous groups about the approach proposed by the CBD – some have turned their backs on the Convention, while others are actively working with national governments to develop workable access laws – there is naturally widespread scepticism about how Article 8(j) will be interpreted to ensure fair treatment and meaningful benefits for communities.

In 1993, the Draft United Nations Declaration on the Rights of Indigenous Peoples confirmed their right to 'own, develop, control and use the land and territories, including the total environment of the lands, air, waters, coastal seas, sea ice, flora and fauna and other resources which they have traditionally owned or

Box 3.1 Plant Precedents on Sharing Genetic Resources: The International Treaty on Plant Genetic Resources for Food and Agriculture

The CBD's recognition of national sovereignty over genetic resources represented an about-face from another international agreement more than a decade earlier. In 1981, member countries of the UN FAO adopted the International Undertaking on Plant Genetic Resources as an instrument to promote international harmony in matters regarding access to plant genetic resources for food and agriculture. The purpose of the Undertaking, to be monitored by the Commission on Genetic Resources for Food and Agriculture (CGFRA), was to 'ensure that plant genetic resources of economic and/or social interest, particularly for agriculture, will be explored, preserved, evaluated and made available for plant breeding and scientific purposes' (CGFRA, 2002).

The International Undertaking's recognition of genetic resources as the 'common heritage of mankind' was in large part a response to a demand from developing nations to keep plant genetic resources in the public domain and to put a brake on further privatization of agricultural genetic resources. Their concerns included gene banking in northern countries of seeds produced by southern farmers; the accumulation of seed companies under the control of transnational corporations; and the implementation of monopoly Plant Breeders' Rights (essentially a patent) over crop varieties, limiting farmers' access to breeders' lines and finished varieties.

Conflict over access to plant breeders' lines in the years following the approval of the International Undertaking led to a 1989 annex recognizing farmers' rights as a counter-balance to plant breeders' rights. Among other things, farmers' rights established the rights of farmers and their communities to participate fully in the benefits derived from plant genetic resources. By the early 1990s, as the privatization of agricultural research and patenting of plant genetic resources in industrial countries increased, developing countries were expressing disillusionment about the effectiveness of the International Undertaking and promises to implement farmers' rights. Consequently they proposed replacing the concepts of common heritage and open access with national sovereignty and benefit sharing to allow nation states to better control and benefit from their biological resources (GRAIN, 2000a). The enshrinement of these principles in the CBD necessitated a renegotiation of the International Undertaking to ensure harmony between the two agreements.

The result was the International Treaty on Plant Genetic Resources for Food and Agriculture, approved by FAO member countries in 2001 after seven years of difficult negotiation. The treaty is intended to meet the needs of both plant breeders and farmers, guarantee the future availability of plant genetic resources for food and agriculture, and ensure fair and equitable sharing of benefits. The agreement, which covers 64 food crops accounting for 85 per cent of global human nutrition, places some constraints on intellectual property over the seeds in the multilateral system and imposes obligations for benefit sharing when accessed seeds are commercialized. Civil society organizations such as Genetic Resources Action International (GRAIN) and the Erosion, Technology and Concentration Group (ETC), while acknowledging the treaty as a step forward, also criticize it for not guaranteeing farmers' rights and doing too little to ensure equity and benefit sharing.

The history of the International Undertaking illustrates the increasing tension between developed and developing countries over the expansion of intellectual property rights and the demands of developing countries and farming communities for greater control over their genetic resources and the use of traditional knowledge developed by farmers. It also underscores the almost exclusive emphasis on plant genetic resources in international negotiations on access and benefit sharing. The International Undertaking and the treaty that succeeded it were made necessary by the interdependence among countries for access to crop germplasm needed to ensure global food security.

> **Box 3.1** continued
>
> While there is currently no parallel interdependence in access to fish germplasm, the expanding importance of aquaculture in meeting global food needs may ultimately create the need to address similar issues to those that have dominated the negotiations towards the revised International Undertaking – most notably the compatibility between intellectual property rights protection and the protection of communities providing aquatic genetic resources for international aquaculture development.

otherwise occupied or used'. In 2001, the International Indigenous Forum on Biodiversity (IIFB, 2001) told the CBD Working Group on Access and Benefit Sharing that the 1993 UN Declaration represented the minimum acceptable standards and that the trust needed to meet the CBD objective of access, and that benefit sharing wouldn't come without recognition of the rights of indigenous peoples. How far to go in that direction remains a challenge for countries intent on facilitating access to genetic resources. Some indigenous groups see the CBD encouragement of benefit sharing with communities as a way to avoid tackling the hard issues that come with recognition of indigenous rights, especially if benefit sharing is limited only to those communities that can prove genetic resources users need their knowledge – and if benefits are solely tied to conservation objectives. The growing litany of 'biopiracy' complaints suggests that countries may find it increasingly hard to separate access issues from indigenous rights issues.

THE PRICE OF INVENTION: Intellectual property law and aquatic genetic resources

Patent applications have caused no end of controversy in the use of plant genetic resources. Naturally, a seed company that develops a genetically modified strain of millet resistant to a fungal infection, for example, considers it a top priority to protect its invention so that competitors don't copy it and flood the market with a cheaper version. But what if the company came up with the idea by modelling its invention on another strain developed by farmers in a traditional agricultural community? The last few years have seen a succession of international disputes – a notable example being the outcry that arose when a US company attempted to patent Basmati rice despite its long history in south Asia. What if a pharmaceutical company succeeds in developing and patenting a pain-killing drug after hiring a researcher to visit shamans in the Amazon, learn about their healing practices, and bring back samples of their medicinal plants for analysis in the US?

Obviously, the ownership of ideas (whether scientific inventions or traditional knowledge) has been the source of far more wealth than the ownership of genetic resources in their physical state. The global trade in plant genetic resources is big business, estimated by ten Kate and Laird (1999) to be several billion dollars annually, so it's hardly surprising that the scramble to get legal protection for products and processes has had some significant impacts on developments in intellectual property law – developments that have been almost entirely shaped by plant genetic resources issues.

As we mentioned in the previous chapter, the number of genetically modified fish strains developed in the past couple of decades is infinitesimal compared to the number of plant strains. Pharmaceutical companies are struggling to find powerful cures based on marine organisms, but the vast majority of drugs inspired by compounds existing in nature are based on plants – by 1996, only two of the top selling 150 pharmaceuticals were derived from marine organisms (Brush and Stabinsky, 1996). Nevertheless, there may be sufficient parallels between some uses of plant and aquatic genetic resources – for example, between plant and marine bioprospecting and between farmed fish and crop enhancement – that patent law agreements can safely accommodate both types of activity.

Where the intellectual property comparisons between the two fields diverge most dramatically is in the area of traditional knowledge. There is simply no parallel in traditional fishing villages to traditional farmers' knowledge of crop breeding and to other communities' knowledge of medicinal plants. This might seem a matter of no great note were it not for the fact that several emerging national biodiversity laws, based loosely on the CBD guidelines, spell out the rights of traditional communities in terms of the knowledge they contribute to the use of aquatic genetic resources. There is no doubt that traditional fishing communities have a wealth of knowledge that comes from the importance of fish as food or ceremonial object – including knowledge of fish life cycles, migration habits, habitat preferences and of techniques for catching fish – yet it is likely to be largely irrelevant to uses for breeding. As we'll show in this and the following chapters, a too rigid interpretation of laws tying community rights to traditional knowledge could mean significant future conflicts (as the trade in aquatic genetic resources becomes more common) and run counter to the CBD's objectives of promoting conservation, sustainable use and equitable sharing of benefits.

Pandora's patent box: Fighting for the right to own genes and genetic inventions

By protecting the ideas of inventors from unauthorized use by others, intellectual property law (including patents, copyright, trademarks, industrial designs and trade secrets) protects an inventor's economic interests and the interest of society in encouraging new inventions that may benefit the public. A patent is a legal certificate that gives an inventor exclusive rights to produce, use, sell or import an invention for a fixed period, usually 17 to 20 years. A patent application must demonstrate that an invention is useful (have industrial application), novel (recent, original and not already publicly known), not obvious to a person skilled in the technology and more inventive than mere discovery of what already exists in nature. Patents can be granted for products, specific uses of products (eg use of a drug to cure cancer but not for purposes yet to be discovered), and processes used to create a product.

The law of patents was developed in 19th-century Europe to protect inventions of factory machinery and excluded the protection of living materials, foods and medicines. However, demands for protection of inventions related to commercial uses of genetic resources have revolutionized patent criteria, and the state of the law remains in flux in the wake of new scientific advances and amid controversies about the patenting of life and the role of traditional knowledge in invention. In the 1960s, the US legislated the right of plant breeders to patent seeds, preventing others from selling the same variety, and in 1980 the US Supreme Court accepted the first patent on a genetically altered micro-organism. By 1997, the US had granted 69 patents on animals (Correa, 1999).

Keeping track of the current state of the law is further complicated by the fact that different countries take different approaches to patent law. The European Patent Convention provides that microbiological processes are patentable but 'essentially biological processes' are not, thereby excluding plant varieties obtained by conventional breeding. No such restriction exists in the US (Crucible Group, 1994). Decisions by the US Patent and Trademark Office to grant monopoly rights over plant, animal and human genetic materials have sparked a rush to collect, map and patent genes, based largely on their potential. Developing countries have been under pressure to recognize US patents, although many developing countries exclude patent protection for plant varieties and animal races (Correa, 1999). Both the scope of protection and the rights of patent holders continue to be expanded as the law continues to evolve in industrial countries. By contrast, developing countries such as Argentina, Brazil and India have set limits by allowing patents on processes but not products and by requiring patent holders to make socially useful products available in the domestic market (Grenier, 1998).

Genetic modification of animal life (the 'Harvard mouse' is a controversial example) has drawn attention to the need to address demands to allow patents on living creatures. Pharmaceutical companies and bioprospectors collecting on their behalf have been actively patenting processes to develop drugs and cosmetics derived from research based on aquatic genetic resources that range from marine invertebrates to algae. Patenting of new fish varieties (such as the Super Salmon and Arctic char varieties) and of processes used in their development has been more limited but can be expected to increase significantly as the aquaculture industry expands. The US Patent and Trademark Office led the way by approving a patent protecting a method of increasing the growth rate of a transgenic salmon (Correa, 1999).

The adaptation of patent laws to cover genetic resources is still controversial. A cotton gin is a very different type of invention from a cotton (or catfish) gene. Patenting of living materials not only raises ethical questions, it also frequently raises concerns about the novelty of 'inventions', especially when an inventor may have relied for inspiration on traditional knowledge. Historically, while technology exporting countries have been quick to develop patent legislation to promote new development, technology importers have had little reason to develop their own patent laws. Developing countries have been understandably reluctant to embrace universal patent laws relating to uses of genetic resources (as TRIPS proposes) because applicants from industrialized countries are the primary beneficiaries (GRAIN, 1998a). As Halewood (1999) notes, the net effect of globalization of intellectual property laws through agreements such as TRIPS and the North American Free Trade Agreement has been primarily to benefit developed countries in the use of genetic resources.

Plant breeders have pushed for an extension of intellectual property rights to include new varieties produced by breeders. There are no equivalent mechanisms for aquatic genetic resources, but these are likely to develop, albeit with modifications that reflect the fact that few aquatic animals have been domesticated (Bartley and Pullin, 1999).

TRIPS: Controlling access to genetic inventions

All countries that are members of the World Trade Organization (WTO) are obliged to implement TRIPS. The agreement focuses on the importance of intellectual property rights in promoting trade liberalization. The emphasis on intellectual property in WTO agreements is a response to the explosive growth in information technology and biotechnology in international trade as well as the desire of some industrial countries to protect products from intellectual 'piracy' in foreign markets (Crucible Group, 2000).

TRIPS requires all member states to set minimum standards of intellectual property protection, thereby ensuring a far higher degree of global uniformity than previously existed. Patents must be available for inventions in all fields of technology without discrimination, whether products are imported or locally produced. Article 27 requires member states to adopt national level intellectual property systems for all products and processes, including pharmaceuticals, modified micro-organisms and microbiological processes. Unlike the earlier international undertaking, TRIPS clearly applies to inventions derived from aquatic genetic resources.

Negotiations on the passage of TRIPS highlighted the very different viewpoints of industrial and developing countries on the extent to which patenting of biological diversity-related inventions should be permitted. The most controversial section of TRIPS has been Article 27.3(b). While it allows countries to exclude plants and animals as well as essentially biological processes from patentability, WTO members must provide protection for plant varieties either by patents and/or by an effective *sui generis* system – that is, a unique system of rights for a specific item or technology. The exemption for plants and animals remains a controversial issue, with some developed countries facing strong pressure from industry to push for the removal of the exemption. Some critics of TRIPS argue that doing so would undermine the CBD by depriving countries of the right to prohibit IPRs on life forms and by diminishing their ability to negotiate a fair share of benefits arising from the use of genetic resources (GRAIN, 1998a). During a 1999 review of TRIPS, a group of least-developed countries proposed, unsuccessfully, that TRIPS should contain a provision that patents must not be granted without the prior informed consent of the country where the genetic resources originated (Martinez, 2002). In 1998, an Organization of African Unity (OAU) model law proposed a prohibition against patents on inventions derived from biological resources obtained from member countries.

In essence, developing countries were pressured into accepting TRIPS in return for the promise of the economic advantage created by improved opportunities for trade. Some developing countries objected to the imposition of Western notions of 'inventions' in parts of the world where many important innovations had occurred in an evolutionary and informal manner in farming and other local communities. While TRIPS has helped allay industrial countries' concerns about foreign piracy of corporate inventions, it has simply fuelled concerns in developing countries that Westernized patenting law may simply accelerate biopiracy of the types of traditional innovations described in Chapter 4.

Indigenous groups have condemned TRIPS as flying in the face of indigenous traditions of treating community knowledge as a shared resource and as essentially forcing indigenous peoples to adopt Western patent laws in order to prevent the commercial appropriation of their own knowledge. In the opinion of one group, TRIPS pushes indigenous peoples to 'play in a game in which the rules are defined by the opponents' (Tauli-Corpuz, 1999).

WHO OWNS TRADITIONAL KNOWLEDGE?

What happens if, without a community's permission, a company patents a product or process made possible by the use of the community's traditional knowledge? While it is true that many indigenous communities have a history of freely sharing their knowledge about wild plants and animals, they may have concerns about the unauthorized use of their knowledge that have nothing to do with compensation but a lot to do with issues such as a lack of respect for a living creature or deceitful dealings with a community, etc. Patent offices rarely require applicants to disclose whether an idea has been appropriated from a traditional community. Even if a traditional community wanted to seek recourse, using the avenues of Western legal systems might be both contrary to its beliefs and unaffordable (Box 4.2 below illustrates a notable exception, in which an indigenous group felt so betrayed that it took the patent holder to court).

Interest in access to traditional knowledge about plant genetic resources has grown by leaps and bounds as the gene rush seeks out new sources of potentially valuable information – like the gold rushes of earlier centuries, making a valuable find may be a long shot, but the potential rewards may be so high that it's worth the effort and the risk. That's why the question of who owns traditional knowledge and how communities can control its use has become such a big issue in recent years, as illustrated in the section below on biopiracy. It's also why international agreements like the CBD have placed so much emphasis on using the demand for traditional knowledge as a rationale for the expansion of community rights. As we'll see in the next chapter, while this may be a sensible approach in the plant world, it may have little relevance for aquatic genetic resources.

Box 3.2 The Wapishana Go to Court: The Case of the Fish Killing Plant

The Wapishana are experiencing what many other indigenous groups and local societies are suffering with alarming frequency throughout the tropics: the appropriation of traditional knowledge by pirates passing for scientists, researchers, missionaries, environmentalists, activists of indigenous people's rights, and other disguises.

JULIO CESAR CENTENO (CENTENO, 2000)

Several Wapishana indigenous communities living in the Amazon basin along the Brazil-Guyana border have long used their knowledge of the toxic properties of the cunani bush to catch fish. When the chewed leaves are thrown into a river, fish in the immediate vicinity reportedly leap out of the water and soon die. The fish can be eaten immediately, with no alteration in their taste and no side effects on humans.

A British biochemist who had spent years living with the Wapishana and studying their traditional uses of plants heard about the unusual properties of the cunani. After he left the country, he undertook extensive research to isolate active ingredients of some of the plants he had collected. He then registered patents in the US and Europe on active ingredients in cunani that are believed to act as powerful stimulants to the nervous system or as neuro-muscular agents that can prevent heart blockages. He also patented active ingredients of tipir, the nut of the greenheart tree, which the Wapishana had long used to stop bleeding and prevent infection and is being investigated for anti-malarial properties.

When Wapishana chiefs heard what the biochemist had done, they accused him of stealing the knowledge of their ancestors and elders in order to sell it to pharmaceutical companies. As one Wapishana woman put it, 'This knowledge has always been with the Wapishana. It's part of our heritage and now is being taken from us without any payment'.

The biochemist expressed puzzlement at the uproar. He pointed out that his discoveries were the result of a lifetime spent decoding the ingredients in traditional Wapishana remedies. The patents were justified, he argued, by the results of his own intellectual effort (Singh, 2000a; Veash, 2000). After an extensive campaign, the Wapishana people eventually succeeded in overturning the cunani patent but not the tipir patent. In addition, at least one chief prohibited all future visits by researchers, whatever their purpose might be.

Drawbacks of IPRs protection of traditional knowledge

The TRIPS agreement sparked considerable protest among advocates of indigenous and local communities who believed that it would erode the already fragile rights of communities to control the use of their knowledge. One of the biggest issues has been whether a product derived from traditional knowledge can truly be called an invention – one of the prerequisites for the right to patent. After the TRIPS agreement, the World Intellectual Property Organization (WIPO) attempted to address the issue through its Intergovernmental Committee on Intellectual Property and Genetic Resources. The Committee looked at ways to take traditional knowledge systems into account in the development of IPRs systems through *sui generis* approaches – that is, unique mechanisms for providing legal protection for holders of traditional knowledge.

Some indigenous movements have been sharply critical of the WIPO approach, arguing that *sui generis* protection of traditional knowledge rights is nothing more than an attempt to assimilate indigenous rights into 'Western' property systems and bypass the real issue – the rights of indigenous peoples to direct control over lands and resources in traditional territories.

Opinions are divided about the usefulness of IPRs in protecting community interests. Some people believe that IPRs as they currently exist can serve the purpose by allowing users of genetic resources to generate revenues from their inventions and share the revenues with countries of origin or local communities. Others believe that existing IPRs are not only inadequate to protect the rights of indigenous peoples but also represent one of the greatest threats to the conservation of biodiversity (Crucible Group, 2000). Indigenous and local peoples generally express a desire to link the protection of indigenous and local knowledge with territorial rights and the right to self-determination – a position that has been reiterated in a wide variety of international and local peoples' declarations and in statements in international multilateral fora (Halewood, 1999).

Theoretically, IPRs could be used to protect the knowledge and innovations of indigenous and local communities. However, differences in Western and indigenous legal concepts make it impractical. Communal property is the prevailing system used in most traditional societies to control access to basic resources, and even in cases where esoteric knowledge is the exclusive intellectual property of individuals, families, shamans, clans or lineages, these owners cannot necessarily commercialize the knowledge without the permission of the whole community or tribal elders (Posey and Dutfield, 1996).

The use of patent law as it currently exists is also problematical because of the difficulty of defining the source of traditional knowledge, accumulated over generations, and therefore its novelty. Use of customary laws is another option, but many nations do not recognize customary law and national legal systems may conflict with unwritten customary laws. Finally, indigenous peoples view any use of intellectual property law with deep suspicion because of its association with past exploitation of traditional knowledge. Shiva (1997) characterizes intellectual property law as a modern form of colonization extended to the interior spaces, the 'genetic codes' of life forms, made possible by the treatment of genetic resources as a common heritage – a view that resonates with many indigenous rights groups.

Sui generis protection of community rights

The inadequacy of patent law as a means of protecting traditional knowledge has led some community rights advocates to propose the use of *sui generis* alternatives to achieve the same end. '*Sui generis*' refers to rights that are designed to be unique for a specific purpose and are not covered by existing legal systems. The TRIPS agreement requires WTO member countries to protect plant varieties either by patents or an effective *sui generis* system, but does not define what that means. The term has become common jargon without any universal understanding of its definition, perhaps in large part because *sui generis* systems are largely still in the formative stages. Canadian land claims agreements with indigenous peoples, referred to in Case Studies 2 and 3, are one recent example of *sui generis* recognition; recent laws in countries like the Philippines that are specific deal to the protection of community rights are another.

One proposed model for *sui generis* protection is a system of community intellectual property rights that would establish the legal right of communities to protect knowledge developed communally rather than by an identifiable individual – primarily to protect farmers' rights to control access to seed. The Crucible Group (1994) suggested that, in order to be effective, community intellectual property rights need to be entrenched in national legislation with reciprocal recognition by other countries, supported by an international database for tracing germplasm. Under such a system, plant varieties developed by communities might be deposited in germplasm banks along with registration data (such as the date, place and community of origin), enabling the source to be determined if complaints arose about appropriation of traditional knowledge by outside interests.

While there are no analogous issues in the use of fish germplasm, a community IPRs system could conceivably be useful for the protection of other types of traditional knowledge of aquatic genetic resources – for example, by providing for the documentation of knowledge of medicinal uses. One model community intellectual rights act, suggested by a Third World Network discussion paper, proposed meeting the patent law novelty requirement by describing indigenous peoples as innovators because they have developed knowledge unknown to the outside world (Singh Nijar, 1998). Posey and Dutfield (1996) suggest that such a law would be compatible with the TRIPS call for *sui generis* IPRs protection and with Article 8(j) requirements. As discussed in the following chapter, this type of legal protection has far more relevance for terrestrial than for fishing communities because examples of traditional innovations using aquatic genetic resources are far less frequent.

Posey and Dutfield (1996) propose a more expansive system of 'traditional resource rights' that moves beyond the narrow limitations of knowledge protection. In their view, existing international agreements (eg on human rights, right to self-determination, land and territorial rights, and intellectual and cultural property rights) provide the basis for overlapping and mutually supportive 'bundles of rights' that would encompass not only IPRs protection but also the control of resources, which indigenous peoples view as central to self-determination. Posey points out that while the privatization or commoditizing of property is often contradictory to indigenous peoples' spiritual beliefs, indigenous and traditional communities are increasingly involved in market economies, and that the right to development and conservation are mutually supportive. Traditional resource rights would also recognize the inextricable link between cultural and biological diversity. Posey suggests that they could be implemented locally, nationally or internationally and could guide both international law and national legislation.

BIOPIRACY: Plain dealing or patent theft?

The urgency of addressing the question of community rights over genetic resources has been heightened in recent years by a flurry of complaints about biopiracy. The Crucible Group (2000) defines 'biopiracy' as the taking of genetic or biological resources without the prior informed consent of local people or a competent state authority for access and benefit sharing under mutually agreed terms.

Most frequently, charges of biopiracy are related to the use of plant genetic resources and often are spurred by patents of discoveries that are in some way related to the use of traditional knowledge of farmers or of indigenous communities. One much publicized example was the attempt by a US company to patent Basmati rice. Another was the dispute between the pharmaceutical company researcher and the Wapishana people, described in Box 3.2.

Had there been an access and benefit-sharing law in place, the Wapishana might have negotiated an agreement with the biochemist to share in the profits from any future royalties or obtain some other more immediate reward, or they might simply have denied him permission to make collections or refused to give him any information about their traditional uses. They might also have demanded benefits that he felt unable to provide without knowing whether his research might lead to a deal with a pharmaceutical company or the development of a marketable product. Article 8(j) of the CBD is intended to deal with exactly this type of situation. Situations like the one involving the Wapishana have occurred many times in different parts of the world, as traditional communities attempt to earn recognition for the value of their plant knowledge, and examples of benefit-sharing agreements are beginning to occur with more and more frequency.

Biopiracy and aquatic genetic resources

It's hard to imagine aquatic resources parallels for the biopiracy examples described above. One might have occurred if Aqua Bounty had developed and patented the 'Super Salmon' after learning from indigenous people about the anti-freeze properties of the ocean pout, which were used to create the new strain. Even then, the company might have argued that the desirable characteristics of the pout were obvious to any observer. Traditional knowledge of aquatic biodiversity may be abundant but is not necessarily relevant to uses of aquatic genetic resources such as aquaculture and the development of pharmaceutical products from animals that live in areas that are inaccessible to local people.

Nevertheless, complaints about biopiracy of marine organisms are not uncommon. Indeed, one of the main catalysts for the passage of access legislation in the Philippines in 1995 (see Case Study 5) was a series of newspaper articles on biopiracy of marine invertebrates (and of plants) by foreign collectors. After the law came into effect, the complaints continued, and communities began targeting the government for not properly enforcing the law and for its lax requirements for obtaining community consent.

When the US-based pharmaceutical company Neurex Inc isolated and patented the toxin SNX-111, produced by the Philippine sea snail *Conus magnus*, civil society organizations took both the company and government to task. The stakes were large: sales of the pain-killing drug derived from the toxin reportedly earned Neurex more than US$80 million during the first year of marketing. Critics charged that the government supported biopiracy by funding research by scientists at the Marine Science Institute (MSI) who collaborated with the University of

Utah in collecting specimens, isolating the toxin and forming a private company to capitalize on the snail (Bengwayan, 2001).

Previously, collectors for the MSI would purchase specimens from fishermen in several areas of the country, who gather different varieties of cone snail for their ornamental value and have no use for the meat.[1] Philippines law (Executive Order 247) now requires foreign collectors to partner with Philippines research institutions, which must get community consent for collections (whether or not traditional knowledge is needed by collectors). To comply with regulations under the law, MSI holds public information sessions in communities where collections of marine organisms are proposed and must also obtain permission from local government representatives. Critics of the process note low turnouts at information sessions and suggest that local people may not even be aware that marine bioprospecting is taking place in their communities (Batungbacal, 2000).

Making informed consent requirements both fair and feasible is a tough challenge. If the consent process is too cumbersome and expensive, collectors may simply go to other, more 'friendly' countries if the organisms they're looking for can be obtained elsewhere. For both countries and communities, it's a question of how to develop effective regulations without killing the goose that might lay a golden egg.

The Philippines law distinguishes between collections for academic and commercial purposes. Getting a fair share of whatever profits may arise from research by foreign collectors continues to be an issue for countries that have not yet passed laws regulating access. In the Bahamas, University of California researchers obtained a permit for the collection of soft coral, without charge and with only the condition that they file reports on their work. The university subsequently obtained a patent on a production process that was in turn sold to a company that marketed it to the cosmetic company Estée Lauder, which used it in the development of beauty products. The Bahamian government unsuccessfully attempted to negotiate royalty payments from the extracting company, which responded that it might simply move its collection activities to more accommodating Caribbean countries where the same species is abundant. The Bahamian government is now in the process of developing legislation to govern access to genetic resources.

University of California researchers have also been criticized for patenting the anti-inflammatory agent pseudopterosin, a compound found in sea whips in the Caribbean and subsequently incorporated in a skin cream also marketed by Estée Lauder. The average annual royalty income received by the university for patented pseudopterosins is reported to be more than US$750,000 (Singh, 2000b).

While bioprospecting for marine invertebrates gets most of the attention, biopiracy concerns sometimes extend to fish as well. The Amazon region has been hard hit by illegal trade in wildlife, and the Brazilian government attempts to be vigilant in stemming its flow. However, given the size and remoteness of the region, enforcement of environmental law is a stupendous task. In another example of suspected aquatic biopiracy, a German aquarist who planned to breed ornamental cichlid varieties (cichlids include important food fish such as tilapias and tiny ornamentals prized for their bright colours) travelled to Brazil to collect

Box 3.3 Biopiracy Debates in Brazil

The chief prosecutor for the Brazilian State of Amazonas, who opened an inquiry into biopiracy in 1997, estimates that about 20,000 individual plant samples are illegally removed from the country every year. Scientific laboratories generally receive the samples and information from third parties who don't say where they came from.

How is the information obtained? A representative from IBAMA notes: 'The scientists congregate in small frontier towns. Then they ask the Indians what they would do if they had a headache, muscle pains or a bad stomach. The local people then take them into the jungle and show them which plant they would use to cure those symptoms. The scientists pay the Indians a little money, then take the plant back to their labs. There, they discover the principle by which the plant works and sell their preliminary research on to the pharmaceutical companies for development'.

Robert Smeraldi, director of the Friends of the Earth Amazon programme, notes: 'There is widespread smuggling of genetic material by unauthorized companies. I'm not talking about respectable pharmaceutical companies being directly involved, but I do believe they could benefit from illegal research'.

A Brazilian cancer specialist was sharply criticized by the media after receiving close to US$1 million from the American National Cancer Institute to analyse a number of Amazonian plants. His critics argued that if information taken from indigenous peoples is used to develop the world's first anti-cancer drug, the Indian tribes might lose out even if the cancer specialist himself does not profit. In his defence, the researcher noted: 'While we continue to talk and worry about biopiracy, fewer people are out there actually studying the Amazon, which is a serious form of scientific neglect. Of course biopiracy happens, but we have to balance this against not researching the rainforest at all. Ultimately that is much more damaging to mankind' (Veash, 2000). We will return later to the subject of 'research chill', particularly in Case Study 5.

wild specimens in the middle Rio Negro. When apprehended by a representative of IBAMA, the Brazilian Institute responsible for enforcement of protected species laws, the collector was examining the viscera of cichlids to determine their natural diet. He had apparently obtained written permission from the nearest municipality but had not sought the necessary approvals from IBAMA. He was deported and ordered not to return.[2]

The money that changes hands in the collection of ornamental fish can stymie the most determined efforts at enforcement, especially in areas like the Amazon – the largest and perhaps most ungovernable river basin in the world. Rohter (2001) reports that zebra fish from the Xingu River are so valuable that specimens are used as local currency and that dealers' profit margins are comparable to those in the cocaine trade, with a particularly rare specimen bringing as much as US$600 from a Japanese collector. Although Brazil has attempted to control sales to prevent rare species from being wiped out, black market dealers continue to thrive. Rohter quotes a regional IBAMA representative as stating that, with only five agents to monitor all wildlife in an area twice the size of New Jersey, little can be done to protect illegal traffic. A tropical fish expert at the Emilio Goeldi Museum in Belem notes that tropical fish dealers routinely file false customs declarations and shipping waybills to get around restrictions, yet that there is little public interest in the problem (Rohter, 2001).

Stopping unauthorized collection of aquatic genetic resources is a challenge at the best of times. Access laws are unlikely to work unless government has the political will and provides the necessary funds for enforcement. This support may be absent in both developed and developing countries depending on the degree of cooperation among different levels of bureaucracy and of coordination among policy structures. Bribery of officials may create an additional impediment in countries where it is a common tradition.

Opposing views on biopiracy

Even when the approval of national agencies and indigenous communities is received, charges of biopiracy may still arise. Indigenous communities may grant permission for collections to occur without understanding (or in some cases being adequately informed of) the true purpose of the collection, as in the case of the Wapishana and the cunani plant. Collectors may take unfair advantage of communities that lack the capacity or the necessary information to negotiate fair deals. Even if the purpose of collection is fully understood, agreements may be perceived to be grossly unfair. Indigenous people may receive a pittance for the right to collect or may be offered royalties that never come to pass or are minuscule in relation to profits. A 1998 estimate placed annual global sales of pharmaceuticals at US$300 billion, of which between 25 and 50 per cent are derived from genetic resources (ten Kate and Laird, 1999). With almost 70 per cent of the total number of ethnolinguistic groups in the world living in 225 regions of the highest biological importance (WWF, 2000), it may be assumed that indigenous communities have been and will continue to be primary sources of the genetic resources needed for pharmaceutical development.

As the Wapishana example illustrates, biopiracy applies both to physical resources and the knowledge that makes their value immediately evident to collectors. Communities face challenges on both fronts: protecting their knowledge against misuse or appropriation under foreign intellectual property laws; and protecting resources over which they may have no legal authority. Very often, in the eyes of communities, the greatest perpetrators of biopiracy are not foreign interests but levels of government in their own countries that exercise authority over 'public' resources nationwide and deny indigenous and other communities a say in who collects plants, fish and animals in community territories. In several countries, struggles for the right to self-determination are fuelled in large part by frustration over lack of access to traditional resources and exploitation by outside interests who have no obligation to seek community consent once having received the consent of governments. Corporations may face accusations of biopiracy even when they have conscientiously complied with all government regulations or have negotiated with communities in what they believe to be good faith. So may collectors from scientific institutions who depend on access to genetic resources for basic research, and whose findings are freely published.

Accusations of biopiracy may relate to activities ranging from the collection of individual animals (eg rare Brazilian ornamental fish) to the entire system of collection of biological and genetic resources – what Shiva (1997) describes as the sequel to colonization of countries, in which 'colonies have now been extended to the interior spaces, the 'genetic codes' of life forms from microbes and plants and animals, including humans'. As Dutfield (n.d.) points out, noting that exploitation of genetic resources has even been called 'the slavery of the new millennium', such rhetoric may in fact undermine legitimate efforts to gain fairer treatment for countries and communities that seek a more level playing field. While the term 'biopiracy' may sound inflammatory to some, the issue raises legitimate questions about fair play for countries and communities that provide aquatic genetic resources.

CASE STUDY 3. AN INDIGENOUS COMMUNITY SAYS NO: Negotiating access to charr broodstock in northern Canada

Countries take many approaches to the recognition of indigenous rights of ownership and control over aquatic genetic resources. Canada has been actively involved in the negotiation of treaties with indigenous peoples. The Inuit, a people along the Arctic coast, recently completed an agreement that recognizes both land and resource rights. The Canadian DFO retains a role in the management of seagoing fish, but communities have the right to prior informed consent to collection of fish broodstock.

Arctic charr, the northernmost species in the family Salmonidae, has long been a staple in the diet of Inuit peoples on the coast of the Arctic Ocean in Canada. While some charr inhabit landlocked lakes, most are anadromous, migrating in late summer from the ocean to rivers and lakes to spawn, and reaching a weight of up to 11.3 kg. During recent years the popularity of the fish in urban markets has increased, creating an additional source of income for Inuit fishers in northern Canada. But charr are slow growing, and the genetically unique subpopulations or stocks of charr are extremely sensitive to overfishing. Consequently, Inuit communities developing sustainable management plans have had to grapple with how best to conserve a diminishing resource while supporting local fishing economies (eg Holman Hunters and Trappers et al, 1994).

The Northwest Territories Scientists' Act requires consent of local communities before any scientific research is undertaken in the Territory. Enacted in 1974, the Act was one of the earliest examples in a developed country of legislation that reflects emerging international principles for respecting indigenous knowledge and returning benefits to knowledge holders and their communities (Mann, 1997). In 1993, Canadian Inuit concluded negotiations of a land claim agreement with the government of Canada. The Nunavut Land Claims Agreement established principles of Inuit priority in the harvesting of marine resources and of ownership over the resources in Inuit-owned land and marine areas.

Soon after the 1993 land agreement came into effect, Canada's DFO began refusing fish harvesting, research and farming permits in the Nunavut region unless the prior consent of local communities had been obtained. Icy Waters, the major charr farming company in the Arctic, proposed a joint venture with Inuit communities and an Ontario university research group to set up a new company, Suvaaq Inc., to improve the company's existing broodstock that were based on previous DFO collections. Under the proposal, each of seven participating Inuit communities would receive a 5 per cent equity stake in the new company in exchange for sperm from six male Arctic charr from two separate stocks found in waters near the communities. Icy Waters suggested that Inuit communities would also benefit through education and practical experience in fish farming and access to genetically improved stocks as these were developed. The business proposal provided that each community would own its original fish contribution but that hybrid lines resulting from cross breeding would be owned by Suvaaq (Mann, 1997). The proposed project would result in Icy Waters gaining access to a total of 14 genetically distinct charr stocks through local communities.

Final approval of the proposed project required consent from the communities (through local Hunters and Trappers Associations), DFO and the Nunavut Wildlife Management Board (Mann, 1997). The latter body, established under the land claims agreement to oversee the protection and wise use of wildlife and wildlife habitat for the benefit of the Inuit and other residents, advises the governments of Nunavut and Canada, which maintain decision-making authority. The nine-member board includes four Inuit representatives and four from the Canadian and Nunavut governments.

Several difficult issues emerged during negotiations on the proposal. Local fishermen worried that the sale of genetically improved farmed fish would have a negative effect on markets and prices for wild caught fish (Nunavut Wildlife Management Board, 1998). Icy Waters attempted to allay this fear by suggesting that successful farming could benefit local fisheries by reducing commercial harvesting pressure on wild stocks, ensuring a valuable sport fishery, and increasing consumer awareness of charr.[3] Ownership issues added a further complication. These included not only concerns about Suvaaq ownership of successive generations of charr hybrids but also the possibility that the university research group might try to obtain a process patent based on genetic mapping of charr (Mann, 1997). Mapping would accompany the collection of genetic resources and was necessary in order to ascertain whether the genetic differences between the collected populations were significant. Finally, some Inuit expressed concern that the project showed a lack of respect for charr and that the spirit of the charr might take revenge on the Inuit people if the project went ahead, a not unusual sentiment among native people who may accept technologies as a necessary evil yet still feel uncomfortable with the spiritual implications of altering nature.

Ultimately, communities withheld their consent and the Wildlife Management Board turned down the proposal. Icy Waters was later able to obtain broodstock from two charr stocks from one community that had consented to their collection prior to the land claims agreement, and the company still pays royalties to that community. These broodstock were subsequently cross-bred with the company's base stock.[4]

Icy Waters described the failed negotiations as expensive and time-consuming, complicated by the difficulty of dealing with several different levels of authority, the need to negotiate with several communities over a vast land area, a high level of confusion about the implications of fish farming, and a long history of local suspicion of southern interests.

Some of the issues that characterized the Icy Waters negotiations – such as the patenting of products and processes – surface frequently in negotiations of agreements for access to genetic resources. However, the Icy Waters example also illustrates that collectors of aquatic genetic resources may face extra complications that are unlikely to occur in negotiations for access to plant genetic resources. For example, the need for genetic diversity of broodstock may necessitate negotiations with several communities over a wide area (because genetic differences, at least in salmonids, usually reflect geographic separation), and in different government jurisdictions, adding to the cost and complexity of negotiations. Indigenous communities may also hold spiritual beliefs that create significant concerns about the movement of fish from their natural habitat – in addition to potential environmental concerns about introduction of fish into areas where they are not indigenous. Suspicion or confusion about possible effects of fish farming on local fishing economies is common, and will also hamper negotiations. And because government policies for fish conservation and use are still at the stage where the genetic fine structure of fish populations is poorly represented (and, in fairness, usually not even known), the ground-rules are often less clear than in the plant world. The Icy Waters case is typical in that genetic mapping of the collected stocks would have taken place as they were collected. In other words, the genetic distinctness of the resources in question was not even known.

What chiefly distinguishes the communities involved in the Icy Waters negotiations from many others in the world is that they have substantial degree of control over the of use their genetic resources and the clearly recognized authority to withhold consent.

Most indigenous and local communities around the world (and in Canada, for that matter) have no such authority. This is one among many factors complicating the efforts of countries to develop access laws and policies that acknowledge in a meaningful way the importance of involving local and indigenous communities in decisions regarding applications for access.

Chapter 4

Thinking Locally: Rights of Indigenous and Local Communities

Sorting ornamental fish after the night's catch, Rio Negro, Brazil (Photo by David Greer)

TRADITIONAL COMMUNITY PRACTICES AND BIODIVERSITY CONSERVATION

The CBD came into being because the countries at the 1992 United Nations Conference on Environment and Development (UNCED) acknowledged the need to conserve global biodiversity for the well-being of humanity. The convention notes the importance of helping indigenous and local communities maintain traditional knowledge and practices relevant to conservation, and recognizes the need to encourage the equitable sharing of benefits derived from the use of community knowledge and innovations.

Acknowledging the rights of communities to control access to genetic resources and receive meaningful benefits is not simply a question of fair treatment or political pragmatism. The simple fact is that rural and indigenous communities also have the motivation and the knowledge to make conservation happen – provided they have the authority to watch out for the health of local ecosystems and the wherewithal to make a sustainable living from them. And therein lies the problem.

Studies in Latin America, Africa, and the Asia-Pacific region have noted that global biodiversity is most highly concentrated in areas inhabited by long-term communities, many of which have developed stable and sustainable resource management systems (Posey, 1993). The same areas also contain a high concentration of poor communities. Economic desperation is a powerful disincentive to conservation where the choice is between protecting nature and feeding the family. This is nowhere more true than in fishing communities, which figure prominently in any list of the poorest communities in the world (FAO, 1998). Eating or bartering the last sea turtle egg is still preferable to starving, no matter how many conservation NGOs would like you to stop.

There are dangers to romanticizing the historical relationship of rural and indigenous communities with their natural environment, and to oversimplifying changes to that relationship. Nevertheless, it remains true that many indigenous and local communities hold a rich store of knowledge about the management of biodiversity and how to sustain the ecosystems that support it. Communities that have been devastated by the loss of autonomy and by subsequent poverty may still maintain practices that make an important contribution to biodiversity conservation. It is important also to remember that community conservation approaches, methods and priorities in conservation may be very different from those promoted by national agencies. This does not mean that traditional community conservation practices are less effective, but may simply reflect the fact that local custom derives from a different knowledge base and is less subject to influence from complex and competing political agendas.

Box 4.1 Managing Fisheries Abundance: Traditions of the Nuu-chah-nulth in British Columbia

The Nuu-chah-nulth peoples of Canada's west coast once enjoyed a stable and prosperous economy based on an intricate knowledge, developed over thousands of years, of the natural cycles of marine life. In February, families moved into the inlets for the herring spawn. Spring was the best time for halibut fishing and seal hunting and brought the migrations of humpback and gray whales, which the Nuu-chah-nulth hunted by canoe. In midsummer, the focus turned to salmon returning to spawn in the rivers and streams of Clayoquot Sound – first the sockeye, and later chinook and chum. Throughout the year, regardless of what other foods were available, shellfish were always abundant.

The Nuu-chah-nulth passed their knowledge of marine species from one generation to another through an elaborate system of songs, dances, masks and medicinal arts that were protected as inherited family rights. Equally important in ensuring the careful management of resources was the system of property rights. An extended family lived in a house under the leadership of a chief who acted as custodian of salmon streams and other resources. Rather than concentrating wealth, the structure of rights was designed to ensure the sharing of resources throughout the community. The position of chief was considered to be more a responsibility than a privilege. This was reflected in the potlatch ceremony, in which elaborate gift giving demonstrated the wealth and prestige of a chief, but more importantly, encouraged the continuing distribution of wealth throughout the community.

By the late 19th century, the Canadian government had banned the potlatch, removed Nuu-chah-nulth children to residential schools to encourage their assimilation into Canadian society, and confined the Nuu-chah-nulth people to small 'reserves', limiting their access to the fisheries that had sustained their economy for many thousands of years. Today the Nuu-chah-nulth, like many other west coast indigenous peoples, are involved in lengthy land claims negotiations with the provincial and federal governments. These negotiations will help define the nature and extent of aboriginal rights already recognized by the courts and in the Canadian Constitution (Ecotrust Canada, 1997). In the meantime, indigenous communities remain, by and large, the poorest in Canada.

Traditional practices are far more prevalent in some communities, especially in developing countries, than in others. In common with many other indigenous peoples that depend on fisheries, the Nuu-chah-nulth in recent years have formed management partnerships with other fisheries stakeholders to take advantage of many of the scientific tools of fisheries management, including sophisticated research techniques such as DNA fingerprinting and gene banking of salmon stocks. Hatcheries, which run counter to some indigenous beliefs, are nevertheless a tool used by several First Nations in the Nuu-chah-nulth Tribal Council; even salmon farming, controversial throughout the west coast of Canada, has been accepted by some groups within the council. Obviously indigenous communities cannot simply return to a simpler time when respect for nature happened to coincide with abundance, and there is not always unanimity on how to respect traditional beliefs and practices while living in modern times.

The poverty barrier in fishing communities

The poverty of many traditional communities is rooted in the loss of ownership or control over traditional lands, especially in developing countries. In many cases, land held in common by villagers or indigenous peoples has throughout history been taken over by governments or lost to colonial powers, local elites or military juntas. Often the result has been the loss of traditionally sustainable livelihoods and a resulting dependence on outside economies. This in turn has often led to the break-up of traditional communities or the erosion of traditional cultures as rural people migrate to cities or struggle to maintain economic and cultural stability against the pressure of dominant cultures and in the face of depletion of or lack of access to traditional resources. The pattern recurs time and again.

In the Philippines, a 1992 survey by the National Statistics Office found that 95.3 per cent of 718,267 fishing families in the country were in the low-income group (Herrin and Racelis, 1992). The widespread degradation of freshwater, marine and coastal resources, a low level of education, lack of skills for participating in alternative livelihoods, and lack of political empowerment all contribute to the poverty of fishing communities. Any attempt to address poverty must address all of these issues.

In some cases, poverty may have origins in the loss of traditional lands; in others it may be a result of overfishing by roaming industrial fishing fleets that depopulate local stocks in any number of communities. Often landlessness and overfishing are linked in a vicious cycle. In Bangladesh, many rural fishing communities have lost their lands to conversion for agricultural purposes by 'patron classes'. This loss of land has led to a greater reliance on fish for food, and the resulting overfishing has depleted fish stocks in rivers, lakes and ponds, and damaged aquatic ecosystems. Increasing landlessness and poverty have also resulted in the incidental loss of traditional pond aquaculture, as poorer farmers can no longer afford to grow the larger carp species that form the mainstay of the aquaculture network (Lewis et al, 1996).

From one perspective, the recurring pattern of poverty and landlessness of fishing communities may simply be a cold historical reality – the way of the world. Obviously issues of poverty, domination and exploitation have neither easy explanations nor easy solutions. The impact of trade liberalization on poverty has been the subject of intense debate in recent years. Although proponents of trade liberalization argue that rural communities will benefit through the trickle down effect of lower prices, others (eg Madeley, 2000) are equally adamant that liberalizing trade rules has reduced food security and exacerbated poverty in developing countries in addition to loosening environmental protection regulations. They argue that rather than moving the world towards sustainable development, trade liberalization has in fact hampered it, and that the real solution lies in revitalizing communities.

On 23 September 2000, *The Economist* argued in an editorial that trade liberalization can only benefit the poor by advancing the sharing of technology and encouraging higher incomes. It concluded that reversing the trends of globalization would be 'an unparalleled catastrophe for the planet's most desperate people, and something that could be achieved ... only by trampling down individual liberty on a daunting scale'. The real question here is whether individual liberty or the liberty of communities to control their own environment and economic opportunities is more likely to alleviate poverty. Community advocates who criticize the impact of globalization are quick to point out that the roots of poverty often lie in the loss of control over resources and the loss of sustainable livelihoods as a result of dependence on a market economy and legal system that elevates individual rights over what is good for the community. As Berlin (1997) notes, people are being asked to replace the idea of the common with the concept of individual well-being, rather than simply giving one more emphasis than the other, with the result that individual citizens feel estranged from their community to the detriment of both.

Providing indigenous and local communities with the means and incentive for effective biodiversity conservation cannot be achieved unless the poverty cycle is broken. Sharing benefits from the use of aquatic genetic resources can be a useful tool for improving the economic and social well-being of communities provided that benefits are carefully designed to address the root causes of poverty rather than the symptoms. Benefits that achieve this objective may be non-monetary – for example, programmes to promote alternative fisheries livelihoods that are sustainable and strengthen the social fabric of a community. A community that has the right to informed consent to the collection of aquatic genetic resources must also have the right to decide what type of benefits it wishes to negotiate, but governments designing benefit-sharing frameworks should take the initiative to plan for a broad range that takes into account the relationship between poverty and threats to conservation.

The sustainable development debate makes it clear that the role of traditional communities must be reconsidered for the sake of future economic and social security. Increasing their ability and incentives to ensure conservation of aquatic genetic resources will ultimately depend on innovative solutions that depart from past practices, including:

- Restoration or enhancement of rights of access and ownership where possible.
- Meaningful participation in aquatic genetic resource management decisions and policy development.
- Appropriate mechanisms for maintaining and protecting traditional knowledge of genetic resources.
- Policies on informed consent for access to aquatic genetic resources and equitable benefits.
- Capacity to develop sustainable fisheries livelihoods.

Women's participation in community fisheries

Women dominate key subsectors in fisheries (Townsend, 1998). Although the participation of women in community fisheries may be less visible than that of the men who bring in the catch, it is usually significant, whether it involves net mending, processing, marketing or catching fish. In the freshwater ornamental industry, for example, women may play an active role in the collection of fish. A study in Malawi found that about 30 per cent of fish processors along Lake Malawi are women and 21 per cent of fish farmers in the country are women (Brummett, 1994). In Bangladesh, notes White (1992), the participation of women in marketing has consistently been underestimated; women's mobility has restricted their participation in the marketplace but has not necessarily constrained their activities in less visible market transactions, where they may play an entrepreneurial role. In poor rural households in countries like the Philippines, women in fishing villages may undertake multiple fishing-related activities in addition to household management (Illo and Polo, 1990).

Some critics of globalization suggest that trade liberalization has accentuated gender inequality in developing countries and has generally had a negative impact on the lives of women involved in food production in developing country communities. Madeley (2000) notes that in most African countries, women produce 60 to 75 per cent of food and have been disproportionately affected by the drying up of credit and the surge of food imports resulting from trade liberalization. Migration of male workers in some countries has generally increased the workload of women carrying both domestic and economic responsibilities. Vandana Shiva (2000) comments that, under economic globalization, women who produce for their families and communities are treated as 'non-productive' and 'economically' inactive. In her view, the devaluation of women's work, and of work done in sustainable economies, is the natural outcome of a system constructed by a capitalist patriarchy. Because many women in the rural and indigenous communities work with nature's processes, their work is often contradictory to the dominant market-driven 'development' and trade policies. 'Feeding the world' becomes disassociated from the women who actually do it and is projected as dependent on global agribusiness and biotechnology corporations.

Townsend (1998) notes that concerns about gender discrimination include the propensity of development agencies to focus on male activities. He suggests that plans for development in any sector, including fisheries, must take account of differences in gender roles and the fact that the relative lack of influence of women in decision-making makes them particularly vulnerable. In the design of benefits for fishing communities – especially benefits oriented towards the promotion of sustainable livelihoods – it will be important to ensure that women's as well as men's livelihoods are taken into account. And in the end, it is probably less important that everyone involved in some aspect of fishing on the Sao Francisco River in Brazil be called a 'fisher' than that the women processing and marketing the fish have their labour officially recognized as contributing to the pension that is every Brazilian's right.

Distinctive cultures of fishing communities

A study commissioned by FAO (2001) found that the degree to which fisheries management practices and policies strengthen or weaken small-scale community fisheries is directly related to the level of understanding of community fishing cultures. The study found that communities that have relied on fishing through many generations generally share two characteristics:

- Small-scale fishermen develop intimate, detailed, and function-oriented knowledge about the aquatic systems in which they operate and about the species of importance to them.
- Participation in fishing often involves the entire community. While the primary producers are usually men, women play a dual role in household maintenance

and in fish processing, marketing and distribution. The systematic division of labour also includes roles for children and the elderly.

Communities take a collective approach not only to the sharing of labour but also to the sharing of the catch and the development of systems of community-based management, which may be very different from 'scientifically based' management by government authority. By focusing on individual rather than community interests and on conservation of stocks of importance to outside commercial fishermen, government policies may disrupt community management systems.

Anything that affects traditional fisheries systems is likely to affect the entire community. Small-scale fishing cultures adapt to risks and uncertainties by taking a conservative approach to fishing, maintaining occupational pluralism, establishing share payment occupational systems, and developing beliefs, taboos and ceremonies that support the maintenance of traditional fishing livelihoods.

The disruption of small-scale fisheries by high-technology competition often leads to a vicious cycle of fisheries depletion, poverty, and loss of cultural identity. Over harvesting by 'outside' fishermen under state licensing frequently destroys traditional livelihoods. In addition, many communities lose access to their traditional fishing grounds. The progression of industrial development towards isolated communities adds the threat of pollution of aquatic ecosystems in addition to opening up access routes from the outside world. Even coastal tourism industries can contribute to the disruption of traditional economies. The increasing dependence of fishing communities on outside work and distant markets can further erode lifestyles and cultures.

Communities dispersed along coastlines and mainly dependent on marine ecosystems close to home are particularly vulnerable to resource depletion. The limited political power of small communities makes them particularly vulnerable to external threats, especially from large-scale fisheries that may get substantial subsidies from the home country or may even be foreign vessels. The inability of poor community fishermen to obtain financing for technological innovations constrains their ability to remain competitive and is often another factor contributing to poverty. The scenario of fishing communities being deprived of traditional, collective fishing lifestyles and cultures, and lacking the means to adapt to competitive market economies is all too common.

Lewis et al (1996) shows how the problem of maintaining traditional lifestyles is not restricted to capture fisheries. Many traditional pond farmers in Bangladesh, one of the poorest countries in the world, have lost their livelihoods as a result of state support for 'more valuable' agricultural production of monocultured crops. Rural fish farmers have had little say in the transformation of ponds to farmland, because they rarely own the land. Those losing their livelihoods include not only pond farmers and their families but also the people who collect the wild fingerlings needed to supply them. Pond farms that survive tend to be run by large landowners and supply more lucrative urban markets rather than the needs of rural local communities.

Development projects to improve fisheries livelihoods may have unanticipated negative effects if traditional cultural practices are not taken into account. A case study by J Kurien (FAO, 2001) describes the decline in the well-being of communities in a coastal region of India as a result of policies supporting the expansion of a modern shrimp exporting industry. Previously, access to fisheries and the allocation of fisheries resources had been regulated by communal traditions and institutions that emphasized the sharing of seafood and of incomes, as well as promoting community-based participation in fisheries management and providing an effective means of conflict resolution. Not only did shrimp exporting provide comparatively little employment, but it resulted in the degradation of marine ecosystems, a consequent reduction in traditional catches, and loss of employment for women in seafood markets. Other development efforts, promoting competitive individualism oriented to markets rather the communities themselves, led to the erosion of cultural traditions that had long guided social and economic life in the region, resulting in new social and political divisions.

Technological advances can be blamed for much of the damage to aquatic ecosystems in the past. Fisheries policy makers are gradually moving towards an ecosystem-based approach rather than simply focusing on commercially valuable species. However, protecting the interests of communities and small-scale fishing may be as important as protecting aquatic ecosystems, and indeed will likely hold the key to ecosystem health in the long run. The real challenge for policy makers will be how to do so in the face of pressures from large-scale fisheries operations and in political systems that are driven by the guiding principles of individual competition and economic growth.

The important role of traditional community practices in maintaining aquatic biodiversity has been clearly recognized in the CBD and other international agreements, and it is arguable that future fisheries policies should make the promotion of the well-being of small-scale fishing communities their first priority. Even if this doesn't occur, it will be crucial to design policies (both for biodiversity management and for access to genetic resources) that are beneficial to small-scale community fisheries. At the very least, this will require paying close attention to the cultural characteristics of fishing communities, making every effort to revitalize traditional management practices and knowledge systems, and promoting participation in policy making.

A few of the new national laws and regional guidelines on access to genetic resources (discussed in Chapter 5) make a point of guaranteeing access for indigenous and local communities to biological resources in their territories. Constraints on access have long been a sore point in fishing communities that have effectively been denied access under fisheries regulations. Communities whose traditional fishing cultures and practices have eroded during recent decades may also need assistance restoring and enhancing small-scale fisheries. National access policies and access agreements can help the development of sustainable fisheries livelihoods in concert with other benefits such as the improvement of community health and education.

INDIGENOUS VIEWS ON THE COLLECTION AND USE OF AQUATIC GENETIC RESOURCES: A workshop in Canada

If the right of indigenous communities to provide or withhold access to genetic resources is taken for granted, as it is in several emerging national laws, then access policies and parties seeking to obtain access will need to respect indigenous views on the use of aquatic genetic resources. Obtaining consent from indigenous communities is not simply a matter of negotiating acceptable benefits. Negotiators and policy makers need to be aware that, while indigenous peoples may bring a variety of different perspectives to the negotiation table, their views on the use of fish may be different from the 'Western' concept of resources to be gathered, bought and sold. In addition, indigenous approaches to negotiations may be complicated by broader concerns about indigenous rights. The tension between indigenous peoples and the Canadian government is instructive in this respect.

To date, collection of aquatic genetic resources in the waters of western and northern Canada has largely been restricted to obtaining broodstock for salmon farming and enhancement of wild stocks, with limited collection of samples of marine organisms for screening by pharmaceutical companies. The rules for collection in traditional territories of indigenous peoples (now known as First Nations) can be complicated. The federal government has the authority to manage ocean resources (as well as sea-going fishes and their inland habitat), while other inland fisheries are the bailiwick of provincial governments.

Anyone (including First Nations people) wanting to collect fish germplasm or broodstock for aquaculture or wild stock enhancement must:

- Apply for and obtain a scientific collection permit from DFO, Canada. The permit identifies the stock or species that may be taken, where and when it may be collected, and the objectives of the collection.
- Obtain a permit from the federal/provincial Introduction and Transfers Committee if the collector intends to move broodstock or germplasm from one watershed to another.

Although there is no formal requirement for collectors to consult with indigenous peoples before applying for a scientific collection permit, DFO, Canada expects them to do so. If a collector fails to provide proof of adequate consultation, it is unlikely that a permit will be provided.[1]

How land claims negotiations affect access

Canada was the first country to ratify the CBD and soon afterwards established an 'ad hoc open-ended working group', including strong First Nations representation, to discuss ways of implementing Article 8(j) – the requirement for indigenous community consent and benefit sharing. As First Nations become more familiar with Canada's legal commitment to implement the convention and

Article 8(j), it is possible that they may use it as a bargaining chip during treaty negotiations.

The current absence of formal policy requiring First Nations consent to collections is in large part a result of the uncertainty surrounding these negotiations. With few exceptions, representatives of colonial governments did not negotiate treaties with indigenous peoples in western Canada. Instead they appropriated indigenous lands and designated small 'reserves' for First Nations peoples to live on. For the past several decades, the federal and provincial governments have been engaged in arduous negotiations with many First Nations to negotiate treaty rights for ownership and control of traditional lands and natural resources. Control over access to fisheries in traditional territories is almost always an issue on the table.

The first successful land claims agreements were implemented in the early 1990s with the Inuit peoples of northern Canada. These agreements provide for fisheries co-management between the federal government and the Inuit and require prior informed consent from indigenous communities for access to aquatic genetic resources. Subsequent negotiations with other First Nations have proven to be far more complicated, partially because of the central involvement of provincial governments (northern Canada, home of the Inuit, has always remained under the sole jurisdiction of the federal government). Traditional territories claimed by First Nations in British Columbia for the purposes of treaty negotiations, for example, cover almost the entire area of Canada's westernmost province.

First Nations priorities

In 1999, WFT hosted a First Nations workshop in Victoria, British Columbia, to discuss principles that need to be taken into account in the formulation of community and government policies on aquatic genetic resources management and access. Participants included fisheries commission representatives from seven First Nations in British Columbia, Yukon Territory and the Northwest Territories: Carrier-Sekani, Gitxsan, Haisla, Nisga'a, Shuswap, Teslin-Tlingit and Inuvialuit. Also attending were representatives of the Yukon Salmon Committee and Northwest Territory Fisheries Joint Management Committee, both of which include indigenous members.

While there was consensus on some issues, workshop participants were reluctant to agree on a set of principles without the approval of their elders. Instead, they suggested that the workshop be used as an opportunity to identify starting points for further discussion among First Nations about access policies. The workshop focused primarily on five questions:

• What are aquatic genetic resources?
• How should they be used?
• Should they be moved from their place of origin?
• How should traditional knowledge be treated?
• How should First Nations deal with requests for access?

The following is a summary of key points made by participants, and provides a valuable insight into the indigenous view of genetic resources.

What are aquatic genetic resources?

- Aquatic genetic resources include all aquatic biological diversity, freshwater and marine, living and non-living. The elders say we can't separate the living from the non-living in the web of life.
- Distinguishing between 'living' and 'non-living' resources is artificial – we consider all things to have life; even the earth is alive with micro-organisms.
- Calling aquatic creatures 'resources' suggests a hierarchy that is not part of our beliefs. We coexist with all creatures and look on them as equals – not 'resources'. Instead of being asked to adapt our thinking to the 'European' way, we should ask the international community to adapt their thinking to the indigenous way. Imagine replacing 'aquatic genetic resources' with 'people' – we don't put one in authority over the other. That concept needs to be fully understood.

What uses of aquatic genetic resources are acceptable?

- The further you move towards DNA identification, the further you move from an indigenous perspective. Categorizing organisms into small boxes is a 'European', not an indigenous, approach. Ecosystems are complex, and policies for managing creatures must show an understanding of the whole – not just the pieces.
- When people talk about sperm cells and genetic resources, we see fish. The environment is like a whole body – if you remove a toe, then you have to learn to walk again.
- Uses of aquatic genetic resources must respect all components of aquatic biological diversity.
- Genetic resources come from living beings, and we have been taught not to interfere with animals at that level. Animals and fish must be treated with respect. This has implications for everything from handling fish to genetic transfers. Many indigenous people believe that genetic manipulation and moving fish away from their natural territory is the highest form of disrespect.
- Removing genetic resources and raising fish in culture is against the beliefs of the elders because they don't have the power to 'give away' genetic resources. If they go along with it and receive some benefit, it's only because it might happen behind their backs if they didn't.
- Gene banking is a useful way of rehabilitating declining stocks, but the emphasis should be on conservation-based fish management, based on genetic diversity, rather than on the yield-based management approach that government uses. Maintaining genetic diversity is integral to indigenous rights and title.
- We need to increase escapement of stocks to traditional fisheries areas instead of focusing only on areas of heavy commercial use. While supplementation of

stocks is acceptable, our people are opposed to genetic alteration or manipulation.

- It is questionable whether genetic material should be used to restore an extinct species. Species evolve naturally to adapt to changing conditions – and some naturally disappear. To understand the traditional perspective we need to include ourselves. We are not above the salmon – yet we wouldn't store our own DNA in case our people become extinct.
- It is important to consider whether genetic materials should be collected at all. As soon as we start collecting them, we create the potential for companies to come in and scoop them up.

Should genetic resources be moved from their place of origin?

- Genetic resources are inextricably linked to their origins. Genetic materials should not be used anywhere outside the watershed from which they are taken.
- Government agencies and groups that collect fish make decisions on where to transplant stocks based solely on management perspectives without always considering genetic implications. Indigenous communities must have a say in where the material goes.
- Those who control access have a responsibility to people elsewhere. Great Lakes natives say we have a responsibility to make sure no more Pacific salmon stocks get into Atlantic areas. We also hear concerns about Atlantic salmon being moved into the Pacific. The position of First Nations, as articulated by the British Columbia Aboriginal Fisheries Commission, has been to oppose the introduction of exotics. Within the freshwater domain, similar opposition could reasonably be expected with respect to Arctic charr.

How should traditional knowledge be respected and protected?

- Many people assume traditional knowledge is from centuries ago, but it can also mean current practices. It's not just an old way of doing things but a very successful base of knowledge that has allowed people to survive and flourish for thousands of years.
- In some cases genetic resources may have no clear link to community uses. However, it may be wrong to assume that there is no local or traditional knowledge of marine animals collected for pharmaceutical research. It may simply be that indigenous peoples are reluctant to share their knowledge, even though they have uses for a creature. Even if they don't, it is still necessary to tell them how a genetic resource will be used in order to get prior informed consent for its collection.
- Elders are often reluctant to share information with outsiders when they see their knowledge exploited and distorted. They want to ensure that traditional knowledge is not misused.
- Traditional knowledge can empower indigenous people to dictate their own policies based on their traditional needs. Government fails to recognize the importance of traditional knowledge in the management of resources and often

conducts studies and research without consultation. Proper consultation and respect for traditional knowledge are essential.

- We shouldn't filter traditional knowledge through science. Traditional ecological principles are spiritual in nature, and we can't look at them scientifically. We send our young people to universities to try to understand the European view, and it's just as important for governments to learn about and understand the view of indigenous peoples. Science has helped provide an understanding of ecosystems, but this needs to be reconciled with the holistic understanding that indigenous people have.

How should access to genetic resources be controlled?

- No one owns genetic resources – only the Creator.
- Genes and can't be owned – patent law isn't relevant. Nor is patent law meant to apply to material we process without knowing its applications. With many different groups involved in the management of genetic resources, adequate planning is needed to avoid ad hoc responses to proposals. Indigenous peoples are in the best position to ensure responsible uses of resources in their territories. In the absence of tools to deal with ownership of genetic resources, indigenous peoples are in the best position to exert fiduciary control.
- Indigenous people should have the first right to say what is done with genetic materials. They should have control over access, use and distribution.
- The rights held by indigenous and local communities are primary but not exclusive. In the Inuvialuit Territory, for example, the hierarchy of rights and responsibilities is as follows: community, Inuvialuit people, people of Canada, world.
- Some companies put pressure on governments to provide access by what is essentially blackmail – eg by threatening to stop research. Before permitting access, communities must know what will be done with a genetic resource. Companies such as pharmaceutical firms may only care about the product, whereas indigenous communities may give priority to process. If the integral nature of physical and spiritual healing is important, they may not wish to let resources from their territory be turned into pharmaceutical products.
- Indigenous peoples should consider creating corporations to protect their rights to control access.
- Resources should not be bought, sold or traded without community approval. Applications for use of genetic resources should go through each First Nation's resource council.
- Many indigenous communities are reluctant to approve access to genetic resources without honourable agreements, based on thorough consultation, that ensure an adequate return of appropriate benefits to communities.
- Indigenous communities need to develop policy principles especially to deal with problems associated with bioprospecting, collection of broodstock and outplanting.

Many of the views expressed by participants in the workshop are probably typical of indigenous communities anywhere in the world. Government policy makers setting guidelines for access to aquatic genetic resources in indigenous communities need to take into account significant differences between the worldviews of indigenous and mainstream societies. This is not an easy task, and the propensity for rhetoric is strong, on both sides of the table. In the workshop summarized above, for example, the stated abhorrence of DNA identification techniques needs to be reconciled with one British Columbia First Nation's interest in using those same techniques to analyse ancient salmon remains in order to establish territorial use patterns and so strengthen its treaty case. First Nations are caught between strong traditional beliefs and a deluge of technologies their elders never envisioned, and these kinds of inconsistencies need to be taken in good faith if any progress is to be made.

The worldviews of indigenous peoples are shaped by their continuous occupation of the same ecosystems since the earliest times. They take a holistic approach to the management of aquatic ecosystems, based on the belief that humans are equal to and do not rule over other species. Consequently, the concept of species as 'resources' for human use is a foreign notion. So are the concept of private ownership of resources and of ideas pertaining to their use. Historically, the survival and prosperity of indigenous peoples depended on sharing ecological knowledge within and among communities and on respecting the natural balance of ecosystems without placing human uses first. To indigenous peoples, 'sustaining' ecosystems does not mean determining how much you can take out without doing damage but rather living harmoniously with other species, receiving nature's surplus as a gift. In this sense, the 'ecosystem approach' to conservation that is increasingly gaining favour originated with indigenous peoples. Hence the value of maintaining and promoting traditional ecosystem management practices.

Traditional knowledge of ecosystem management was preserved through generations by incorporating it into cultures – through song, dance and art, for example. Today, indigenous peoples may be reluctant to share traditional knowledge with outsiders (or to provide consent to access to resources) not only because they want to ensure reasonable compensation but also because of cultural beliefs about respect for species and about treating them simply as raw material for human invention. These beliefs also may explain in large part indigenous peoples' scepticism about scientific research in their territories and about the validity of scientific knowledge based on reducing ecosystems to their basic elements. Monetary (or non-monetary) benefits may seem meaningless to a community that objects to the basic premise of treating fish as genetic resources. All too often the real incentive for indigenous communities to consent to the taking of genetic resources is desperation to find ways out of poverty brought on by the erosion of their cultures and loss of traditional livelihoods. Indigenous peoples of the world continue to push for the recognition of their rights to self-determination and control over genetic resources in their traditional territories. Even where this recognition has not been achieved, it is important that national governments promote benefit-sharing arrangements that are acceptable to indigenous communities.

THE KNOWLEDGE KNOT: Traditional knowledge and access to aquatic genetic resources

Article 8(j) of the CBD requires national governments to encourage the equitable sharing of benefits arising from the use of the knowledge, innovations and practices of traditional communities. Traditional knowledge is especially important for the use of plant genetic resources. New crop varieties developed by seed companies may be based on strains produced by generations of traditional farmers. Similarly, traditional knowledge of medicinal uses of plants may provide a shortcut for pharmaceutical companies making decisions to invest in research and development of new products, either by synthesizing or modifying compounds found in plants used by indigenous peoples or by marketing botanicals.

Although some countries have a lengthy history of pond aquaculture, industrial aquaculture is a relatively new activity, and the enhancement of farmed fish strains relies almost exclusively on collection of wild broodstock. There is no real parallel in fish farming to the situation in the plant world, where the experience and knowledge of traditional farmers makes a major contribution to crop development. Nor is there any strong parallel in marine bioprospecting to the need for indigenous knowledge in developing drugs based on traditional uses of medicinal plants.

As following sections in this chapter indicate, traditional communities have extensive knowledge of aquatic genetic resources. It's not a question of whether the knowledge exists but what type it is and whether collectors need it for the most predominant uses of aquatic genetic resources – aquaculture and pharmaceuticals development. Fish breeders may look to local communities for help in finding and catching broodstock. In some cases as well, they may tap into local knowledge of physical characteristics – for example, colorations and markings of prized ornamentals in remote jungle rivers. However, the bottom line is that there's no comparison between aquatic and plant genetic resources uses in the type and level of dependence on traditional knowledge.

The reason this distinction is so significant is that Article 8(j) of the CBD has become the baseline for the development of several national laws regulating access to genetic resources in indigenous and local communities. The implementation of Article 8(j) has for many years been the subject of many at CBD meetings involving not only national governments but also advocates for indigenous and local communities. Discussions have focused primarily on how to set up effective guidelines for community consent and benefit sharing, with little attention paid to the issue of how governments will define what types of knowledge confer the right for benefits or what happens when community knowledge is *not* relevant to the use of genetic resources. As Chapter 6 demonstrates, lack of clarity about these issues continues in the laws that have been developed to date.

With plant issues dominating the debate over Article 8(j), community knowledge of fish genetic resources hasn't made it into the agenda. That will undoubtedly change once collection of broodstock from communities becomes more common and the question arises: if community knowledge isn't essential for the actual use of aquatic genetic resources, what rights do communities have to provide informed consent for access or to receive benefits? In the meantime, those involved in the making of access policy need to be aware of fish and plant distinctions and ensure that policies take those distinctions into account.

Traditional knowledge of aquatic biodiversity

Traditional ecological knowledge (sometimes referred to as indigenous knowledge or local knowledge) is a term commonly used to describe community knowledge, in some cases evolving over hundreds or thousands of years, of local ecosystems. It may form the basis for local decision-making for all facets of community life, including natural resource management, nutrition, food preparation, health, education, and community and social organization (Warren et al, 1995).

Indigenous knowledge of aquatic resources and ecosystem relationships has been passed orally from generation to generation and may be incorporated into cultural practices (eg songs, dances and art) that ensure its preservation and continuity. Typically, indigenous knowledge of aquatic resources includes fish location, movements, and other factors explaining spatial patterns and timing in aquatic ecosystems, including sequences of events (such as fish catches, marine mammal sightings, aquatic blooms), cycles (eg fish migration, spawning, tidal changes, lunar influences), and trends (eg decreases in catches, early thaws, rainfall patterns, and changes in migration and spawning patterns; Posey, 1999). Although discussions of traditional knowledge often focus on indigenous peoples, the ecological knowledge developed by non-indigenous fishing communities with a lengthy history is also substantial.

The relevance of traditional knowledge to conservation

Many fisheries managers (as well as scientists and policy makers) have been sceptical about traditional knowledge. Indigenous knowledge tends to be holistic in nature (in contrast to the reductionist scientific approach) and closely tied to beliefs about the unity of nature and spiritual qualities of animal life. Many indigenous peoples strongly object to describing aquatic life as 'resources' because the term justifies human domination of nature and implies a lack of appreciation of living creatures as equals with a spiritual life of their own.

Scientific scepticism about the mingling of practical knowledge and spiritual beliefs has been heightened by the romanticizing of traditional knowledge in support of indigenous rights movements. Commentators unconcerned with political correctness have asked, did indigenous peoples practise sustainable management because they purposefully lived in harmony with nature, or simply because they lacked the technology to exploit natural resources beyond sustainable limits? And has the level of traditional fisheries knowledge been exaggerated to increase its effectiveness as a negotiation tool? Johannes and Ruddle (1993) noted that environmentally destructive practices coexisted with conservation efforts in indigenous societies just as they did in all other societies. Blench (1998) rejects the image of indigenous peoples as natural conservationists, and cites numerous instances where the disappearance of megafauna in recent prehistory was the direct result of human activities. For example, fossil evidence suggests to some researchers that the Polynesians had severe impacts on local fauna as they colonized the Pacific (Pimm, 1995). Some anthropologists reject the notion of the 'ecologically noble savage' and argue that expecting indigenous peoples to continue using only traditional technologies and low-impact subsistence strategies places an unfair responsibility on them and denies their right to develop according to their own preferences (Dutfield, 1999).

Nevertheless, many indigenous and traditional societies do have a history of living sustainably, in part as a result of the perception that all components of natural landscapes are directly useful or usable resources – in contrast to the prevailing economic view that few resources have production value (Toledo, 1991). From that perspective, the effectiveness of some indigenous peoples in conserving aquatic genetic resources, while it may be linked to spiritual beliefs, is rooted in a very practical understanding of the importance of protecting ecosystems. The suddenly popular 'ecosystem approach' to resource management – basing management decisions on the ability of ecosystems to support resource use without damage – is not so different from long-standing principles held by indigenous peoples (although it is exceptionally difficult to achieve in practice). These principles in turn are based on and support an understanding of aquatic resources and ecosystems that, while not scientific in nature, can nevertheless be comprehensive.

The simple truth is that, to live sustainably from resources that are not pushed to the limit requires little more than experience and common sense; it's only when multiple users push resources to the breaking point that science needs to be enlisted.

Fisheries management that emphasizes commercially important species over ecosystem interactions bears much of the responsibility for diminishing fish stocks. The more recent move to 'ecosystem-based management' has produced some innovative results. Protected areas have proved a useful conservation tool, although limited by the fact that they tend to be small and scattered. The highest aquatic genetic diversity is often located in traditional communities simply because people naturally set their roots down in areas with the greatest natural abundance. It therefore stands to reason that promoting the restoration and maintenance of traditional knowledge and practices, as Article 8(j) seeks to do, is a useful conservation objective.

While much attention has been focused on the importance of traditional knowledge for conservation, its economic value to communities is also vital. Many activities and products based on traditional knowledge are important sources of income, food, and health care for large parts of the populations in developing countries (UNCTAD, 2000). Moreover, many of the cultures from which traditional knowledge is collected are more endangered than the ecosystems in which they reside (Reid et al, 1993), and there is increasing recognition that the loss of cultural diversity is intricately linked with the loss of biological diversity (Crucible Group, 2000). Consequently, conservation of aquatic genetic resources and conservation of communities cannot be considered in isolation from one another.

The continued availability of aquatic genetic resources will depend on conservation at the community level. As Dutfield (1999) has pointed out, there is no need to provide moral justification for compensation, as industrial users of genetic resources would benefit, as would the biosphere and humankind. When genetic resources in communities are treated as a common heritage while those in industrial laboratories are treated as private property, the burden of conservation falls unfairly on communities; in this context, compensation should be defined as payment not for past services but for future options (Brush and Stabinsky, 1996). While such arguments are generally made on behalf of rural farmers, they are just as valid for fishing communities.

The relevance of traditional knowledge for collectors

Collections for pharmaceutical and industrial use

In inland indigenous communities, medicinal uses of plants have always been vital to the well-being of local people. The same holds true for uses of plants by fishing communities. However, for obvious reasons, fishing communities may have little familiarity with the types of marine organisms sought by pharmaceutical companies. In the first place, the organisms may inhabit relatively inaccessible sea beds. Second, while many marine organisms have enormous potential for medicinal uses, it usually takes sophisticated scientific knowledge to tap into them. Familiarity with the toxic characteristics of cone snails or corals doesn't necessarily lead to the knowledge needed to use them for healing.

Collections of ornamental fish

Traditional knowledge is more relevant to the ornamentals trade than for any other use of aquatic genetic resources. Many ornamental stocks are highly localized in remote areas and because their activity is often nocturnal, they can only be captured by local people thoroughly familiar with their habits and habitat. In addition, aquarium hobbyists are prepared to pay high prices for wild specimens from strains that haven't previously been distributed. Collectors, whether their purpose is breeding or distribution of wild specimens, need information about the characteristics of local populations (such as coloration patterns, shapes and growth characteristics) that may make them attractive to buyers. They also need information about where to find the fish.

Breeders of some species may collect all the broodstock they need from the live trade in ornamental fisheries. Or, as in the case of species such as guppies, mollies and neon tetras that have been cultured for years, breeders may never need to collect more specimens from the wild. The biggest demand for wild specimens for breeding – and for the traditional knowledge that facilitates collections – will likely occur for species or populations previously unknown to collectors or previously considered too difficult to breed. As Case Study 1 illustrates, the number of species being cultured is constantly expanding as a result of advances in breeding technologies.

One feature that distinguishes the ornamentals trade from collections of plant genetic resources is the coexistence of collections for breeding and for the trade in live fish. Neither government agencies in provider countries nor local fishers may have any way of knowing whether collected specimens will be used for culturing or simply sold to hobbyists that have no interest in breeding fish. Similarly, there may be no way of telling whether collectors are seeking out local knowledge with the intention of trying to breed fish collected from the wild. This simple reality creates a difficult hurdle for policies that work on the assumption that the purposes of collections of genetic resources are well understood and that the only challenge is determining whether access to traditional knowledge is needed for their use. In the case of the ornamentals trade, neither of these facts can be easily ascertained.

Collections for food fish farming

While industrial aquaculture has a very brief history, rural pond farming has occurred for hundreds of years in some developing countries – thousands in the case of carp in China. Even though local communities involved in pond farming may have developed a substantial body of knowledge, a shorter history is not the only factor differentiating traditional knowledge in fish farming communities from that in crop farming communities. While it is possible for new strains to evolve in pond farming, their appearance may just as easily occur by accident as by design. At any rate, it is highly unlikely that breeders involved in industrial aquaculture would choose to collect broodstock from pond farmers rather than simply collecting fish from the wild.

Collectors of wild broodstock for food fish farming may be looking for a different type of knowledge than that supplied by ornamentals fishers. In addition to knowledge of fish habitat, migration routes, life cycles and fishing techniques, communities with a lengthy history of fisheries dependence may also supply useful information about characteristics such as nutritional value (taste and oil content, for example), rate of growth, and hardiness. However, as in the case of the ornamentals industry, food fish breeders are far less likely than collectors of plant genetic resources to actually need access to this local knowledge. The British Columbia salmon farmer (Case Study 2) who planned to enhance his stocks with broodstock from the Yukon River didn't need anyone to tell him that a salmon population from cold northern waters would have the high oil content that he needed for the Japanese market. Similarly, when Aqua Bounty inserted a gene from the ocean pout to develop the 'Super Salmon', it was already obvious that the pout was capable of surviving in freezing waters. And the Icy Waters Company (Case Study 3) had no real need to tap into the knowledge of Inuit communities of local populations of Arctic charr that the company wanted to collect to improve its farmed stocks.

There are three basic reasons why the need for access to traditional knowledge for the enhancement of farmed stocks is likely to be limited:

• Community knowledge of wild populations primarily relates to fish habits rather than the characteristics of interest to breeders.

- Scientific knowledge of desirable characteristics of wild populations may already be well developed.
- Communities may have no traditional use for some species or populations of current or future interest to farmers (eg some marine species that inhabit waters far removed from any traditional communities).

The type of traditional knowledge most likely to be useful to breeders is how to catch and collect broodstock. For example, some large-scale pond owners in Bangladesh hire people in traditional fishing communities to collect fish from the wild because they know where and how to set nets for hatchlings and what types of hatchlings are most desirable for farming (Lewis et al, 1996). Broodstock sought for selective breeding are also often more easily found by local people. The situation is somewhat parallel to the ornamental industry's reliance on the traditional knowledge of local fishermen about catching fish for breeding and sale. Does this type of knowledge contribute to the use of aquatic genetic resources? That might be considered a stretch, but the question is important for three reasons:

- With few exceptions, it's the only type of traditional knowledge that's particularly relevant to the collection of aquatic genetic resources.
- Article 8(j) can be read to mean that countries only need to share benefits from the use of genetic resources with communities whose traditional knowledge has made their use possible.
- Consequently, if national access laws base the consent and benefit-sharing rights of communities on provision of knowledge associated with the use of genetic resources, fishing communities could be shut out of the benefit-sharing equation.

Who needs traditional knowledge? A do-it-yourself guide to biodiversity

Years ago, when international travel was the province of the wealthy, tourists needed a local guide to find the best hotels, the most interesting hikes, and the special restaurants where only the locals ate. Now that air travel is affordable, bookstores have entire sections devoted to local lore; some, like the very successful Lonely Planet and Rough Guide series, even specialize in taking the tourist off the beaten track. The new guidebooks are a direct result of market demands.

Local people know their way around; nobody would argue with that. Tourists and hunters do better if they have guidebooks or guides. It's not surprising that, when it comes to biodiversity coveted by 'outsiders,' local people are presumed to be the fastest way to the source. They've been husbanding or harvesting obscure plants and animals for generations, the argument goes, and their traditional knowledge of which organisms do what, and where to find them, is the best possible database for anyone wanting access to that biodiversity. That's the reasoning of the CBD, whose Article 8(j) has established traditional knowledge as the linchpin of access and benefit-sharing arrangements. Traditional knowledge, says the CBD, is the key. Bioprospectors need to work with traditional knowledge. From traditional knowledge flow the benefits.

But what if there *is* no traditional knowledge of an interesting piece of bio-diversity? Or, what if there is, but it's not the *only* knowledge? Does that mean the plant or animal can't be collected, analysed, copied? Not at all – but it may mean that, since benefit sharing is so closely wedded to traditional knowledge by the CBD, and since national governments are all tailoring their access policies to the same pattern, the community can be bypassed.

Collecting biodiversity by relying on traditional knowledge is like turning back the clock on international tourism. It assumes that local guides are the only ones. They aren't. For a hundred years, scientists have been studying plants and animals in faraway places. Enthusiastic academics captivated by nature's infinite variety have spent entire careers collecting and describing biodiversity. There is much that they don't know, but the cumulative body of academic knowledge of biodiversity should not be underestimated. Graduate students without the slightest interest in profiting from their research have crawled through the rainforest and dived on tropical reefs for decades and continue to do so for the simple reason that the eating habits of a fire ant or the defence mechanisms of a rare nudibranch are fascinating to them. Financial gain doesn't enter into it.

So if the bioprospector – the 'biodiversity tourist' – is looking for, say, a tropical plant that produces a potent insecticide, or a wild tilapia strain that could be used to breed a superior animal for farming, does he have to go to the local village authority or medicine man in Thailand, or to the family in Ghana who knows about the tilapias that have been there for centuries? Not really, because there's an American botanist in Hat Yai who went native years ago and knows every plant in the forest; and there's a professor from a university in Europe who's been studying those native African tilapias for 30 years. By now, *these* people are the local knowledge.

This is the situation policy makers need to grapple with when designing access and benefit-sharing policies. If outside experts are capable of collecting bio-diversity without local help – if, in other words, traditional knowledge can be dispensed with – then invoking Article 8(j) of the CBD in order to restrict access to genetic resources leaves a loophole big enough for a Land Rover full of samples to drive through.

As methods for building biologically active molecules and transferring genes become more sophisticated, the role of wild biodiversity will change. Wild bio-diversity will become more and more of a *starting point* for a drug or chemical or high-yielding broodstock, not a pilot-scale factory that simply needs to be scaled up. And the role of traditional knowledge will decrease accordingly, because the piece of biodiversity that proves useful may have no traditional interest whatever.

It is risky to establish the value of something against a shifting baseline. If access and benefit sharing are tied to traditional knowledge as part of a strategy to promote and protect that knowledge, the strategy may backfire. Traditional knowledge is a cultural legacy that should be preserved and perpetuated, but its advocates cannot afford to link its survival to a market that may not exist much longer. In many cases, for example a bottom-living marine animal offshore from a fishing village, the presumption of local knowledge verges on the ludicrous.

Benefits to traditional communities can play a vital role in promoting the conservation of aquatic genetic resources, especially when tied to the building of sustainable local economies. But if the right to receive these benefits is based solely on the contribution of traditional knowledge, then provider communities may be able to claim no right at all. Other access and benefit-sharing rules need to apply.

No knowledge, no benefits?
The shortcomings of Article 8(j)

As discussed in the following chapter, many countries are in the early stages of developing access and benefit-sharing laws to meet their CBD commitment. How to draft provisions related to community consent and benefit sharing remains one of the most difficult issues to address. The handful of countries that to date have developed or implemented legislation have taken different approaches to the question of whether community rights to consent to the collection of genetic resources depends on the contribution of traditional knowledge to their use of genetic resources. The Philippines and Costa Rica require community consent for all requests for access to genetic resources. By contrast, Brazil and Peru tie the right of consent to the provision of traditional knowledge.

At meetings on the implementation of the CBD, Parties to the Convention have wrestled for years with how to interpret Article 8(j) in national legislation and what requirements to make for informed consent by communities. Finally, in 2001, the Sixth Conference of the Parties (COP) to the CBD approved the 'Bonn Guidelines' on access and benefit sharing. The guidelines recommend that informed consent of indigenous and local communities be required for collection of genetic resources with or without associated knowledge, 'in accordance with their traditional practices, national access policies and subject to domestic laws'. This is encouraging news for fishing communities whose aquatic genetic resources may be sought by collectors in the future. However, as neither the CBD nor the guidelines are binding on Parties to the Convention, it remains uncertain whether different governments will follow the Philippines or the Brazilian route.

Many countries fear that the right to informed consent to access may be the thin end of the wedge for community demands (especially among indigenous peoples) for extended rights of ownership and control of lands and biological resources and a consequent erosion of national sovereignty and control. While such concerns may be justified (especially in light of international human rights agreements supporting such an extension in the case of indigenous peoples), the main reason for ensuring that communities have the right of consent with or without knowledge associated with the use of genetic resources is that the objectives of the CBD won't be achieved if countries don't acknowledge that right. This is the major shortcoming of Article 8(j) – by implying that benefit sharing should be limited to communities providing knowledge, it fails to recognize that the conservation and sustainable use of genetic resources will be attained only if indigenous and local communities have the incentive and wherewithal to carefully manage biological diversity. But consent and wherewithal depend on being able to negotiate benefits that alleviate poverty and build the capacity to develop sustainable livelihoods and healthy economies and cultures. This is especially true for fishing communities and the conservation and sustainable use of threatened aquatic biodiversity.

CASE STUDY 4. GENETIC IMPROVEMENT OF FARMED TILAPIA: Lessons from the GIFT project

ICLARM, now the World Fish Center works with farmers, scientists and policy makers to help the rural poor increase their income, preserve their environment, and improve their lives through the sustainable use of aquatic resources. An ICLARM project for the development of improved strains of tilapia for rural pond farmers reveals the complexity of issues that policy makers face when developing regulations for access to aquatic genetic resources. It also illustrates the limitations of thinking of benefits strictly in monetary terms.

Background

Tropical finfish currently account for about 90 per cent of global aquaculture production for food. Most species currently farmed are genetically very similar to wild, undomesticated stocks. For aquaculture to be able to meet the expected global increase in demand for fish protein, there is a need for improved strains that are faster growing, resistant to disease, and suited to a variety of pond farming conditions. The situation is analogous to the early days of agriculture.

In developing countries, small-scale pond farming can provide nutrition and income in addition to recycling otherwise wasted nutrients to improve soil fertility and subsequent crop production. Many attempts at pond farming fail because of inadequate knowledge of sound farming practices, poor water quality, and lack of access to fish that are adapted to pond farming conditions. Tilapias, for example, mature and reproduce so quickly that, even if a farmer overcomes other obstacles, he may end up with a large population of fish too small to be marketable.

Although the majority of Africans rely on fish as their primary source of animal protein, pond farming has generally failed to flourish in Africa. Yet tilapia, a species native to the continent, has proven to be one of the biggest success stories in pond farming in many Asian countries (particularly the Philippines, China and Thailand). Tilapias are a major source of protein for the poor in Thailand because they cost half as much as other freshwater species such as catfish and snakehead. The fish is also widely and profitably farmed in the southern US.

Some of the recent success of farmed tilapia production in Asia is a result of a breeding programme by ICLARM. In the early 1990s, ICLARM developed a new strain of tilapia by cross-breeding several strains of Nile tilapia (*Oreochromis niloticus*). Neither genetically modified nor transgenic, the new strain has been developed using traditional selective breeding methods under the Genetic

Improvement of Farmed Tilapia (GIFT) programme. Tilapias were first introduced from Africa to Southeast Asia in the 1970s, and the GIFT strain was developed from collections made in four African countries in the late 1980s and from four existing collections in the Philippines. Two decades later, following a further series of ICLARM projects, tilapia farming in rural Africa may finally be about to get a fresh start.

The beginnings of GIFT

In the mid-1980s, ICLARM developed an aquaculture programme based on the recognition that more productive and profitable aquaculture in developing countries would depend on development of better breeds of farmed aquatic organisms and better farm environments. Tilapias were chosen as test species because of their importance in warm water aquaculture and their usefulness in investigating the application of genetics in aquaculture. The proposed programme, which employed both in situ and ex situ conservation of genetic resources, would proceed in three phases: documentation of genetic resources (wild and farmed); evaluation of their culture performance; and the use of germplasm in breeding programmes. This programme became the foundation for the GIFT project, which was started in 1988 with the objective of developing more productive stocks of tilapia by selection for high growth rate and other economically important traits (eg disease resistance and maturation rate), and providing the improved strains to national and regional testing programmes and thence to fish farmers (Pullin et al, 1991).

The GIFT project involved a collaboration between ICLARM, Institute of Aquaculture Research of Norway (AKVAFORSK), and three Philippine institutions: the Freshwater Aquaculture Centre of Central Luzon State University, the Marine Science Institute of the University of the Philippines, and the Bureau of Fisheries and Aquatic Resources. The Philippines was chosen as the site for GIFT because of farmers' need for more productive fish, a well developed national seed supply system, and availability of technical support. AKVAFORSK would contribute practical experience in fish breeding programmes.

Initial steps in the GIFT project included the documentation of tilapia genetic resources in Asia and Africa, establishment of a collection of promising strains of Nile tilapia from Africa and from existing Asian cultured stocks, and evaluation of the wild Nile tilapia germplasm from Africa, along with existing cultured stocks in the Philippines in a wide range of farming systems and agroclimatic conditions.

In 1988, the GIFT team travelled to Africa to collect breeders and fingerlings of Nile tilapia in Egypt, Ghana, Kenya and Senegal. This was done in collaboration with national research institutions in each of the four countries (Gupta et al, 2000) as well as the University of Hamburg; the Musée Royale de l'Afrique Centrale in Tervuren, Belgium; the Ghana Institute of Aquatic Biology; the Suez Canal University in Egypt; and Baobob Farms in Mombasa, Kenya. The eight tilapia strains eventually used for the GIFT study included four African wild strains and four domesticated strains from the Philippines. Three of the African strains (Egypt, Kenya and Senegal) were found to perform as well as or better than domesticated strains used by Philippine fish farmers. Combining germplasm from the African strains with the farmed Philippines strains formed the basis for creation of a gene pool for selective breeding, with positive results (Pullin et al, 1991; Eknath et al, 1991, 1993).

International concerns about the use of aquatic germplasm

In 1992, ICLARM organized a meeting on International Concerns in the Use of Aquatic Germplasm, with the objective of providing clear priorities and directions in fish-breeding research and approaches that would benefit small-scale, resource-poor fish farmers in developing countries (ICLARM, 1992). The group recommended that GIFT undertake a further sampling of wild tilapia populations in Africa, with guidance from the FAO Code of Conduct for plant genotype collection, in order to reexamine the potential benefit of cross breeding. It noted the potential of GIFT to significantly improve the productivity of tilapia farming and the intention of GIFT trustees that the improved strains be freely provided, through the appropriate national authority, to tilapia farmers in participating countries. The primary beneficiaries would be five Asian countries with significant tilapia production.

As African access to the GIFT strain would not be likely in the short term, the group suggested that ICLARM recognize the African contribution by increasing its commitment to African aquacultural development, although there was much uncertainty about how this might be done (ICLARM, 1992). One meeting participant later commented: 'The Biodiversity Convention does not provide regulations for compensation for past contributions. However, as it is important that Africa conserves wild tilapia relatives to keep them available for future use, some benefits accruing from utilization of tilapia germplasm must be returned' (Rosendal, 1992).

The group considered the need to safeguard innovations through patenting but concluded it was not likely to become an issue in the foreseeable future (ICLARM, 1992). It also noted the lack of recognition by researchers of the importance and relevance of local knowledge of fish genetic resources and habitats and suggested that ICLARM explore ways to disseminate information on the existence and possible usefulness of local knowledge.

Distribution of GIFT strain to farmers

By the fifth generation of selection, the GIFT fish had achieved an average genetic gain of 12–17 per cent per generation and a cumulative increase of 85 per cent in growth compared to base populations. Testing of the second generation in four other countries (Bangladesh, China, Vietnam and Thailand) also revealed higher growth rates and better survival rates than in local strains. Dey (2000) concluded that 'the adoption of the improved strain will increase tilapia production and consequently the total fish production in a country, enhance profitability of fish farming, decrease tilapia prices, increase consumption of tilapia and other fish for non-fish farming producers and GIFT adopting farmers and increase the welfare of the country's economy as a whole'.

Prior to the official termination of the GIFT project in 1997, its partners decided to establish a private, non-profit foundation called the GIFT Foundation International to commercialize the GIFT strain in the Philippines through partnerships with the private sector, thus generating funding to continue with selective breeding and research on GIFT fish. ICLARM provided germplasm to the Foundation and to a Philippine institution. Later ICLARM provided breeders from the sixth generation to a Norwegian aquaculture company, GenoMar ASA, for further improvement and marketing. At the same time, the GIFT Foundation was selling/disseminating the GIFT strain in the Philippines and ICLARM was providing it, through the International Network on Genetics in Aquaculture (INGA), to other Asian countries that requested it.[2]

The GIFT Foundation established six accredited hatcheries in the Philippines near the greatest concentration of tilapia grow out production farms. Small-scale farmers (operating ponds ranging from 2000 to 3000 m²) can now buy GIFT fingerlings from these hatcheries, although the cost is higher than other available tilapia strains.[3] As poor farm practices or environmental problems can inhibit the effective use of the improved GIFT strains, the Foundation has begun providing technical support to Philippine farmers of the GIFT strain. Farmers in other countries can obtain the GIFT strain through government agencies that have received breeding material from the GIFT project or through INGA at no cost. In addition, the Foundation has entered into a commercial relationship with GenoMar, which is expected to make the GIFT strain available in other countries through hatcheries set up for the purpose.[4] In 1999, GenoMar obtained commercial rights for further improvement of the GIFT strain, and the brand name 'GIFT Super Tilapia' was registered in the Philippines.[5] ICLARM retained the right to distribute the germplasm it had improved through the GIFT project.

Returning benefits to Africa

In 2000, ICLARM began a project to transfer GIFT's selective breeding technology from the Philippines to sub-Saharan Africa and Egypt. The objectives of the new project were to train African scientists on the use of the selective breeding technology that is the basis for GIFT, initiate national breeding programmes, and develop strategies for the dissemination of the GIFT technology and the genetically improved fish resulting from it. With the assistance of INGA, national research institutions in 13 developing countries in Asia, Pacifica and Africa have now used the selection methods developed through the GIFT project to initiate national breeding programmes for genetic improvement of their indigenous cultured species (Gupta et al, 2000).

Under its Biodiversity and Genetic Resources Research Program (BGRRP), ICLARM followed the GIFT project with another in the coastal zone of West Africa to facilitate the conservation and sustainable use of the brackish water black-chinned tilapia (*Sarotherodon melanotheron*), with the objective of improving fish supply and providing livelihood opportunities for fishermen and farmers. *S. melanotheron* has long been an important resource for poor fishermen using a variety of fishing gear and traditional methods of fisheries enhancement, the so-called 'brushparks'. However, indigenous knowledge and the management practices that have traditionally been used to conserve its populations are breaking down because of human population increases and habitat degradation. *S. melanotheron* is not currently farmed, but the national institutions in Ghana and ICLARM believe it has potential for both brackish water and freshwater farming and that its development for this purpose would reduce importation of exotic species for aquaculture, which could have adverse environmental impacts.

Activities under the *S. melanotheron* project in 1998 included: collection of more than 400 tissue samples in several countries by national institutions to determine the genetic diversity of the subspecies; obtaining indigenous knowledge on the biology, ecology and use of the brackish water tilapia; identifying locations in Ghana with the potential for community-based sustainable aquaculture and/or fisheries development; and starting an aquaculture development programme in one of these locations (ICLARM, 1999). The live germplasm is being maintained by the national institutions.

Case study conclusions

For certain purposes, genetic resources may be collected from – and benefits may flow to – many communities in many countries. In the case of GIFT, ICLARM had great ambitions to improve conditions for raising farmed fish and increasing food supplies in developing countries, and to a large extent succeeded. While there is no indication that the communities from which tilapia were collected received any direct benefits, African countries did eventually benefit from the research conducted under GIFT and subsequent projects. While none of this occurred under the types of access and benefit-sharing arrangements envisioned by the CBD, it provides a useful illustration of the types of non-monetary benefits that may be useful to communities.

Access to broodstock in communities

When the original GIFT collections occurred, several years prior to the CBD, genetic resources were considered common property and it would have been rare indeed for collectors to seek the consent of provider communities. National institutions in the provider countries made the collections on ICLARM's behalf, and none of the countries involved had requirements for obtaining the consent of or sharing benefits with communities from which aquatic genetic resources were obtained.

Ten years later, when ICLARM returned to Africa to obtain broodstock for the BGRRP project, not much had changed. Once again government institutions from African countries made the collections, and none of the countries had developed access laws. As a CGIAR centre, ICLARM is obliged to follow CGIAR collection policies, which state that centres must obtain formal permission from the relevant authorized government body prior to making a collection (CGIAR,

2001). Although the OAU model law clearly confirms the need for laws requiring collectors to obtain consent from local communities (OAU, 2000), no African country has yet made it a legal requirement.

The few access and benefit-sharing laws already in existence generally require community consent for collections – without saying how to obtain it. What are the implications when projects require collections in many communities scattered over several countries? As in the case of the ICLARM projects, organizations planning to select fish populations suitable for aquaculture may need to make numerous collections to determine genetic variability and identify desirable characteristics for breeding. In this respect, collections for aquaculture are like bioprospecting for marine organisms – they may require collections from a variety of populations over a wide area. Collections for aquaculture development require much greater effort than collections for crop breeding, which often have the benefit of generations of farmers' experience and knowledge. The fish farming industry is starting from scratch – attempting to accomplish in a few decades what crop farmers may have taken thousands of years to achieve. Many fish species currently being tested for aquaculture potential have never been farmed before.

As more and more national access laws come into being, organizations like ICLARM may need to obtain consent from numerous local communities for collections of broodstock or even DNA samples. The impact of such a requirement on research and development can be imagined.

Academic versus commercial collections

Even if laws distinguish between academic and commercial research, the consent process is still likely to be onerous. The only distinction the OAU model law makes is that academic users may pay lower permit fees. Then there's the difficult question of the potential for overlap between academic and commercial research purposes. Philippine law requires institutional collectors to switch from an academic to a commercial permit if it becomes apparent that research may lead to commercial prospects. The OAU model law prohibits collectors from applying for IPR protection over biological resources or their derivatives without the consent of provider communities. In the GIFT case, ICLARM had no direct commercial objectives when the project started yet, ten years after the initial collections, a private company obtained the right to commercial activities made possible by the GIFT development of a new tilapia strain. As the GIFT example illustrates, the link between the collector (national institutions), the user (ICLARM), and eventual commercial use (by GenoMar) can cover a lot of time and territory. Clearly, social benefits do arise from GenoMar's work, which could not effectively proceed without some form of intellectual property protection.

More than anything else, the GenoMar link illustrates the complexity of issues that policy makers must take into account when developing laws on access to genetic resources and their commercial use. Laws that are too zealous can severely impede the work of institutional collectors whose ultimate goal is to improve conditions in local communities, and they can also hamper commercial opportunities which may be in the public interest. Nevertheless, if governments are serious about ensuring benefits to communities that provide broodstock, they will need to carefully consider how far reaching laws will be with regard to commercial profits that may be only tenuously linked to initial collections and may not occur until the distant future.

Benefits to communities

Obtaining the consent of each community providing aquatic genetic resources could be relatively straightforward if fair and efficient processes are developed with national assistance. The most difficult obstacle may ultimately be the negotiation of benefits acceptable to communities. The OAU model law, like some other proposed or existing laws, makes only one requirement: the payment of royalties. This provision probably originated with concerns about bioprospecting for medicinal plants or the use of the traditional knowledge of agricultural communities for commercial gain. However, the narrow legislative focus on monetary compensation may be both short-sighted and counterproductive. Non-monetary benefits directed towards improving the economic and social well-being of communities may be far more useful in the long run not only for the communities themselves but also for the promotion of sustainable development – the ultimate objective of the CBD. The ICLARM projects provide an innovative example of how access to genetic resources in a variety of communities can result in the creation of sustainable fishing and fish farming livelihoods on a broad scale, potentially resulting in far greater benefits for rural communities and countries than cash payment. The GIFT example has no clear parallel in the collection of plant genetic resources. Although Asian rather than African farmers were the initial beneficiaries of the development of improved tilapia strains, the GIFT project provides a useful model for innovative uses of farming technologies for the benefit of local communities.

A legislative focus on benefit-sharing agreements between a provider community and a collector may be too narrow to accommodate projects such as those conducted by ICLARM and those that will be needed in the future to improve the productivity of rural pond farms in developing countries. It may be that national governments need to facilitate broader-scale agreements involving groups of communities. In the case of GIFT, not every community in which collections were made directly benefited from the results of the ICLARM development of new strains and training for rural fish farmers. They may benefit in the long run, however, through the efforts of national breeding programmes assisted by GIFT. Alternatively, governments could take steps to ensure that communities providing aquatic genetic resources share in revenues created in other communities – for instance, through the establishment of national trust funds to help provider communities enhance sustainable fishing livelihoods (eg through restoration of fish habitat, revival of traditional fisheries practices, improvement of marketing skills, etc).

Pond farming and capture fisheries

In some northern countries, capture fisheries organizations fiercely oppose competition from industrial aquaculture, arguing that it will not only put them out of business but also have an adverse effect on aquatic biodiversity. But equating the industrial aquaculture of species like salmon with rural pond farming of species like tilapia is comparing apples and oranges. The need for a massive increase in the availability of fish protein to feed growing populations in developing countries is undisputed, and to ensure food security, governments will need to do everything they can to promote both sustainable capture fisheries and pond farming. Small-scale pond farming can substantially benefit the economies of the smallest villages and communities, some of which may rely on capture fisheries as well.

Chapter 5

Acting Globally: National Laws on Access to Aquatic Resources

Farmed Atlantic salmon broodstock, British Columbia (Photo by Monica MacIsaac)

THE COLLECTOR'S CONUNDRUM: What's the law?

In May 2002, the US Department of State (2002) issued the following guidelines to American researchers collecting plant, animal and microbial genetic materials in other countries:

> *Before collecting any genetic resources abroad, a researcher should have a written agreement that includes these key provisions:*
>
> * *prior informed consent of the national government;*
> * *access to the genetic resources or 'traditional knowledge' of an indigenous community or communities will normally require obtaining the prior informed consent of that community(ies);*
> * *the non-monetary and/or monetary benefits the collector will provide, and whether, and under what conditions, the collector may transfer the collected genetic resources to another party.*

Basically, the guidelines sum up the essence of the access provisions of the CBD – no more collection of genetic resources without a solid agreement with the country and community where you're collecting them. The US Department of State noted that many countries have either introduced or are developing national access regimes and that the CBD creates an obligation to obtain the prior informed consent of source countries whether or not they have such regimes in place. Somewhat ironically, the US is one of a handful of countries that have yet to ratify the CBD.

Imagine you're a researcher hired by an aquaculture company to collect, say, tilapia broodstock from several locations in Africa or catfish broodstock from different rivers in Asia. Or let's say you're with an ornamental fish consortium in Florida and you want to enlist the help of villagers in a South American country to collect live specimens so you can transport them back to the US and try breeding them. Or perhaps, as a researcher for a pharmaceutical company, you know that a new type of sponge has been discovered in Caribbean waters, and you want to collect samples for testing. Or you're doing a PhD study on genetic variability in freshwater turtles, and you'd like to travel to remote areas catching turtles in the wild, scraping off DNA samples, and freezing them for later analysis back home.

At present, you or an intermediary might just go and collect the animals or genetic material, pay whomever helped you catch them, make the appropriate arrangements for safe transportation, maybe buy a gift for a minor official or two if necessary and if your conscience would allow it, and go about your business. But all that has changed with the CBD, and you want to make sure you're in compliance with the US Department of State guidelines. Where to start?

Wanted: A guidebook for collectors

It would make the job of researchers a lot easier if there were the equivalent of a Lonely Planet Guide to access and benefit-sharing laws in every country. The guide might answer such questions as:

- Does the country have any laws regulating the collection of aquatic bio-diversity?
- What's the scope of the law? Does it make any distinction between biological and genetic resources?
- Whose permission do I have to get and how do I get it?
- If I need to get the prior informed consent of an indigenous community, how do I tell what the community is and who speaks for it?
- What happens if the community has no knowledge of the fish I'm collecting – or at least no knowledge that I need for breeding or other research? Do I still need to get its consent?
- What does prior informed consent mean, anyway? How much information do I have to reveal and how can I make sure the community understands what I'm talking about?
- What kinds of 'benefits' will I be able to and need to provide? What if I'm not planning to use the material commercially or, if I am, I won't know whether there's likely to be any money it for years?
- If I do pay the community something for the right to collect fish broodstock, can I patent the new strain I develop and be done with any future obligations to the community?
- I'm a scientist, not a negotiator. I know nothing about the indigenous communities in the region where I'll be working and I don't even speak the language. How can I get help negotiating an agreement?
- Why can't I just buy the fish or marine organisms I need from a local fisherman?
- If I do get consent, what am I allowed to do with the material I collect?
- What if a community says no? Can I just move to another part of the river inhabited by the fish I'm looking for and make a deal with another community?

If such a guidebook did exist right now, it would be a very slim volume. The CBD obligates all its member countries (188 in 2004) to develop access and benefit-sharing measures. Ten years after the coming into force of the CBD, not a single developed country has such a law in place. This may not be surprising given that southern countries are where genetic resources are in greatest demand – though it is a matter of some concern to indigenous peoples in northern countries. In the South, as we'll see below, several countries are experimenting with new laws governing access to genetic resources, community rights, and biodiversity management generally. At the moment, that's largely all they are – experiments in the form of regional model laws that countries might draw upon (eg OAU), provisional presidential decrees (eg Philippines and Brazil) that lack the weight of congressional statutes, and innovative but unimplemented proposals (eg Peru's law for the protection of indigenous knowledge).

In essence, the world has been adopting a wait-and-see attitude towards making clear rules regarding the conservation of biological diversity, the sustainable use of genetic resources, and sharing the benefits from their use – the three goals of the CBD. Certainly the objectives of the CBD are no less important than they were at the time of the Earth Summit in 1992 – quite the contrary. So why the delay?

The hold-up in developing access laws

One body of opinion has it that industrialized countries, through the Agreement on TRIPS, have hijacked the CBD. From this perspective, developing countries put all their effort into gaining CBD recognition of national sovereignty over genetic resources, only to find that what really mattered was ownership of the ideas that makes possible particular uses of genetic resources. In other words, if a southern country has sovereignty over a medicinal plant or toxic marine organism, but a transnational company holds the patent on the process of using the genetic resource to make a medicine – or, indeed, a patent on a naturally occurring gene that enables a fish or plant to live in icy conditions – then sovereignty over natural resources may be virtually valueless compared to the right to profit from invention. Developing countries that thought that the CBD was merely setting the stage for new rules have discovered to their consternation that the playing field has shifted under their feet thanks to the pressures of corporate globalization.

The TRIPS syndrome is certainly not the only factor holding back the development of access and benefit-sharing laws, but it has made developing countries think very carefully about how to get the most bang from their legislative buck when it comes to regulating genetic resources. Some countries are also taking it slow and easy in order to learn from the painful experience of the Philippines, the first country out of the starting blocks in the initial eagerness to translate CBD theory into legislative action (see Case Study 5 at the end of this chapter).

The approximately 50 countries currently in the process of developing access and benefit-sharing laws are asking themselves questions such as the following:

- How do we define the right of indigenous and local communities to negotiate access to genetic resources? Do we base that right on their contribution of traditional knowledge, or should any community have the right?
- How do we balance our CBD obligations to protect traditional knowledge against industrial country pressures to protect the IPRs of users of genetic resources?
- How do we give communities a right to negotiate access to genetic resources without bringing commercial and academic research to a virtual halt? How do we distinguish between commercial and academic research?
- How do we build and finance the infrastructure needed to implement and enforce new laws?
- What kinds of benefits should be negotiated with collectors at the national and community levels? What kinds of benefits are meaningful and achievable, and how can they promote the conservation and sustainable use of biological diversity?
- Should there be broad stakeholder participation in the development of access laws, or will that just lead to gridlock and no result at all? If we want to get stakeholder input, how should we go about it?

In the meantime, while the parties to the CBD try to decide how to implement access and benefit-sharing laws, confusion reigns. Ten Kate and Laird (1999) note that the most common industry complaint about the CBD and its implementation is the lack of clarity about access procedures. Companies say that while the CBD (and existing access laws) may be fine in theory, there is no practical way to implement, monitor and enforce them. As one researcher put it, 'The access and benefit sharing discussion is not really moving, and companies and collectors are operating in a vacuum.'

What makes the situation even worse for collectors of aquatic genetic resources is that the development of new access laws is almost exclusively shaped by plant issues such as the use of farmers' traditional knowledge about crop lines or access to plants that may have medicinal values. In countries such as the Philippines, collection of marine organisms for sampling by pharmaceutical companies has certainly been in the minds of policy makers, but there's little evidence of much thought being given anywhere to the application of access laws to collections for aquaculture, whether for food fish or ornamentals. This will undoubtedly change during the next two decades for two primary reasons: increased pressures for rapid global growth in food fish aquaculture to provide food security, especially in southern countries, and the continuing momentum of the indigenous rights movement.

This chapter and the two succeeding chapters discuss:

- Progress to date in the development of laws related to the availability and use of aquatic genetic resources.
- Possible frameworks for the negotiation of access agreements with fishing communities.
- Fundamental principles that may need to be met to ensure the effective sharing and conservation of aquatic biodiversity in the future.

FINE-TUNING THE CBD: The Bonn guidelines

The US Department of State memo described above appeared shortly after the parties to the CBD had agreed on a set of general guidelines for access and benefit-sharing legislation. By November 2001, 58 parties had submitted their second national reports on their progress in implementing the CBD. We have already seen in Chapter 3 what a generally low importance these national reports placed on aquatic biodiversity. Regarding Article 8(j), 25 placed a high priority on implementation. Seventeen others described it as a medium priority, and 13 called it a low priority. Slightly more than half of the countries that submitted reports indicated that some actions were either being taken or contemplated to implement Article 8(j). Others indicated that they were waiting for further guidance from the CBD Working Group on Article 8(j) before proceeding (World Fisheries Trust, 2002b).

In the spring of 2002, the Sixth COP of the CBD approved the Bonn Guidelines on Access to Genetic Resources and Fair and Equitable Sharing of the Benefits Arising out of their Utilization (CBD, 2002). Like other CBD products, the guidelines represent a hard won consensus among countries with very divergent interests and consequently take the form of general principles rather than a detailed policy framework. It can be expected that countries may take very different approaches on specific legislative provisions.

The Bonn Guidelines address the question of access to genetic resources in indigenous and local communities in several sections dealing with prior informed consent and benefit sharing.

Prior informed consent

- Respecting the established legal rights of indigenous and local communities associated with the genetic resources being accessed or where traditional knowledge associated with these genetic resources is being accessed, the prior informed consent of indigenous and local communities and the approval and involvement of the holders of traditional knowledge should be obtained, in accordance with their traditional practices, national access policies and subject to domestic laws (31).
- Access to genetic resources should be facilitated at minimum cost (26).
- Any change in use for which consent has been granted, including transfer to third parties, may require a new application for prior informed consent (34).
- Countries of origin should support measures to enhance indigenous and local communities' capacity to represent their interests fully at negotiations (16).

Benefit sharing

- Countries of origin, or other countries that have acquired genetic resources in accordance with the CBD, should ensure the fair and equitable sharing of benefits in conformity with mutually agreed terms established with indigenous and local communities (16).
- Benefits should be shared fairly and equitably with all who have contributed to the resource management, scientific and/or commercial process – including governmental, non-governmental or academic institutions and indigenous and local communities. Benefits should be directed in such a way as to promote conservation and sustainable use of biodiversity (48).
- Benefits may be monetary or non-monetary (Appendix II of the guidelines includes an extensive list of each type).

The Bonn Guidelines appear to move beyond Article 8(j) of the CBD by suggesting that the right of communities to prior informed consent exists whether or not collectors of genetic resources rely on the use of traditional knowledge, and that benefits should be shared with any community that has contributed to the management of the genetic resource. This provision, if translated into national legislation, may prove particularly relevant for fishing communities that may not contribute knowledge vital to collectors but may nevertheless have a long history of sustainable management of aquatic ecosystems.

What legal rights do communities have?

The Bonn Guidelines' suggestion that the right to prior informed consent be based on 'established legal rights' of communities is likely to be contentious in many countries. Municipalities may, for example, include a range of distinct fishing villages that may object if the right to consent to access rests with a distant mayor – as indeed they have under Philippine access legislation. In the case of indigenous communities, what the state recognizes as established legal rights may differ widely from those claimed by indigenous peoples. Under Canadian law, for example, many indigenous fishing communities (and First Nations) have no legal right even to be consulted in the collection and use of aquatic genetic resources. The Supreme Court of Canada has recognized the existence of aboriginal rights in areas where no treaties were signed before Canada became a nation. As a result the federal and provincial governments have been embroiled for years in negotiations with dozens of First Nations to create treaties that will define the nature and extent of aboriginal rights, including ownership of land and control over biological and genetic resources. While a few treaties have been signed (Case Studies 2 and 3 refer to two of them), most are years away from being finalized. As Canada has discovered, negotiating the legal rights of indigenous peoples may be the best way to secure a fair and stable result, but the path is long and arduous.

Some countries, such as the Philippines and India, have opted instead to define community and/or indigenous rights by statute. Others are still exploring other options for *sui generis* protection of community rights and traditional knowledge. Typically, the few national laws on community rights emphasize intellectual property protection. In most nations, indigenous and local community rights remain ill-defined at best, and national governments are approaching the issue with extreme caution. The concept of 'established legal rights', while it may sound relatively straightforward, could be a powder keg when it comes to working out the details of prior informed consent requirements in national legislation.

NATIONAL AND REGIONAL APPROACHES TO ACCESS LAWS

Countries developing access and benefit-sharing laws are likely to look for guidance beyond the generic provisions of the Bonn Guidelines to the experience of the few countries that have already embarked on legislation. Countries that have drafted or enacted legislation have taken widely varying approaches to access. For example:

- Costa Rica and India have embedded access and benefit provisions in comprehensive biodiversity management laws rather than as separate legislation. The advantage of this approach is that it recognizes the integral relationship between access policies and those for the management of biological and genetic resources generally.
- The Philippines and Brazil have enacted laws specific to access and benefit sharing.

- Peru has proposed a separate law that deals specifically with the protection of knowledge of indigenous peoples and recognizing their rights to control the use of their knowledge.

The only countries with access and benefit-sharing laws currently in force are Costa Rica, the Philippines and Brazil. Of these, only the Costa Rican law has been approved by the national legislature. The Philippine and Brazilian laws are presidential decrees that can be terminated by order of the president; in both countries, bills have been presented to congress but not yet passed.

Some southern countries have been hesitant about putting rigorous access requirements in place simply because of the fear of losing business and potential revenues. If a desired species or population is widespread, collectors faced with what they perceive to be onerous regulations may simply move their operations to more 'friendly' jurisdictions. Partially to avoid such scenarios, three regional groups of southern countries have prepared guidelines for member states both to encourage consistency in approaches and to join forces in the challenge of preparing very complex legislation with numerous possibilities for error. The regional groups and the guidelines they have adopted include:

- The ASEAN: includes all South east Asian countries: Indonesia, Malaysia, Singapore, Philippines, Thailand, Brunei Darussalam, Lao People's Democratic Republic, Myanmar and Cambodia. (Model law: ASEAN Framework Agreement on Access to Genetic Resources.)
- The Andean Pact: Bolivia, Colombia, Ecuador, Peru and Venezuela. (Model law: Decision 391 – Common Regime on Access to Genetic Resources.)
- The OAU (predecessor of the African Group), including more than 50 African countries. (Model law: African Model Legislation for the Protection of the Rights of Local Communities, Farmers and Breeders, and for the Regulation and Access to Biological Resources.)

The regional guidelines set minimum standards for national laws and take somewhat different approaches to the recognition of community rights:

- The OAU model law specifically recognizes community rights over biological resources and traditional knowledge and practices as expressed in customary community law.
- The principles established under the ASEAN Framework Agreement (2000) echo the language of Article 8(j) on traditional knowledge and practices and call for 'the fair and equitable sharing of benefits arising from the utilization of biological and genetic resources at the community, national and regional levels'.
- The Andean Pact Decision 391 deals with agreements between the state and collectors and makes no specific reference to consent by communities.

COMPARATIVE ANALYSIS: How the new laws deal with access to genetic resources in communities

Not surprisingly, southern countries have been first off the mark to embark on the development of access and benefit-sharing legislation. As the primary providers of genetic resources, they have the most to gain by negotiating benefits in return for permitting access. Northern countries have a far bigger stake in expanding patent protection for users of genetic resources and consequently have been much more actively involved in pushing for global standards for the other half of the equation, namely for IPRs.

The three regional associations described above and several countries in Asia, Africa and South America have taken different approaches to the regulation of access to genetic resources in indigenous and local communities. Some countries appear to limit the right to informed consent and benefit sharing to those communities whose traditional knowledge is needed for the use of genetic resources, while others assume the right of communities to grant or withhold consent regardless of whether such knowledge is a factor. As the previous chapter noted, this distinction is far more crucial for traditional fishing communities than for farmers and for indigenous groups familiar with medicinal uses of plants. Assuming that the law does require community consent for access to aquatic genetic resources, several other issues are important for both communities and collectors:

- What procedures should be followed to obtain consent?
- Should academic researchers be treated differently from commercial collectors?
- What types of benefit are most appropriate?

The following synopsis compares how the three regions and several countries (Brazil, Costa Rica, India, Peru and the Philippines[1]) have addressed these questions. The Philippines – the first country to pass access and benefit-sharing legislation after the CBD came into force – has the most experience with implementation. Case Study 5 at the end of this chapter provides a detailed look at the challenges the Philippines has faced. The Philippine experience holds important lessons for other countries – and for communities and collectors – about what works and what doesn't.

Numbers in parentheses refer to the article or section number of regional model laws and national laws.

The scope of access laws: Biological and genetic resources

As Glowka (1998b) notes, drafters of legislation should be encouraged to use definitions that already appear in international agreements such as the CBD, since the terms and definitions used in such documents reflect a broad international consensus. The CBD defines biological resources as including 'genetic resources, organisms or parts thereof, populations, or any other biotic component of ecosystems with actual or potential use or value for humanity'. Genetic resources are defined as 'genetic material of actual or potential value', and genetic material

---

Box 5.1 Comparing Laws: Defining the Scope

Do access laws and guidelines apply to genetic resources, biological resources and/or knowledge? As the following summary shows, different countries and regions take different approaches:

OAU

Applies to biological resources and knowledge or technologies of local communities in any part of the country (s. 3). Biological resources are defined to include genetic resources, organisms or parts thereof, populations, or any other component of ecosystems (s. 1).

Andean Community

Applies to *in situ* and *ex situ* genetic resources, defined as all material that contains genetic information of value or of real or potential use (1).

ASEAN

Defines 'bioprospecting' as the search for wild species with genes that produce better crops and medicines, or the exploration of biodiversity for commercially valuable genetic and biological resources (3).

Brazil

Applies to access to components of 'genetic heritage', defined as 'information of genetic origin'.

Costa Rica

Applies to samples of components of biodiversity, whether *in situ* or *ex situ*. Biodiversity includes the variability of living organisms of any source, whether found in terrestrial, air or marine or aquatic ecosystems or in other ecological complexes (s. 7). Access sections (ss. 62–85) apply only to genetic components (containing functional units of heredity) and biochemicals.

Philippines

Applies to biological and genetic resources.

---

means 'any material of plant, animal, microbial or other origin containing functional units of heredity'.

Most laws do not distinguish between biological and genetic resources, or, as in the case of the OAU model law, define biological resources to include genetic resources. The access provisions of Costa Rica's biodiversity law apply only to genetic components (containing functional units of heredity) and biochemicals. In all cases, the scope of the laws is broad enough to include all forms of aquatic genetic resources, although nowhere is it apparent that collection for aquaculture has been contemplated. For example, the ASEAN framework defines 'bioprospecting' as the search for wild species with genes that produce better crops and medicines, or the exploration of biodiversity for commercially valuable genetic and biological resources. Collections of broodstock for industrial aquaculture haven't yet become an issue in developing countries.

Prior informed consent by communities

The primary authority for approving applications for access lies with national governments, which the CBD recognizes as having sovereignty over genetic resources. Each country designates a 'Competent National Authority' to oversee the approval process. Typically, under proposed and existing access laws, the national authority requires proof of consent by indigenous and local communities, although specific requirements vary considerably.

But what is a local community? Brazilian law defines it as a 'human group, differentiated by its cultural conditions, which is traditionally organized along successive generations and with its own customs, and conserves its social and economic institutions' (Article 7). Philippine law describes it simply as 'the basic political unit where biological and genetic resources are located' (2). The OAU model law describes it as 'a human population in a distinct geographical area, with ownership over its biological resources, innovations, practices, knowledge and technologies governed partially or completely by its own customs, traditions or laws' (1). It is not yet clear how different countries will translate such broad definitions into practice both in regulatory frameworks and in dealing with groups whose concept of themselves as a community may differ a great deal from that of a government agency.

There is no consistency among countries on the issue of whether collectors need consent for all collections of genetic resources or only when seeking access to traditional knowledge. Peru and Brazil specifically link the requirement to obtain indigenous community consent to access to traditional knowledge. Countries such as the Philippines require consent for access to genetic resources without limiting the right to communities whose knowledge is required for the use of genetic resources. The OAU model law recognizes the rights of communities over their biological resources, innovations, practices, knowledge and technologies and the right to benefit from their use (16).

Notable in some laws are the restrictions on the authority of communities to withhold consent. The Costa Rican law recognizes the right of communities to oppose any access to their resources or associated knowledge, whether for cultural, spiritual, social, economic or other motives (66). In Brazil, however, access may be permitted without consent 'in instances of relevant public interest' (17). Under the OAU model law, communities can refuse access if it will be 'detrimental to the integrity of their natural or cultural heritage' (19). It remains to be seen how different countries will handle refusals of consent by communities that are simply unsatisfied with the benefits offered to them, or give no reasons for refusal, and what impact such refusals are likely to have on both academic and commercial research. There are still too few instances of negotiations with communities to determine whether the withholding of consent is likely to be a common trend. As discussed below, bureaucratic hurdles under the new laws have already led to 'research chill' even before negotiations with communities become a reality.

Regional guidelines and national laws spell out principles but generally don't provide specific guidance on procedures for obtaining community consent. As the majority of laws discussed here are either in draft form or very new, regulations

Box 5.2 Comparing Laws: Community Right to Consent

OAU

Access to biological resources, knowledge and/or technologies of local communities is subject to the written prior informed consent of the Competent National Authority as well as that of concerned local communities, ensuring that women are also involved in decision-making (s 5). An access permit is granted through a written agreement between the Competent National Authority, concerned local communities and the applicant or collector (7). Local communities can refuse access if it will be detrimental to the integrity of their natural or cultural heritage (19) and can withdraw consent or place restrictions on activities relating to access if they are likely to be detrimental to their socio-economic life or their natural and cultural heritage (20). Women are to fully and equally participate in decisions about prior informed consent for access (18).

Andean Community

Parties to access agreements are the state and the applicant (32). Applicants may make ancillary contracts with the owner, possessor or manager of the land where the biological resource containing the genetic resource is located (41). No specific mention of communities.

Brazil

The state recognizes the right of the indigenous communities and of the local communities to decide on the use of their traditional knowledge related to the genetic heritage of the country (1).

Peru

Collectors wishing to obtain access to collective knowledge for scientific, commercial or industrial purposes must request the prior informed consent of one or more indigenous peoples possessing the collective knowledge (7).

Costa Rica

Prior informed consent for access to genetic components and biochemicals must be obtained from representatives of the place where access will occur, whether regional councils of Conservation Areas, owners of farms, or indigenous authorities (s 63). Local communities and indigenous peoples can oppose access to their resources and associated knowledge for cultural, spiritual, social, economic or other reasons (s 66).

Philippines

Prospecting within ancestral lands and domains of indigenous cultural communities is allowed only with their prior informed consent, obtained in accordance with customary laws. Prior informed consent must also be obtained from concerned local communities, defined as basic political units where the biological and genetic resources are located (2). Research proposals must be submitted to the recognized head of any affected local or indigenous cultural community (4).

implementing national laws are virtually non-existent outside the Philippines. Under the Philippine regulations, a collector must obtain consent from the mayor of a local community or head of an indigenous people, hold a community assembly, fully describe the research proposal in a language or dialect understandable to local people, and describe proposed benefits. As Case Study 5 illustrates, community advocates have criticized these provisions for not requiring sufficient consultation with communities that don't believe a municipal mayor represents their interests. In addition, local people may not fully understand the implications of proposed activities and uses of genetic resources, and may lack the capacity to conduct negotiations effectively without assistance.

Protection of traditional knowledge

In some cases, access and benefit-sharing laws have made efforts to address potential conflicts over rights to knowledge by providing for *sui generis* protection of traditional knowledge. The advantages of unique legal forms of protection for community property rights have been much discussed, but how they will be crafted to fit into existing legal systems remains to be seen.

Costa Rica's biodiversity law recognizes and protects *sui generis* community intellectual rights over knowledge, practices and innovations related to the use of components of biodiversity and associated knowledge (82), and provides that no form of intellectual or industrial property rights protection can affect these historic practices. The law provides for a participatory process with small farmer and indigenous communities to determine the nature and scope of *sui generis* rights (s 83).

The OAU model law also takes a step towards the enshrinement of *sui generis* rights by providing that the Community Intellectual Property Rights of local communities are inalienable (23). Community Intellectual Property Rights are defined as those rights held by local communities over their biological resources or parts or derivatives thereof, and over their practices, innovations, knowledge and technologies. The state recognizes and protects community rights as enshrined under the norms, practices and customary law, whether written or not (17). The Philippines, in addition to its bioprospecting law, has adopted separate legislation for the protection of Community Intellectual Property Rights.

Some community advocacy groups have criticized the concept of *sui generis* rights for trying to fit traditional knowledge into a property rights model that has no relevance to traditional community governance systems. Indigenous communities with long traditions of sharing all community resources, including knowledge, may be suspicious of *sui generis* initiatives based on IPRs models based on individual rights. For some groups, recognition of rights over genetic resources can only be settled through acknowledgement of full rights to manage and control local ecosystems and the biological and genetic resources within them. The Costa Rican and OAU initiatives are the most progressive among access and benefit-sharing laws to date, but it remains to be seen how they will work in practice. Bangladesh and the Philippines have moved a step further by drafting stand alone community rights legislation.

One of the primary incentives for national initiatives to protect traditional knowledge is to provide a legal barrier against its unauthorized use by collectors of genetic resources. As discussed in previous chapters in this book, *sui generis* protection of traditional knowledge bolsters the rights of plant communities but may be largely irrelevant to the collection of aquatic genetic resources in fishing communities. This is because, while dependence on traditional knowledge may be the rule in the use of plant genetic resources, it's the exception in the use of aquatic genetic resources. Consequently, drafters of laws that apply to the collection of genetic resources in general need to consider very carefully the implications for both plant and aquatic collections.

Intellectual property rights protection

Most developing countries are amending their patent laws to comply with the WTO TRIPS Agreement, which requires all countries to extend their patent systems to include all technologies and all inventions. This includes the patenting of micro-organisms and microbiological processes, although countries can exclude plants and animals. In addition, developing countries are facing pressure to go beyond the TRIPS agreements. For example, preferential trade, aid, investment or technical assistance privileges may be tied to a commitment from developing countries to adopt more hard line standards for IPRs on life forms, including International Union for the Protection of New Varieties of Plants (UPOV) standards of plant variety rights or industrial patent rules over plants and animals (GRAIN, 2002a).

The tension between TRIPS and CBD commitments is reflected in differing approaches taken by access and benefit-sharing laws. The Brazilian law notes that protection of traditional knowledge 'shall not affect, damage or limit rights related to intellectual property' (8) and requires that access and benefit-sharing contracts include provision for IPRs (28). By contrast, the OAU model law provides that collectors must agree not to apply for intellectual property protection over a biological resource or its derivatives without community consent (8); it also prohibits patents on life forms and biological processes (9). Costa Rica provides for the protection of IPRs with several exceptions, including the prohibition of IPRs for 'inventions which, to be commercially exploited through a monopoly, can affect farming or fishing processes or products which are considered basic for the food and health of the inhabitants of the country' (78).

The question of IPRs is a sore point for many indigenous peoples, not only because of understandable suspicions about the unauthorized appropriation of traditional knowledge, but also because the concept of private ownership of ideas directly contradicts indigenous traditions of sharing knowledge for the benefit of all members of a community. Case Study 3 describes negotiations for access to charr broodstock that failed in large part because of indigenous communities' discomfort with proposals to patent processes for gene mapping. In this example, there was no relationship whatsoever between the IPRs sought by the user and the traditional knowledge held by Inuit communities. What will happen if indigenous communities demand a prohibition on IPRs as a condition for providing consent for access, even though the collector's invention owes no debt to traditional knowledge? It's a stalemate that is especially likely to happen during negotiations for access to living creatures as opposed to plants, and policy makers would do well to anticipate such scenarios. The right to intellectual property protection to inventions is frequently one of the key benefits collectors expect to take away from what may prove to be very expensive negotiations.

Treating academics like commercial collectors: A recipe for research chill

Some laws distinguish between applications for commercial and academic research purposes. The OAU model law simply provides that applications must state the relationship of the applicant with industry (11) and that permit fees may differ depending on whether the research is for commercial or academic purposes (12). Brazilian law appears to require an access and benefit-sharing contract only when there is a possibility of commercial use (16). The Philippine law uniquely provides for separate commercial and academic research agreements – the latter being restricted to institutions within the country (3). Academic research agreements can be broader and more general in character (4), with each agreement covering all scientists and researchers at an institution. If it later becomes evident that academic research resulting from collections has commercial prospects, a scientist must reapply for a commercial agreement (5). Under either type of agreement, collectors must obtain the prior informed consent of communities where collections take place; under academic agreements, collecting institutions can develop their own internal guidelines for obtaining prior informed consent.

Drawing meaningful distinctions between academic and commercial research is one of the most difficult challenges that policy makers face. Obviously, encouraging pure academic research is absolutely vital for countries that are serious about developing the comprehensive knowledge needed not only to conserve biological and genetic diversity but also to explore new uses that may be either commercially valuable or in the public interest. This is even more important in the aquatic than in the plant world given the current state of understanding of (and growing commercial interest in) aquatic ecosystems. The very activity of research also builds important technical capacity in the country.

Unfortunately, the days of independent research institutions appear to be numbered and the boundaries between academic and commercial activities are becoming less and less clear. In these days of downsizing, many research institutions both in government and in the academic world are forced to become ever more dependent on corporate support just to survive – and consequently may face pressure to focus on research with promising commercial applications. A scientific institution that collects sponges for taxonomic purposes may also have an agreement with the American Cancer Institute to provide samples for screening. The conundrum for policy makers is how to design processes for approval for access to genetic resources that ensure a fair return from commercial applications without being so onerous that they shut down scientific research altogether. As Case Study 5 at the end of this chapter illustrates, the distinctions between

---

Box 5.3 Comparing Laws: Academic vs Commercial Uses

OAU

Research applications must state the objective of the research and the relationship of the applicant to industry (s. 11). Permit fees may differ depending on whether research is for commercial or academic purposes (s. 12).

Philippines

Research for commercial purposes, directly or indirectly, requires a Commercial Research Agreement (CRA). Application for Academic Research Agreements (ARAs) is restricted to Philippines universities and academic institutions, domestic governmental entities and inter-governmental entities (3). ARA proposals can be broader and more general in character than CRA proposals (4). One ARA can cover all scientists and researchers at an institution (5). Scientists operating under an ARA must later apply for a CRA if it becomes clear that research and collection has commercial prospects (5).

---

academic and commercial research under Philippine law appear to have done little to facilitate academic research and indeed have hindered it.

In addition to distinguishing between academic and commercial purposes, some laws also differentiate between nationals and foreigners. India's law specifically notes that no non-Indian person can obtain any biological resource or associated knowledge without approval of the National Biodiversity Authority (3). Under Philippine law, foreign applicants must apply for collection in partnership with a Philippine national research institute or university. Their research applications must include a proposal stating the purpose, source of funds, duration and a list of biological and genetic materials and amounts to be taken (4).

Sharing benefits with communities

Defining the nature, amount and method of delivery of benefits to communities will likely be the greatest challenge of all for both policy makers and those involved in access negotiations. Some laws mention benefits in the most general terms without elaboration; others, such as Philippines Executive Order 247, specifically mention benefits such as royalties. From the viewpoint of communities, the drawbacks of limiting benefits to royalties have long been apparent because the likelihood of developing a marketable product from a single collection (at least in the pharmaceuticals field) is so low. The Philippines legislation has been sharply criticized by civil society organizations for providing only for royalties and for not specifying how they will be divided between communities and government. The OAU model law, which appeared three years later, addressed this concern by requiring at least a 50 per cent share for communities.

Non-monetary benefits, such as technology transfer, training and employment can ultimately be not only far more useful to communities but also more effective in facilitating sustainable, conservation-based economies. Generally, under existing and proposed laws, the responsibility to determine appropriate types of benefits and the manner of ensuring their delivery lies primarily with national authorities. The effectiveness of access and benefit-sharing legislation will consequently depend to a large extent on the ability and motivation of governments to work with communities and collectors alike to facilitate creative solutions.

One important question that appears to remain largely unresolved is whether benefits should be distributed only to those communities in which collections occur, or on a broader scale. Peru, recognizing that collective knowledge may be shared among a variety of indigenous groups, takes the approach of providing for the transfer of monetary benefits to a general fund for the development of indigenous peoples. (This in some ways resembles a similar approach taken in the corporate world by Shaman Pharmaceuticals, which decided to divide a portion of its profits among all communities where collections took place, whether or not any given community's contribution led to the development of a marketable product.)

Governments that adopt such an approach could follow up with institutional arrangements for promoting community development and biodiversity conservation through, for example, transfer of small-scale technologies (and training in their use) to support sustainable livelihoods, help in the development of marketing skills and mechanisms, and assistance in the development of conservation strategies that contribute to economic well-being. In fishing communities, this might include, for example, providing help with the development of sustainable fisheries that may or may not have been traditionally practised. Costa Rica's biodiversity law promotes community participation in the conservation and sustainable use of biological diversity through technical assistance and special incentives, especially in areas with rare, endemic or endangered species. To this end, it requires the Ministry of Environment and Energy to give priority to projects for community management of biodiversity (102). Using this type of model, governments elsewhere might channel a portion of benefits received at the national level to local and indigenous communities, to the advantage of the country as a whole.

Such a broad-based approach to benefit sharing makes sense because it can enable national authorities to use the proceeds from the use of genetic resources for the benefit of many communities rather than just the few that may be involved in negotiating agreements. It may also help avoid the detrimental effects that might arise if one community's benefits place it at a significant advantage over neighbours who may share similar genetic resources (and knowledge) but weren't party to an agreement. This could conceivably happen to communities that negotiate in good faith, only to discover that the collector moves to another community that can meet his needs with fewer demands – just as collectors may avoid a country with strict regulations (like the Philippines) in favour of a nation with fewer restrictions.

As discussed earlier, while the general trend in access legislation has been to require prior informed consent of communities whether or not their knowledge contributes to the use of a genetic resource, not all countries take this approach. The effect of some current laws could be to leave fishing communities entirely out of the benefit-sharing equation and to create an imbalance in which objectives for the conservation of terrestrial biodiversity are met at the expense of aquatic

Box 5.4 Comparing Laws: Sharing Benefits with Indigenous and Local Communities

OAU

Under the agreement with the Competent National Authority and communities, the collector undertakes to: provide for the sharing of benefits; inform concerned communities of all research and development findings; contribute economically to community efforts to regenerate and conserve the biological resource collected and to maintain the innovation, practice, knowledge or technology to which access is sought (s. 8). Communities are entitled to a share of earnings derived when any biological resource and/or knowledge generates a product used in a production process (12). The state must ensure that at least 50 per cent of benefits so derived are channelled to concerned local communities in a manner that treats men and women equitably (22).

Andean Community

Applications for access and access contracts shall include conditions for strengthening and development of the capacities of the native, Afro-American, and local communities with relation to the associated intangible components (know how, innovations, practices), the genetic resources, and their by-products (17). Access contracts shall stipulate fair and equitable distribution of profits from the use of genetic resources or by-products with an intangible component (35).

Brazil

Indigenous and local communities that create, develop, hold or conserve traditional knowledge associated with genetic heritage have the right to receive benefits from the economic use by third parties of associated traditional knowledge to which they hold rights (9).

Costa Rica

Requirements for access include technology transfer and equitable distribution of benefits, as agreed in permits, agreements and concessions (63).

India

National Biodiversity Authority approval of access depends on securing equitable sharing of benefits arising from the use of biological resources, their by-products, innovations and practices associated with their use and applications and knowledge related thereto (21). Required benefits may include: joint ownership of IPRs with benefit claimers; technology transfer; location of production, research and development units in such areas which will facilitate better living standards to the benefit claimers; association of benefit claimers and local people in biological resources; venture capital funds to help benefit claimers; and payment of monetary and non-monetary benefits to benefit claimers (21). 'Benefit claimers' includes conservers of biological resources, their by-products, creators and holders of knowledge and information to use biological resources, innovations, and practices associated with such use and application (21). If approving collectors' applications of IPRs, the National Biodiversity Authority may impose a benefit-sharing fee or royalty or both or impose conditions including the sharing of financial benefits arising from the commercial use of such rights (6).

> **Box 5.4** continued
>
> *Peru*
>
> Whoever gains access to the collective knowledge of an indigenous people must destine at least 0.5 per cent of the value of sales resulting from the marketing of products developed from such knowledge to the Fund for the Development of Indigenous Peoples (7). The Fund will support projects and activities approved by an Administrator Committee.
>
> *Philippines*
>
> Commercial agreements between the applicant and government must include provision for payment of royalties to the national government, local or indigenous cultural community (5).

biodiversity. This is another reason why drafters of access and benefit-sharing laws will need to consider the implications of legislative provisions not just for plant genetic resources but also for aquatic genetic resources and the communities that provide them. Chapter 6 discusses strategies for developing benefits that are appropriate for fishing communities and that can help promote conservation and sustainable use.

Making benefit sharing work: Responsibilities of industrial countries

The CBD states three objectives: the conservation of biological diversity, the sustainable use of its components and the equitable sharing of benefits arising from the use of genetic resources. Achieving the first two objectives logically depends on meeting the third: unless the biodiversity rich countries and communities providing genetic resources benefit by doing so, they will have neither the incentive to make those resources readily available nor the motivation or means to promote their conservation.

Under Article 15(2) of the CBD, each contracting Party (ie the 188 countries that have ratified the convention) must create the conditions needed to facilitate access to genetic resources. That's the commitment developing countries made in return for international recognition of their sovereignty over genetic resources. In addition, under 15(7), each Party is to take legislative, policy or administrative measures with the aim of fairly sharing the results of research and development and the benefits arising from the use of genetic resources with each country providing the resources.

What the CBD recognizes is that it will take a concerted and cooperative effort by southern and northern countries (ie the primary providers and users of genetic resources) to make sustainable development work. Developing countries have made good progress towards putting access and benefit-sharing laws in place; industrial countries, for their part, need to do whatever they can to make sure that laws in provider countries are effective. Why? It's extremely challenging to enforce access and benefit-sharing laws because of the transnational, north-south flow of genetic resources and because governments in many developing countries lack the financial and staff resources to do so. As a result, there's a trend in source countries to establish very restrictive access laws that often unintentionally hinder scientific research as well as domestic and international development.

Laird (2002) suggests that the major industrial nations have abdicated their responsibility to institute measures to ensure equitable access and benefit-sharing arrangements. They have been slow to develop legal measures to ensure that the acquisition and use of genetic material and associated knowledge by persons, institutions and corporations in user countries are carried out in compliance with the laws in source countries and with the provisions of the CBD. For example, none of the IPRs systems of the industrialized countries requires that patent applications for inventions based on genetic inventions or associated knowledge acquired in another country prove that the resources or knowledge were acquired in compliance with the CBD or national law in the source country.

As illustrated in our discussion of biopiracy complaints in Chapter 3, this is an issue that has received considerable attention in the plant world and has largely been ignored in discussions about the commercial use of aquatic resources outside of collections for the pharmaceutical industry. This will undoubtedly change with the global expansion of commercial aquaculture and, with it, an increased interest in international collection of the broodstock and germplasm that might produce the best trains. Case Study 4 describes ICLARM's initiatives to collect tilapia broodstock in several African countries in order to develop new strains in the Philippines that are now widely farmed throughout Southeast Asia. ICLARM did so with the permission of the source countries and for an altruistic purpose – ensuring the availability of more hardy and productive strains for rural fish farmers. At the time of the initial collections, ICLARM did not anticipate that patenting would be an issue, although the 'Super Tilapia' was in fact patented several years later by the GIFT Foundation. Variations of ICLARM's GIFT initiative – considered highly innovative at the time it occurred – will likely appear in the future for other species and other countries as the aquaculture industry becomes more diverse. It will be important not only for source countries to have workable access laws in place but also for recipient countries to support CBD principles by taking legal measures to ensure that collectors comply with laws in countries that provide genetic resources, whether in situ (in the wild) or ex situ (eg from gene banks).

Assuming that northern countries do become more rigorous about lending support to the CBD principles and the access laws of southern countries, a variety of uncertainties specific to aquatic genetic resources will need to be addressed. For instance, Case Study 1 describes recent successes in breeding cardinal tetras in Florida. Cardinal tetras are collected by local fishermen in Brazil and exported for distribution to the aquarium hobbyists' trade – not for breeding but simply for live display. Aquarists who want to breed ornamental fish might simply buy them from the export trade and search out fish with the most desirable colorations or patterns. Does a fish caught for aquarium display (or for food) transform from a biological resource to a 'genetic resource' only at the instant someone decides to use it for reproduction? Is it the intent of the user rather than the physical characteristic of the resource that ultimately matters? This is an especially important question, given the divergent approaches countries have taken to date in defining the scope of new access laws and whether they apply to just biological resources, just genetic resources, just traditional knowledge of resources, some combination of the above or, as in the case of Brazil, the wonderfully ambiguous 'genetic heritage'.

If an aquarist comes to a US patent office to apply for a patent on a strain of cardinal tetra he has 'created', how can he prove the breeding pairs were acquired in compliance with the CBD and Brazilian law? The situation is doubly confusing in Brazil because both the national and some state (eg the state of Acre) governments have independently put forward separate versions of access and benefit-sharing laws. Moreover, the national government's provisional law is so new and lacking in clarity that it's not at all clear how wide its scope is. What is almost certain is that it never crossed the minds of the drafters of the law that it might have relevance for the Rio Negro cardinal tetra fishery.

There are no easy answers to such conundrums. The point is that northern countries, several of which are slowly proceeding with their own versions of access and benefit-sharing laws, need to consider how best to support the efforts of developing countries to control the use of their biological resources in a manner that aims to conserve genetic diversity. To do so, they need to develop mechanisms that take account of inherent distinctions between plant and fish genetic resources; they also need to anticipate new developments in the aquatic genetic resources trade, some of which are only beginning to become apparent.

For a start, the Bonn Guidelines spell out several basic steps that user countries can adopt to encourage compliance with CBD principles for prior informed consent and mutually agreed terms. The measures suggested by the guidelines include:

* Informing potential users about their obligations regarding access.
* Encouraging the disclosure (eg in patent applications) of the country of origin of genetic resources and the origin of traditional knowledge.
* Preventing the use of genetic resources obtained without prior informed consent.
* Cooperating with provider countries to identify infringements of access and benefit-sharing agreements.
* Promoting certification schemes for collecting institutions.

USING FISHERIES CERTIFICATION TO SUPPORT ACCESS LAWS

It's hardly surprising that governments in industrial countries are slow to make rules regarding sustainable development if doing so may affect the bottom line of influential corporations. Yet recently there has been a trend among such governments to embrace forest certification, the main objective of which is sustainable management of forest lands and ecosystems. Essentially, governments and the forest industry have been pushed into doing so by consumer demand shaped by environmental campaigns. Certification has a very long history as a mechanism for ensuring high product standards; adapting it to address conservation and fair trade issues is a relatively recent development. In essence, it has become a tool by which concerned citizen groups can both work with government and industry to secure standards consistent with sustainable development and fair treatment – or, if considered strategically necessary, bypass government and industry by targeting markets and creating consumer demand for products that come with an assurance that those high standards have been met.

Now it appears that the stage has been set for the certification movement to expand its horizons to include the use of genetic resources. The Panel of Experts on access and benefit sharing, appointed by the CBD COP, noted a need to consider multilateral mechanisms to promote support for the prior informed consent rights of provider countries and communities. One possibility suggested by the Panel in its first report was the adoption of certification systems with a focus on access and benefit sharing. This is an option that could prove relevant for some aquatic genetic resources, and in fact is already under consideration in the collection of ornamental fish.

Certification most commonly refers to independent, third party verification that an organization complies with a set of standards and principles based on best practices in the field. In the natural resources field, forestry certification has received much attention in recent years. Increasing interest among forest companies in achieving certification, through bodies such as the Forest Stewardship Council (FSC), has largely been driven by consumer demand for timber products from sustainably managed forests and by scepticism about some countries' government regulations. Forest certification programmes ensure sustainable management by auditing forest companies' on the ground operations or environmental management systems, or both. In addition to providing certificates showing proof of certification, some programmes also provide product 'ecolabels' as an assurance to consumers that a timber product has met objective standards for sustainability throughout the 'chain of custody' from forest to store shelf. Generally, certification standards and principles are developed through multi-stakeholder processes to ensure both credibility and widespread support.

In 1997 the World Wide Fund for Nature (WWF), which had been instrumental in the founding of the FSC, engineered the creation of a parallel body for capture fisheries certification. The MSC seeks to achieve a balance between social, ecological and economic interests in fisheries by evaluating and accrediting certifiers, encouraging the development of national standards for fisheries, and promoting training and education. MSC's Principles and Criteria for Sustainable Fishing are based on the FAO Code of Conduct for Responsible Fisheries. In addition to certifying groups such as fisheries organizations, processors and governmental management authorities, MSC provides chain-of-custody certification.

The MSC still confines itself to capture fisheries. Given the controversy that surrounds some sectors of food fish aquaculture, however, it may not be long before certification systems expand to cover that industry as well. Depending on the level of public awareness and interest, consumers may also begin to demand 'fair trade' fish – that is, fish from stocks developed from fairly collected germplasm. The coffee trade provides a good illustration of the rapidity with which consumer demand can change. Until a few years ago, coffee drinkers gave little thought to the origin of their beans. Then came the demand for 'organic coffee', grown under 'sustainable' conditions. More recently, chains such as Starbucks have begun selling coffee labelled as 'fair trade' in response to consumer demand. A similar trend could occur for farmed fish or even pharmaceuticals once public awareness of access and benefit-sharing issues increases – something that only takes the determined efforts of a few NGOs. While it may be far more difficult to evaluate chains of custody for consumer products containing multiple ingredients (foods containing soybean derivatives, for instance), the process would be more straightforward where there is a clear link between the origin of a genetic resource (fish germplasm obtained from communities either directly or through collaborative gene banks) and the tilapia or salmon at the seafood counter. As we have already seen, both species of farmed fish have already benefited from locally collected germplasm.

Existing models for sustainable fisheries certification could serve as a jumping-off point for fair trade (or, more accurately, fair collection) certification. In 2001 another non-profit international organization, the Marine Aquarium Council (MAC), announced its development of an independent third party performance system to ensure quality and sustainability in the collection, culture and commerce of marine ornamentals in coral reef systems. MAC works with the entire industry chain of custody ('reef to retail') and the retailer can display a MAC logo after certification. MAC certification will be a reality once the organization has provided accreditation to independent certification companies.

Neither MSC nor MAC currently address prior informed consent issues, although MAC has flagged bioprospecting as an issue in the development of standards. MSC's forestry counterpart, the FSC, has begun to address bioprospecting related issues through a working group on non-timber forest products. The group has proposed that FSC Principle 3 (indigenous groups) be adapted to require adequate consultation with indigenous communities and remuneration to indigenous and local communities for the use of traditional knowledge (Glowka, 2001).

Governments are increasingly relying on independent certification to supplement environmental compliance laws, reflecting a general trend away from direct government regulation towards collaborative approaches to environmental compliance. In some cases (for example, Pan-European Forest Certification), national governments work together to accredit independent certification programmes and participate in standard setting. A similar approach to certification for collection of aquatic genetic resources, both within and between countries, could facilitate both the making and enforcement of effective policies for access and benefit sharing in communities.

Glowka (2001) suggests several reasons why an independent certification system for bioprospecting might be a useful complement to access and benefit-sharing laws and policies. Discouraged by past experiences with biopiracy and the failure of some researchers to live up to promises made, provider countries have reason to be suspicious of the integrity of collectors. They may want legitimate transactions to be as fair as possible but may lack the capacity to ensure a fair result, determine what deals might be fair, or determine who might be a reliable long-term partner. Regulatory systems that are too cumbersome may actually discourage genetic resources transactions, with potential users simply moving their operations to other countries, as in the case of some marine bioprospecting projects. Nor do access and benefit-sharing policies necessarily increase the legal certainty of transactions or certainty over the legal status of materials transacted.

Under these circumstances, certification systems applied to users of genetic resources could increase the confidence of provider countries about potential partners; and certification of the legal and institutional systems of providing countries could increase the confidence of potential users. In addition to helping governments ensure that the application of their own laws and policies meets best practices and not too cumbersome, certification systems could provide useful guidance for countries that have yet to develop regulatory systems. At the local level, certification of a collecting company or institution could facilitate benefit sharing by increasing the readiness of a community to negotiate. In addition, communities might feasibly apply for certification as an assurance to collectors of their suitability as negotiation partners. In short, certification systems could be adapted to deal with several types of applicant.

The primary downside of certification is the cost incurred by applicants for certification, costs which may in turn be passed on to consumers. In the forest industry, certification has taken off largely in response to consumer demand for lumber from sustainably managed forests, reflected in the decision of the largest North American home lumber retailers to buy only certified wood. In Canada, after it became apparent that the British Columbia forest industry could only remain competitive by achieving certification, the government started a programme encouraging it to do so (Brown and Greer, 2001). The issue was complicated by competition among certification systems. As the cost to the consumer tends to increase with the rigour of certification requirements, certification programmes need to take into account consumers' willingness to pay for products that are 'environmentally friendly'.

CASE STUDY 5. COMMUNITY RIGHTS VS RESEARCH CHILL: The Philippine experience with access and benefit-sharing legislation

The Philippines became the first country to enact an access and benefit-sharing law, following a cooperative effort among community groups, civil society organizations and the scientific community, strengthened by support from a president who wanted to make his mark at a time when biopiracy had become a hot topic in his country. The challenges the Philippines has faced during the initial years of the implementation of Executive Order 247 hold useful lessons for policy makers generally and for those dealing with access to genetic resources in fishing communities in particular.

Threats to aquatic biodiversity in the Philippines

Coral reefs are among the most biologically diverse of shallow-water marine ecosystems but are being degraded worldwide by human activities and climate change. The waters of the Philippines' more than 7000 islands lie at the global centre of reef building coral and fish diversity. A survey in the late 1970s found that 71 per cent of the country's reefs were either in fair or poor condition and only 5 per cent remained undisturbed (Gomez et al, 1981). Reef degradation and over-exploitation of reef fish species have continued with little abatement since that time.

In the mid-1990s, fishermen in the profitable live fish trade sprayed an estimated 10 to 15 million coral heads annually with sodium cyanide (Barber and La Vina, 1995). The 1998 Philippines Fisheries Code of Conduct prohibits the use of poisons and explosives in fishing. However, many local fishermen have continued the practices because they say it's the only way they can feed their families. In the Philippines, as in many other countries, fishing communities are often among the poorest. Educating people about the importance of biodiversity doesn't mean much if they're too desperate to care. Sharing the benefits from the commercial use of aquatic genetic resources could help make a difference, but only if there's a strong policy framework to ensure that there *are* benefits, and that they are the kind communities want and need.

The world's first access law: Executive Order 247[2]

Two years after the CBD came into force in 1992, the Philippines became the first country to enact access and benefit-sharing legislation. Presidential Executive Order 247 (EO247), issued by the Ramos administration in 1995, contains guidelines and procedures for the prospecting of biological and genetic resources in the public domain.[3] EO247 is administered by the Department of Environment and Natural Resources, which in 1996 issued regulations governing its implementation[4] and established the Inter-Agency Committee on Biological and Genetic Resources (IACBGR) to review requests for access to genetic resources.[5]

Several circumstances created a favourable climate for the drafting of EO247. The overthrow of the Marcos regime in 1987 led to a democratic political system, with NGOs and community advocates playing an influential role in policy development. An increase in exploration by researchers for pharmaceutical companies, especially in coastal waters, culminated in a public controversy, fuelled by media coverage, about biopiracy by foreign corporations. Many policy makers felt that it was important to establish an initial regulatory framework through the executive order process, given the perceived urgency of the situation and the slow pace of congressional legislation. EO247 was developed in 1994 through consultation involving various government agencies, scientific and technical experts and institutions, and NGOs (Barber and La Vina, 1995). The Philippines is one of the few countries to have undertaken a broad consultation process in the development of access regulations and today remains the only country in Southeast Asia with comprehensive access legislation.

While EO247 is comprehensive, efforts to implement the law have been frustrating for researchers, community advocates and government agencies. Their experience can provide useful lessons for policy makers embarking on similar laws in other countries, bearing in mind that different cultural and political circumstances require different approaches. Every country will have to deal with the issues addressed by EO247, including prior informed consent, appropriate mechanisms for benefit sharing, and creating the institutional structure for implementation and enforcement. The Philippines' experience clearly spells out the range of challenges that face policy makers.

The framework for regulating biodiversity prospecting under EO247 contains four basic elements:

- A system of mandatory research agreements between collectors and the national government with minimum terms for provision of information and samples, technology cooperation and benefit sharing.
- Minimum standards for obtaining prior informed consent from local and indigenous communities where collection is carried out.
- An inter-agency committee to review applications and enforce compliance with research agreements and to coordinate further institutional, policy and technological development.
- Minimum requirements for conformity with environmental protection laws and regulations.

Commercial and academic research agreements: A recipe for research chill?

Anyone proposing to collect genetic resources must operate under the terms of a research agreement (commercial or academic) with a government agency. ARAs apply to universities, other academic institutions, government agencies and intergovernmental agencies proposing scientific research with no intention of profit. Any collector with a commercial objective must obtain a CRA. Foreign proponents are required to obtain the collaboration of a Philippines research institution (such as the MSI of the University of the Philippines) in the development of CRAs. If researchers operating under an ARA produce results that turn out to have commercial potential or wish to transfer the collected materials to a third party, the agreement must be replaced with a CRA. (EO247, s 3)

Anyone wishing to obtain either type of agreement must submit an application to the IAC. The IACBGR includes representatives from government agencies as well as a representative from a civil society organization and a member of a 'people's organization' representing the interests of indigenous communities. The application must include a research proposal stating the purposes, source of funds, duration, and a list of biological and genetic materials and amounts to be taken.

ARA proposals can be broader and more general than CRAs (s 4), and a single ARA can cover all scientists and researchers from an institution (eg the University of the Philippines) (s 5), allowing a greater degree of self-regulation for academic research. The purpose of distinguishing between commercial and academic research was to minimize bureaucratic hurdles for academic researchers and to give the IACBGR more time to monitor private commercial parties. Shortly after EO247 came into force, Barber and La Vina (1995) noted that, as foreign commercial collectors of genetic resources often rely heavily on local academic institutions as suppliers, the application of different requirements to commercial and academic research might prove counter-productive and would need to be closely monitored. Since then, suspicions about academic and commercial links have been one of several factors contributing to delays in approvals of applications for research agreements.

Minimum terms of the agreements include:

- Limits on the type and amount of samples collected.
- Deposit of a complete set of all specimens with the National Museum or other designated government entity.
- Access by Philippines citizens and government entities to all specimens deposited abroad, and to relevant data.
- Information about all discoveries that lead to development of a commercial product.
- Regular status reports to the IAC of the research and of the ecological state of the area concerned and/or species collected.
- For endemic species, transfer to a Philippine institution of technology enabling commercial and local use without royalty payments.
- Payment of royalties to the national government and local or indigenous community when a research activity leads to development of a commercial product. (s 5)

Far from facilitating access to genetic resources, EO247 appears to have put a damper on research. More than 30 applications (primarily for ARAs) have been made, but several of these have been withdrawn. By mid-2002, the IACBGR had approved only two ARAs, one covering several campuses of the University of the Philippines and the other for the International Rice Research Institute (IRRI). The only CRA to be approved was a joint undertaking between the Philippines Department of Agriculture, the University of the Philippines and the University of Utah, under a research programme funded by the US National Cancer Institute and US National Institutes of Health. Its research objectives are:

- To collect approximately 200 marine organisms (ascidians, marine invertebrates, marine micro-organisms and sponges) annually from different habitats in the Philippines archipelago, in amounts ranging from 50 to 500 grams
- To isolate active metabolites using bioassay-guided fractionation and to determine the structures of active metabolites

- To perform systematic inventories of biodiversity of various habitats in the Philippine marine ecosystem.

The initial draft of EO247 was prepared by a group of chemists at the University of the Philippines and aimed to regulate the collection and use of biodiversity by foreigners but not by Philippines scientists. The later expansion of its scope to include academic research, in part to comply with the CBD, has been a continuing source of frustration to the academic community. Some academic and applied scientists, as well as conservation NGOs, have argued that EO247 hinders scientific progress and impedes students from obtaining academic qualifications. Some scientists feel particularly disillusioned because they originally proposed the regulation to control the activities of foreign scientists and protect their own interests (Dano, 2001). The National Museum of the Philippines continues to take the position that its legal charter authorizes it to conduct bioprospecting activities without complying with the EO247 requirement to obtain a research agreement (Peria, 2002). This has been a subject of continuing controversy, especially among NGOs that suspect that commercial users of genetic resources may make arrangements with the museum to conduct collections on their behalf.

Prior informed consent: Insurmountable hurdle or far too easy?

One of the prerequisites for approval of an application for a research agreement is proof of prior informed consent by local communities, whether or not traditional knowledge of uses of those resources is evident. Under a separate provision, collections within ancestral lands and domains of indigenous communities require consent to be in accordance with customary community laws (s 7).

The regulations implementing EO247 (Department Administrative Order No 96–20) define prior informed consent as 'consent obtained … after disclosing fully the intent and scope of the bioprospecting activity, in a language and process understandable to the community, and before any bioprospecting activity is undertaken' (DAO, s 2). To obtain the Prior Informed Consent (PIC) Certificate needed for approval of a collection permit (s 7), an applicant needs to take the following steps:

- Provide a summary of the research proposal to the community mayor or head of an indigenous people.
- Inform the community of its intention to conduct bioprospecting, through media advertisements or direct communication.
- Advertise and organize a community assembly to discuss the proposal.
- Provide to the local mayor or recognized head of an indigenous people a summary of the research proposal, in a language or dialect understandable to them, stating (a) the purpose, methodology and duration of the project, as well as the number of species/specimens to be used and/or collected, (b) equitable and reciprocal benefits to parties concerned before, during and after the duration of the bioprospecting activity, and (c) a categorical statement that the activity will not in any way affect the traditional use of the resources.

- Submit the PIC certificate, if issued by the mayor or head of an indigenous people, to the Technical Secretariat of the Inter-Agency Committee on Biological and Genetic Resources (IACBGR), together with proof of compliance with legal procedures.

Researchers have complained that the requirements for prior informed consent are too onerous, while community advocates say they don't go nearly far enough. As straightforward as the steps appear, there are many potential complications. In some cases it may be difficult to identify the recognized head of a community or even to precisely define the identity of a community. Local people may question the authority of a mayor to speak on their behalf, and it may be difficult for the IACBGR to determine whether consent is apparent when communities are strongly divided. Researchers planning projects in indigenous communities may need considerable time and effort to understand and adhere to customary laws of collective decision-making. Translating research proposals into local languages may present a formidable task given the number of languages in the Philippines, but even that may not be enough. One NGO suggests that pictures may be needed to describe the species to be collected and the amounts to be collected.

Are the prior informed consent requirements too demanding or not demanding enough? Both NGOs and academics support the process, but their concerns are very different. Some NGOs point out that the implications of bioprospecting for genetic resources may be virtually incomprehensible in some communities, and that applicants for research agreements need to go far beyond a basic description of a research proposal to ensure that communities have sufficient information and understanding to make decisions about prior informed consent. The sample PIC certificate contained in the regulations simply states that the signer (ie the mayor or head of an indigenous people) has reviewed the research proposal, has understood the implications of the proposed research activity, and has consulted with constituents, who have voiced no objection. One interviewee expressed concern that mayors and fishing organizations are likely to provide consent without sufficiently understanding the consequences.

A researcher studying the toxic properties of cone snails used to simply buy them from fishermen who caught them only for the commercial value of their decorative shells and threw the venom duct away; now she can only obtain the material under the authorization of a CRA with all its lengthy delays and complications. Some researchers worry that publicity about biopiracy and the possibility of large royalties and other substantial rewards has raised community expectations too far, increasing the difficulty of obtaining consent. Communities may have difficulty understanding the difference between academic and commercial research and may expect economic results that simply don't exist. Common suspicions that commercial research may be cloaked under the guise of academic research add to the confusion. One researcher noted that leaders of indigenous communities are reluctant to sign forms because experience has taught them that signing documents means giving up rights.

Scientists are not very good at explaining their work to local people (this is hardly unique to scientists in the Philippines). They just want to get on with their research, and may lack the funding to develop complicated PIC procedures that may need to be adapted to different community cultures. In remote areas, obtaining prior informed consent from communities may take months. With the assistance of social scientists, the University of the Philippines has developed guidelines to help its researchers meet prior informed consent requirements. The perception among many scientists that obtaining community permission is just too difficult has short circuited several proposed research projects. However, as one civil society organization notes, most of those who oppose prior informed consent have not actually tried it (Dano, 2001).

Stronger prior informed consent provisions could act as a further disincentive to researchers who find even the existing administrative requirements too great a burden. Many of the Philippines' marine species can also be readily found in nearby Malaysia and Indonesia, and Philippine enforcement agencies are too weak in most parts of the country to stop commercial researchers from simply collecting in secret. However, advocates for community and indigenous rights are quick to point out that giving communities a chance for greater control over their own destinies is not only a matter of justice but also may be just what is needed for achieving more responsible management of biological diversity. EO247 has opened a Pandora's box that will not easily be shut.

Who speaks for communities? Proposing a voice for fisheries cooperatives

The Department of Agriculture is responsible for fisheries management and policy development in the Philippines. The 1998 Fisheries Code provided for the appointment of an undersecretary of fisheries in the department to oversee fisheries regulation, research and policy development. The Code promotes public participation in policy development through the appointment of a National Fisheries and Aquatic Resources Management Council comprising a cross-section of interest groups including government, small fishermen, commercial fishermen, fish processors, academics, and civil society organizations. At the local level, the Code provides precedence to municipal fishermen and their cooperatives within 15 km of municipal shorelines. It also provides for the creation of local Fisheries and Aquatic Resource Management Councils (FARMCs), with small fishermen making up three-quarters of the membership, in every municipality with fishing activities. The main role of local FARMCs is to help in the preparation of municipal fisheries development plans, recommend the enactment of ordinances, and assist in enforcement of fisheries laws.

The Tambuyog Foundation, a civil society organization that promotes the rights of fishing communities, suggests that requests for prior informed consent should be directed not to mayors but to FARMCs, which, it argues, more legitimately represent the interests of fishing communities and are the keepers of traditional knowledge. Who has the legitimate authority to speak for communities? Although EO247 delegates that authority to heads of municipalities (for local communities), other national access laws have yet to address an issue that will be crucial to the implementation of effective consent arrangements.

Royalties and other benefits – An improbable dream?

A brochure describing the MSI-University of Utah bioprospecting enterprise and aimed at target communities, noted its medical, ecological and scientific benefits and added that the institutions would share any royalty or profit with the Philippine government in the event that a product capable of being patented should be developed. The brochure addressed the question of benefits to the local community as follows:

> At the early stage, the study will find out what is the state of the environment in the study site. The data can help to plan ways of taking care of and preserving the ecology of the place. We can't promise that any drug will come out of the study. But, if there should be any, every effort will be made so that the local community will share in the financial benefits. How exactly will be determined later on.

One of the key benefits of the agreement has been training for University of the Philippines researchers in purification processes.

For communities and national government alike, the promise of royalties is the pot of gold that encourages prior informed consent for commercial collections. Anti-cancer drugs are at the top of the list and, in the event that the identification of an anti-cancer agent leads to the development of a marketable drug, no doubt the returns would be considerable. However, the odds of collections in any particular community leading to commercial profit are extremely slim. In the event that royalties do materialize, it will be up to parties to research agreements to determine how to distribute them. The legislation has come under criticism in some quarters for not precisely defining a royalty split (say, 50–50) between the government and provider communities.

Section 5(e) of EO247 provides that forms of compensation other than royalties may be negotiated where appropriate. As communities are not parties to research agreements, they have no direct role in negotiating benefits. However, under section 8 of the regulations, parties to research agreements must ensure that negotiated benefits also accrue to local communities and indigenous peoples and are allocated for conservation measures. The latter requirement has been a sore point for critics of the legislation who maintain that creating an obligation to aim community benefits in the direction of conservation undermines the sovereignty that the concept of prior informed consent is intended to confer. This illustrates a dilemma likely to face policy makers drafting effective access and benefit-sharing legislation in other countries. To be faithful to the objectives of the CBD, is it enough simply to require equitable sharing of benefits with communities, or should there be strings attached to promote the conservation of biological diversity? To create an incentive, is it also necessary to create an obligation? In the Philippines, much depends on how the requirement for allocation for conservation measures is interpreted. For example, benefits that have no apparent direct link to conservation, such as improved health and education programmes, may still make a significant long-term contribution to conservation of ecosystems by helping a community improve its economic health.

As Batungbacal (2000) points out, economic benefits from bioprospecting do not have to be enormous to create significant environmental, social and economic results in coastal communities, provided they are captured at a local level and are at least partially dedicated to conservation:

> *One hundred thousand dollars in the hands of an NGO, a small business or a local community can go a long way: providing medicines, supporting a nature reserve or an inventory of biodiversity, funding a clinic or processing facilities, and creating employment. These direct benefits can be felt indirectly in other sectors of the economy – for example, in tourism or through providing transferable skills such as information technology – thus contributing to a country's broader sustainable development.*

Various organizations in the Philippines have been actively promoting alternative livelihoods in sustainable fisheries and aquaculture. For example, the SEAFDEC has helped communities on the island of Bohol start up sustainable mud crab fisheries with low-technology support and has worked with other communities to demonstrate the long-term effects of no fish areas in increasing catches (Primavera and Agbayani, 1997). The Haribon Foundation, in cooperation with Project Seahorse, has coordinated the development of seahorse sanctuaries in poorer fishing communities, again with the result of rebuilding populations and catches (Project Seahorse, 2000). And ICLARM's GIFT project has provided improved broodstock and training to rural pond farmers (Pullin et al, 1991). Each of these projects, discussed in the following chapter, illustrates the potential for improving economic conditions in communities in ways that increase awareness of ecological issues.

Biosprospecting for marine organisms in the Philippines often takes place in fishing communities where economic conditions create little incentive for careful management of fisheries resources. For example, the Fisheries Code prohibits the use of explosives and poisons in coral reef fisheries, but local fishermen may flout the law out of desperation to feed their families. Assistance with the creation of sustainable fisheries livelihoods could be one of the most useful forms of benefits to communities providing aquatic genetic resources in the Philippines.

Implementing Executive Order 247 – A bureaucratic nightmare

The magnitude of the difficulties involved in implementing EO247 is illustrated by the fact that only two out of 37 applications for research agreements had been approved five years after the presidential order was issued in 1995. The great majority of these applications for ARAs. It appears that many would-be applicants for CRAs have moved their research activities to more 'friendly' countries or, in some cases, have simply bypassed the legislation by making unauthorized collections.

One of the main reasons for delays in approval appears to have been a lack of financial and bureaucratic support for the IACBGR charged with reviewing and approving applications and for the Technical Secretariat to support its work. One member of the IACBGR notes that, although the Committee was intended to convene monthly, its meetings are irregular because of the difficulty of forming a quorum. She attributed this to the fact that the dealings of the IACBGR have been a low priority for overworked government agencies and to a general lack of awareness in government bureaucracies of the significance of its mandate. Another interviewee noted that the IACBGR had difficulty preparing effective procedures and guidelines because government representatives were too busy to deal with the issue.

An uneasy relationship between NGOs and scientists also appears to have contributed to a rocky start for EO247. Some NGOs remain concerned that there is not a clear enough distinction between academic and commercial research and that EO247 provides insufficient authority and information to communities to secure adequate benefits from collections. One scientist commented that some NGOs seem to take satisfaction in frustrating the efforts of scientists to engage in both commercial and academic research. She added that the anti-biopiracy focus of NGOs distracts the attention of the country from increasing its capacity for commercial development of genetic resources in a manner consistent with bio-diversity conservation.

How can the processing of research applications be made more efficient? Suggestions put forward by representatives from NGOs and the research community included the need for:

- Increased government funding for the IACBGR and to make its work a priority for heads of government agencies
- A 'one-stop shopping' system to expedite the application process with a single agency being responsible for reviewing and approving applications, monitoring and providing guidance for prior informed consent procedures, monitoring compliance with agreement requirements, and enforcing the law
- Increased public and bureaucratic awareness of bioprospecting and biodiversity conservation issues
- A central biodiversity office to promote both the commercial use and conservation of biological diversity.

Executive Order 247 and aquaculture

EO247 was motivated by national concerns about the collection of both sea and plant life whose chemical components might enable the development of new drugs and other pharmaceutical products. The law's definition of 'prospecting' as

> *the research, collection and utilization of biological and genetic resources*
> *for purposes of applying the knowledge derived to scientific and/or*
> *commercial purposes*

could be interpreted to include the collection of wild broodstock for food fish or ornamentals aquaculture. In theory, the provisions might even have applied to the

ICLARM's collection of germplasm from locally cultured tilapia under the GIFT project. However, there is no indication that EO247 was intended to deal to collections for aquaculture, and its application to such collections remains a grey area. The normal practice (by SEAFDEC, for example) is simply to purchase broodstock from local fishermen, who appear to be content with the current arrangement.

Would fishermen get a better deal through formal access agreements between communities and collectors? Perhaps so, if a collection led to the development of a valuable strain with international markets – or perhaps there would simply be an expansion of the 'research chill' that currently appears to inhibit collections throughout the Philippines. Once again, it is important to consider some fundamental distinctions between different uses of genetic resources. Article 8(j) of the CBD was driven by concerns about the appropriation without compensation of traditional knowledge of crop breeding and medicinal uses of plants, and it was initially anticipated that access and benefit-sharing legislation implementing Article 8(j) would tie access agreements to the provision of traditional knowledge enabling the effective use of genetic resources. EO247 moved beyond the expectations of Article 8(j) by requiring the consent of communities *with or without* traditional knowledge, and some other national laws have followed suit.

To the drafters of EO247, there was a clear logic in requiring the agreement of communities for collection of marine organisms that might eventually yield enormous profits in the event of the discovery of, say, an anti-cancer drug. Should the same logic require a collector of broodstock to make an agreement with a community rather than simply buying from a fisher who sells his catch for a living? If so, how? Drafters of access and benefit-sharing policies in other countries face many tough questions, and this is one of the toughest.

Lessons for other countries

As other countries in the ASEAN region develop their own legislation based on the ASEAN Framework guidelines, there may be an opportunity for smoother implementation of EO247 simply because collectors of genetic resources cannot just move their operations to a more accommodating nation. Nevertheless, the Philippine experience deserves careful consideration by other countries. Executive Order 247 was carefully prepared, with participation by a broad range of stakeholders, and at first glance appears to be a logical and straightforward approach to facilitating access to genetic resources. As so often with the implementation of legislation that represents a major change to the status quo, the devil has been in the details, and the details here are many. At the very least, the difficulties experienced in implementing EO247 suggest that to be effective, access and benefit-sharing laws need to:

- Provide for an efficient process without unreasonable delays.
- Ensure the availability of adequate government resources to implement and enforce enabling regulations and to process applications expeditiously.

- Ensure that distinctions between academic and commercial research are clear and that academic research applications can proceed without unnecessary obstacles.
- Provide adequate support for the negotiation of prior informed consent at the community level.
- Clearly define the scope of the legislation with regard to the genetic resources to which it applies.

Chapter 6

Results that Count: Meaningful Benefits for Fishing Communities

Fishing family with traditional fish trap, Marituba wetlands, Brazil (Photo by Brian Harvey)

One of the three objectives of the CBD, the equitable sharing of benefits from the use of genetic resources, is intended to promote the other two: conservation and sustainable use of genetic resources. Ten years after the CBD came into force, there are few publicized examples of benefits to developing countries from the use of plant genetic resources, and virtually none for aquatic genetic resources. The most obvious explanation is the slow progress in the development of access laws and the regulations that define how they'll work in practice. In the meantime, uncertainty about legal requirements for access has had a chilling effect on commercial and academic research and has left many indigenous and local communities uncertain about whether they have any rights to negotiate with collectors and, if so, how to go about it.

Some corporations and research institutions have negotiated agreements with national governments, and occasionally directly with communities, in countries where legislation has yet to be enacted. One of the reasons there has been little public information about such agreements is that many have been negotiated secretly, especially in cases where sensitive commercial information is involved. Martinez (2002) points to the growth of a new profession of 'biotrade brokers' whose job it is to negotiate little-publicized deals between northern organizations and southern biodiversity rich countries, which may share some or many species and compete among themselves for a share of the action. GRAIN (2002a) concludes that the trend towards such bilateral contracts has rarely favoured provider countries. Its study of a number of completed agreements concluded that, in most cases, more than 95 per cent of the benefits derived from biodiversity continue to be captured by industrial interests. Other analysts might use different measuring sticks and come up with different results, but there's no doubt that there is a gap and that it needs to be narrowed.

At the community level, receiving a fair share of benefits will start with legal recognition of the right of informed consent to the collection of genetic resources. However, much more will depend on the types of benefits up for discussion (royalties may have zero value), the support of a sound negotiation framework and the commitment of both communities and collectors to negotiate a workable agreement.

BLUE GOLD OR FOOLS' GOLD? Prospects for benefit sharing

Plant biodiversity has been called 'green gold' because of the potential for bioprospecting agreements to provide lucrative export markets for plants and plant products from southern countries. The high expectations that the CBD created haven't been met so far. Are the prospects for 'blue gold' any better? Chapter 1 details the potential value of different types of aquatic genetic resources. Benefit-sharing agreements will likely vary considerably in nature and scope depending on the types of resource and collection requirements involved.

Marine bioprospecting

Bioprospecting for marine organisms is like panning for gold. It may only take one major find in one location to produce riches. But, just as in prospecting for gold, the disappointments far outnumber the successes.

The odds against provider communities receiving a share of royalties from pharmaceutical companies are extraordinarily high, given the rarity with which samples lead to the development of a marketable product. Moreover, pharmaceutical and other companies are increasingly managing to reduce the need for collection of samples: they synthesize compounds, chemically alter them to make them distinct from the originals and therefore eligible for patent protection, or grow medicinal plants on plantations. By one estimate, the global trade in genetic resources runs to several billion dollars annually (ten Kate and Laird, 1999), but such large figures bear little relationship to amounts received by provider countries. The total profits in worldwide trade in plant seeds in 1993 were about US$700 million. As Pullin and Casal (1996) note, if 10 per cent of that amount came from materials collected under the CBD, there would have been about US$70 million a year in profits to be shared and perhaps US$7 million in royalties to be shared among source countries – an amount that might be exceeded by the cost of estimating and distributing such benefits.

Plant bioprospectors sometimes attempt to negotiate agreements with national governments to obtain samples from parks and other protected areas, either to avoid the need to deal with communities or private landowners or because the rules for negotiation are simply more straightforward. One of the few bioprospecting agreements on aquatic genetic resources provided for the collection of thermophilic organisms unique to the hot springs of Yellowstone National Park. The US Parks Service itself initiated the process with the express intent of discovering applications for products derived through research on thermophilic organisms (so prior informed consent was not an issue), and was to receive US$100,000 annually from the Diversa Corporation for five years of sample collection as well as in-kind services and royalties from any products developed (Columbia University, 1999).

However, most bioprospecting for aquatic organisms will continue to focus on ocean waters, where marine equivalents of parks are so few that collectors don't have the option of obtaining specimens from protected areas even if allowed to do so. Assuming that continues to be the case, what say are communities likely to have in collections off national coastlines? Most bioprospecting for marine organisms is conducted on the seabed of the continental shelf, which falls within national jurisdiction under the UNCLOS. In Fiji, indigenous communities already have certain rights to the seabed. However, this is the exception rather than the rule, and whether communities have a right to benefits from offshore resources is likely to remain a controversial issue that becomes even more complex as scientific knowledge of ocean life expands. Will communities be able to demand a say if micro-organisms found recently in hydrothermal vents on the seabed hold the prospect of commercial development? It sounds unlikely, but territorial claims of some indigenous peoples (like the Haida in Canada's Queen Charlotte Islands, close to some of the vent discoveries) may extend far beyond the coastline.

Traditional knowledge of or uses for seabed organisms is likely to be virtually non-existent in areas where bioprospecting takes place, but this may not be a barrier to community rights in countries that follow the Bonn Guidelines, and appears not to have been an obstacle under the Philippine access law. Future access policies (and land claims agreements with indigenous communities) will need to clearly consider and describe the rights of communities over offshore aquatic genetic resources if contentious disputes are to be avoided.

Food fish aquaculture

Collections of broodstock for development of new food fish strains are more likely to lead to returns, though not of a similar magnitude, to source communities, simply because the odds of creating a successful commercial product are higher. In addition, the research and development phase is likely to be far shorter than the ten to 20 years for pharmaceutical products. Consequently, benefits such as royalties that depend on commercially valuable results are likely to be distributed more quickly.

Collectors of aquatic genetic resources don't have the opportunity, frequently pursued by plant bioprospectors, of drawing upon the extensive holdings of publicly available ex situ collections. The need for wild broodstock could diminish over time as genetically diverse ex situ collections become well established; however, the gradual expansion in the farming of food fish species or populations that have never before been cultured will lead to ongoing demands for wild genetic material. Universities and other national institutions are currently the primary actors in this field and will generally have to meet the same requirements as foreign collectors if current trends in the development of access law continue.

One of the key distinctions between bioprospecting and aquaculture is that the development of promising new strains for farming may require collection from many dispersed locations, so that several communities and in some cases several nations could be involved in the negotiation of agreements. This would have been the case, for instance, if national access and benefit-sharing laws had applied to ICLARM's collections of wild tilapia broodstock in four African countries in the late 1980s (see Case Study 4). Such a diversity of communities contributing to development of a product is unlikely to occur in the plant world, and it raises the question of how benefits can most effectively be shared and how the process of negotiating benefits can most efficiently be carried out in a way that is cost effective for a fish breeder and fair to participating communities.

Those access laws that already exist appear to operate on the assumption that agreements will be bilateral (that is, between a national institution and a foreign collector or between a national institution and an individual community). For the collection of aquaculture broodstock, multilateral agreements may be more cost effective, efficient and realistic, especially for the sharing of non-monetary benefits (such as assistance in the development of sustainable livelihoods) that may be useful in similar ways to the variety of communities providing broodstock.

Breeding of ornamentals

Regulation of the collection of broodstock for the ornamentals industry presents altogether different challenges. For some species, breeders can simply tap into the well established live trade in ornamentals to obtain broodstock without ever going near the community of origin. About 90 per cent of freshwater ornamentals already come from breeders, and cultured populations of popular species like the neon tetra are so diverse that the need for wild broodstock has virtually been eliminated. By contrast, only a handful of marine ornamental species are bred in captivity.

Sophisticated aquaculture technologies are increasingly making it possible to culture species never before bred in captivity, creating new demands for wild broodstock with desirable coloration and markings. However, it may be very difficult for regulatory agencies to make effective distinctions between collections for sale to hobbyists and those that will be used by breeders. Breeders who buy broodstock through existing import and export channels do not necessarily need to make their intent known. Moreover, fishermen already involved in the live trade may be quite happy to meet collectors' needs for a small informal payment.

Another distinction between the ornamental and food fish industries is worthy of note. Paradoxically, NGOs that oppose food fish aquaculture because of its environmental impacts may support the culture of ornamental fish because they assume it will reduce the pressure on wild fish populations. However, competition from breeders may have a grave impact on communities where the capture fishery not only provides a primary way of life but also provides the incentive needed to protect ecosystems from more damaging resource uses. Case Study 1, on the cardinal tetra fishery in Brazil, describes just such a situation. In that instance, as Project Piaba might argue, to support the notion of community benefit-sharing negotiations with Florida fish breeders would be to support the destruction of a local community dependent on capture fisheries. In short, there may be a great danger in focusing obsessively on the rights of communities to negotiate benefits from the use of aquatic genetic resources when what they really need is practical assistance – from any source willing and able to provide it – in protecting existing livelihoods and local ecosystems against the threat of development pressures.

SHARING BENEFITS FAIRLY WITH COMMUNITIES

International legal instruments include two commonly used meanings for 'equitable sharing of benefits'. One refers to equitable sharing among countries regarding the use of natural resources; the second calls for a fair economic return to all state and non-state actors from which resources are obtained (Lynch and Maggio, 1997). Agenda 21, negotiated at the 1992 Earth Summit, provides that governments should 'recognize and foster the traditional methods and the knowledge of indigenous people and their communities ... and ensure the opportunity for the participation of those groups in the economic and commercial benefits derived from the use of such traditional methods and knowledge...'. In

1994, the Desertification Convention went further, expressly requiring equitable sharing with local communities.

What does 'equitable sharing' really mean, and what types of benefits are likely to be practical? As discussed in the previous chapter, while some access laws make specific reference to royalties, others make no effort to define the nature of benefits.

National responsibilities

The CBD calls on member nations to encourage the equitable sharing of benefits arising from the use of communities' knowledge, innovations and practices. As the name of the Convention implies, the primary rationale for Article 8(j) is the recognition that benefits to communities can provide a positive stimulus for the conservation and sustainable use of biodiversity. Under the framework set out by the CBD, each country has the right to prior informed consent to the collection of genetic resources and to negotiate the mutually agreed terms under which collections may occur. Communities are not specifically recognized as parties to these agreements, even by access laws that provide for community prior informed consent. Ordinarily, states and designated national institutions negotiate the benefits they wish to receive and make separate arrangements for distributing a portion of benefits to communities.

In addition to calling for equitable benefit sharing between parties to agreements, the CBD outlines the responsibilities of Parties to the Convention, especially northern countries, for sharing specific types of benefits with developing countries. These include:

- Ensuring access to and transfer of technologies that are relevant to the conservation and sustainable use of biological diversity or make use of genetic resources and do not cause significant damage to the environment (Article 16). Of particular interest to developing countries are technologies that enable them catch up with northern countries in the study and uses of genetic resources in order to advance their own economic development.
- Exchanging publicly available information relevant to conservation and sustainable use, including the results of technical, scientific and socio-economic research (Article 17).
- Promoting technical and scientific cooperation, with special attention to strengthening the national capabilities of developing countries (Article 18).
- Taking legislative, administrative or policy measures to provide for effective participation in biotechnological research activities, especially by developing countries, and promoting access by developing countries to the results and benefits arising from biotechnologies based upon genetic resources provided by those countries (Article 19).
- Providing financial resources to enable developing countries to implement the Convention and benefit from its provisions (Article 20).

Negotiated benefits typically focus on technology transfer (eg training of scientists) and capacity building at the national level, in addition to the standard negotiation of royalties and other financial rewards. What hasn't been addressed in any comprehensive way – either in international agreements or in most national laws – is how to share these benefits equitably with communities providing genetic resources, and what types of benefits will prove most useful and acceptable to those communities. Governments were quick to accept the principle that incentives to conserve resources depend on adequate benefits from their use, but generally haven't embraced its logical extension – that the same principle must govern relationships with local communities. Neither the Bonn Guidelines nor most national laws appear to take for granted that prior informed consent by communities includes direct negotiation of benefits.

Community expectations

In the case of the Philippines, one of the few countries where prior informed consent by communities has been put into practice, it appears to have been treated primarily as an exercise for sharing information about the purposes of proposed collections. The inter-agency committee charged with ensuring the protection of community rights regarding prior informed consent has been hampered by a lack of government commitment, inadequate resources, and agency conflicts (see Case Study 5). Thanks in large part to the strong network of civil society organizations, the Philippines has been among the most progressive of countries in its legislative support of community rights; it is reasonable to assume that other countries with a less impressive record will have more trouble translating rhetoric into action.

Not surprisingly, one of the main criticisms levelled at the CBD by advocates for indigenous and local communities is its failure to provide substantive guidance for the sharing of benefits with local people – that it 'talks the talk' but doesn't 'walk the walk'. Needless to say, achieving consensus among most of the world's countries about specific mechanisms for addressing community rights, even if that's ultimately the key to conservation and sustainable use of global biodiversity, would have been a near impossible task. Access laws that do provide for compensation to communities generally don't specify an effective mechanism for doing so – the Philippine legislation again being a good example.

Dissatisfaction with mechanisms for distributing benefits and the types of benefits themselves has fuelled demands for direct community control over genetic resources rather than simply having a right to prior informed consent. With few exceptions (such as the OAU model law, community rights legislation in the Philippines and Bangladesh, and a few land claims negotiations in Canada and Australia), national governments have shown little appetite for devolving significant authority to communities. Some indigenous organizations have already made clear their categorical opposition to the collection of genetic resources in their territories. While this opposition may be based in part on principled concerns about genetic modification of wild creatures or plants, usually it has far more to do with wanting to be treated fairly and with respect.

It doesn't sit well with indigenous groups that the CBD's attention to rights of traditional communities appears to have more to do with biodiversity conservation and corporate desires for access to their resources than with a sense of fair play. For the most part, national governments continue to pay little attention to international human rights conventions that recognize the right of indigenous peoples to self-determination. It is not surprising, therefore, that many indigenous groups balk at the suggestion (implied or explicit in most national access laws to date) that benefits negotiated with communities should be designed to promote biodiversity conservation and sustainable use objectives. And it is no small irony that indigenous peoples with the longest traditions of practising sustainable use of ecosystems have largely been deprived, through erosion of their cultures and loss of control over their territories, of the ability to continue to do so. Any effort to develop practical frameworks for the negotiation of benefits with communities will need to keep this reality in mind.

A HANDOUT OR A HAND UP?
Royalties vs non-monetary benefits

As discussed in Chapter 5, national access and benefit-sharing laws can set the stage for negotiations with communities by requiring their prior informed consent access, but the types of benefits that result will depend on the nature of the negotiations. From the point of view of a company collecting genetic resources, monetary benefits such as royalties may make most sense, but community negotiators will be well aware that royalties rarely materialize – at least in the case of pharmaceutical bioprospecting. Communities that hope to achieve tangible benefits of a lasting nature may do better by exploring opportunities for non-monetary benefits.

Fishing communities tend to be over represented among the poorest communities of the world because their traditional sources of sustenance and income have been devastated by the impacts of industrial activities such as commercial trawling, pollution of fish habitat by runoff from mining or agricultural activities, destruction of habitat by industrial logging, disruption of fish migration routes by dam building, and loss of physical control over traditional territories. What can truly benefit such communities in the long term is the means to regain an economic footing based on local enterprises with links to aquatic resources, a chance to apply traditional as well as new skills, feasible marketing opportunities, and a cooperative approach. As Schumacher (1973) pointed out more than 30 years ago, long-term prosperity in communities means looking at the real needs of local people, using appropriate low or intermediate technological solutions that are in tune with local resources, means and culture. Creative benefit-sharing agreements are one way of providing a catalyst for such solutions.

Royalties

Royalties are the most common currency of access negotiations and the benefit most likely to be required under national laws. From the point of view of collecting institutions, they're the most straightforward and fair means of compensation for the right to collect. Being forced to 'share benefits' before there's any guarantee of benefits to the collector makes no sense from a business point of view and simply puts a damper on research that may benefit both a company and society at large – provided something comes out of it. Why give something for nothing? Dividing up benefits before there's any proof of the value of a genetic resource, such institutions say, will simply be the thin end of the wedge leading to greater and greater demands from communities caught up in the 'pot of gold' syndrome.

The problem with this argument is that it treats genetic resources purely in economic terms – commodities to be bought and sold, without value until they produce a profit. Apart from the fact that it doesn't take into account other values to communities, the argument ignores a basic premise of the CBD – that genetic resources that were once common property are now subject to national sovereignty, and collectors from northern countries have an obligation to negotiate the right to access. What primarily motivated developing countries to buy into the CBD was the promise of putting an end to the exploitation of biodiversity by industrial countries without adequate compensation. Developing countries also sought to put an end to the assumption that it is their responsibility to conserve the richest areas of biodiversity for the benefit of northern countries. That's why access to technology for the use of genetic resources has been such an important bargaining chip for developing countries. To arrive at mutually agreed terms with provider countries, commercial collectors may need to be prepared to negotiate the full range of monetary and non-monetary benefits outlined in the CBD.

Non-monetary benefits

Typically, collectors will be negotiating with national institutions rather than directly with communities, at least in countries that don't provide full negotiation rights to communities. The types of non-monetary benefits that may be most valuable at the national level (such as technologies for genetic research and modification and training of scientists to use them) may be irrelevant to the needs of indigenous and local communities. If the prior informed consent process is to work smoothly, communities will need assurance that any benefits they receive will be meaningful.

Royalties may seem attractive at first glance, but they can also turn out to be an empty promise that doesn't pay the rent. Monetary alternatives to royalties may include fees per sample collected, milestone payments at each stage during the development of a product, and short- and long-term employment with a collection project. However, the most valuable benefits to communities are often non-monetary ones that strengthen local economies and cultures battered by decades of fisheries depletion, erosion of traditional ways of making a living, and the march of industrial development into once remote indigenous and local communities.

The case studies included in this book, while they do not all focus on benefit-sharing agreements, illustrate how a wide range of non-monetary benefits may be relevant to fishing communities:

Case Study 1 – Project Piaba provides training and technologies to help fishing communities along the Rio Negro maintain a sustainable ornamental fishery (eg construction of a municipal aquarium to increase public awareness of habitat needs of fish populations; teaching fishermen how to reduce mortalities in captured fish; helping fishermen to develop marketing strategies).

Case Study 2 – A salmon farmer offers to help build a fish hatchery in return for access to wild broodstock.

Case Study 3 – A Canadian aquaculture consortium offers indigenous groups part ownership in a fish farming enterprise in return for access to charr broodstock.

Case Study 4 – A fisheries research institute in the Philippines, after developing improved tilapia strains from wild broodstock in four African countries, transfers the breeding technology to African research institutes with a view to helping rural community pond farmers increase fish production.

Case Study 5 – A scientific institute in the Philippines promises communities that (in addition to possible royalties) research associated with collections of marine organisms will facilitate conservation of aquatic ecosystems.

Case Study 6 – A bioprospecting agreement with Fijian communities provides for assistance with the development and management of village-based enterprises as well as the establishment of a marine conservation area to allow fish populations to recover and potential fisheries stocks to increase.

Obviously, a company or research institute may find it far easier to negotiate royalties or other payments directly with a community than to embark on a range of other options outside its immediate expertise. How agreements with fishing communities turn out will probably depend to a large extent on the availability of alternative benefit-sharing models, the skill of negotiators, and support for alternative benefit-sharing arrangements from government or non-governmental institutions. In many cases, non-monetary benefits acceptable to a community might be as simple as employing local people to collect aquatic genetic resources. In other instances, negotiations might consider options for creating longer lasting employment or other benefits such as support for educational or health programmes.

The agreement described in Case Study 6 resulted from an effort by the WWF and the University of the South Pacific to demonstrate best practices under the CBD. While the case study illustrates some of the many benefits that can contribute to a community's well-being and promote conservation, it is unlikely that such comprehensive agreements will become commonplace in the near future without significant guidance and support from governments, NGOs or other bodies with an interest in promoting benefit-sharing agreements and the resources to do so. There are three key reasons for this:

- Agreements require a comprehensive framework to support negotiations with communities that may have no experience dealing with interested collectors.
- Collectors must have the incentive (which usually includes the option of patent protection for any discoveries) to conduct laborious negotiations directly with a community.
- From the point of view of institutional or corporate collectors, it generally makes good business sense to limit benefits to the promise of a share of future royalties rather than becoming involved in the expensive and messy business of negotiating non-monetary benefits (primarily capacity building and technology transfer) that may be of more immediate use to communities.

Governments that are serious about furthering the objectives of the CBD and who recognize the importance of management of biodiversity at the community level will need to determine how to deliver meaningful benefits to fishing communities without making it impossible for collectors to reach a deal. This applies equally to bioprospecting and to collections for aquaculture.

LINKING SUSTAINABLE LIVELIHOODS TO CONSERVATION

Conservation and sustainable use of aquatic genetic resources aren't going to be achieved simply by beefing up governmental policies on harvesting and ecosystem management. Ultimately, meeting those objectives will depend on governments' success in developing strategies for the involvement of communities located in areas of rich biodiversity. The CBD and other international agreements have recognized the importance of encouraging a greater role for traditional communities, but it's a long road from rhetoric to reality.

Some governments have taken tentative steps towards developing co-management agreements with communities, but sharing authority doesn't always address a more fundamental barrier to conservation: widespread poverty among countless communities that prospered before the erosion of their traditional cultures and ecosystem management practices. Aquatic products are the main source of animal protein for most of the world's poor and indigenous peoples, and fishing villages are over represented among the poorest communities in the world. The cause may be industrial development or overfishing or loss of community control over natural resources or any combination of these.

The point is that governments need to develop imaginative and practical ways to enable fishing communities to be more self-sufficient, whether through increased local control, health and education programmes, or assistance with the development of sustainable livelihoods. Obviously, negotiation of non-monetary benefits such as sustainable livelihoods initiatives is likely to be more complex than simply making a deal for royalties or up-front payments. However, if such benefits are likely to be more effective in achieving CBD objectives, it may be worthwhile for national governments, industry and international organizations to cooperate in developing the support systems needed to promote sustainable livelihoods that ultimately create benefits far beyond the local communities that initially receive them.

Where overfishing or habitat destruction have contributed to the loss of traditional fishing practices, the most useful benefits may be building capacity to manage fish stocks more effectively or develop new types of sustainable fishing livelihoods. Community programmes in the Philippines and Fiji have demonstrated that the establishment of no-fish zones, with the agreement of all community interests, can restore fish populations while dramatically increasing catch numbers and sizes in adjacent areas (Aalbersberg et al, 1997; Agbayani et al, 2000). A little bit of training and application of low-technology techniques can go a long way to developing alternative fishing livelihoods that benefit entire communities. Examples include a SEAFDEC initiative to provide training and technology to develop sustainable mud crab fisheries, Project Seahorse's cooperation with the Haribon Foundation in the Philippines to help communities develop sustainable seahorse fisheries, and ICLARM's programmes to help pond farmers in Africa and Southeast Asia raise fast maturing tilapia (see Case Study 6 at the end of this chapter). Innovative projects such as these can have the double benefit of helping to build community stability and conserving aquatic biodiversity.

The two Philippine projects described below, while not the result of access agreements, exemplify how benefit-sharing initiatives that are well planned can be used to promote conservation and sustainable use in fishing communities. They also illustrate several key components to ensuring the success of sustainable livelihoods projects. These include:

- A close link between sustainable livelihoods and traditional fishing occupations.
- Low-technology solutions.
- Community participation in developing and implementing resource management plans.
- Information and education about ecosystem relationships and effective management systems.

Seahorse culture in Handumon, Philippines

> *For aquaculture to contribute to conservation, it must serve as an alternative to fishing, transforming seahorse fishers into seahorse farmers. Aquaculture that does not include seahorse fishers will not reduce pressure on wild populations, because seahorse demand is considered limitless. For seahorse aquaculture to be accessible to seahorse fishers, it must be low technology and low risk to avoid impoverishing them further.*
>
> PROJECT SEAHORSE, 1998.

The Philippines is one of more than 50 countries involved in the trading of more than 20 million dried and live seahorses a year for use in traditional medicine (including aphrodisiacs) and as aquarium specimens and curiosities. Demand far exceeds the supply, yet catches are steadily decreasing because of overfishing, habitat loss (including the destruction of mangrove forests) and unsustainable collection methods such as taking pregnant and immature fish. The dependence of thousands of rural fishermen on seahorses creates an unfortunate pattern common to many other small-scale fisheries: as village populations increase, fishing intensifies, contributing to a decline in seahorse populations. This in turn leads to declining catches and a greater pressure on fishermen to collect smaller and immature seahorses, which are both less valuable, and vital to sustain seahorse populations. Too often the result is increased poverty for villagers together with the loss of one of their most valuable resources, forcing people to look for alternative livelihoods that may worsen the initial problem.

The village of Handumon on the island of Bohol in the Philippines was one of many communities that experienced the vicious cycle described above. Twenty per cent of households in the community depend on seahorses for 40 per cent of their income, and between 1985 and 1995 the catch had declined by 70 per cent. In 1995 Project Seahorse, under the direction of Amanda Vincent of the University of British Columbia, partnered with the Philippines-based Haribon Foundation, developed a proposal for a conservation project to protect and rebuild local seahorse populations. The two groups worked with the villagers to establish a 33 hectare seahorse sanctuary. Pregnant males caught in other locations were placed in meshed underwater cages. Juveniles escaping through the mesh were then held in underwater corrals to grow to maturity before being sold or released to replenish wild stocks. The project trained villagers in the management of seahorse stocks and also encouraged the development of other livelihoods, such as seaweed farming and ecotourism (seahorse watching), to help reduce local dependence on the seahorse trade. In addition, villagers participated in the planting of 15,000 mangroves to reforest the shore of the sanctuary. The end result was stabilization of seahorse populations and increased opportunities for enhancement of a conservation-based community economy.

In addition to establishing the marine reserve, the project provided training in surveying marine ecosystems and recording fisheries data, a public awareness programme, assistance towards the development of a natural resources management plan and identification of alternative livelihood options, and a gender analysis to examine issues such as women's contribution to income generation in fishing villages. Plans were also made to transfer management of the reserve to a new people's organization, Kanagmaluhan. The project also plays an advocacy role with the local and national governments to promote enforcement of fishery laws, develop effective fisheries management policies and build awareness of marine conservation issues (Project Seahorse, 1998 and 2000; Amanda Vincent, McGill University, personal communication).

Community fisheries management, Malalison Island, Philippines

A development project organized by SEAFDEC in the Philippines illustrates the types of challenges that poverty stricken fishing communities may face and the multifaceted approach needed to promote sustainable livelihoods and economic stability. The Malalison example underscores the importance of designing solutions to meet specific local needs and of community ownership of the design process.

Almost three-quarters of the households on tiny Malalison Island (55 hectares) in the central Philippines make at least part of their income from fishing, and 75 per cent live below the poverty level (Agbayani et al, 2000). Serious depletion of local fish stocks began with the introduction of dynamite fishing after the Second World War and has since accelerated as a result of a succession of other factors leading to intensified fishing: the use of sodium cyanide in the capture of ornamentals (a ban on both dynamiting and cyanide in 1976 proved ineffective); the intrusion of commercial vessels using purse seine and bag nets in the 1970s; and local adoption of non-traditional fishing technologies (compressor assisted spear guns and the muro-ami, a type of gill net using weighted 'scare lines') in the 1980s. By the late 1980s, live coral cover was down to 35 per cent and the community catch had shrunk to a small fraction of what it once had been (Baticados and Agbayani, 2000). As in many other rural Philippines fishing communities, the prospect for economic diversification and the alleviation of poverty was hampered by low levels of education, an absence of skills for developing alternative livelihoods, and lack of effective community organization.

In 1991, with funding assistance from the International Development Research Centre (IDRC), the Aquaculture Department of the SEAFDEC began a pilot project in community-based fisheries management (CFRM) at Malalison Island. Its objectives were to develop the community into a strong organization that could be granted territorial use rights to strengthen fisheries management, encourage supplemental livelihoods, regenerate fish habitats, and increase fish stocks. After SEAFDEC and its NGO partner, PROCESS Foundation, conducted initial biological and socio-economic research in the community, the newly created Fishermen's Association of Malalison Island (FAMI) acted as a formal link between the project and the community. The project then provided FAMI members with training in leadership and communication skills development, organizational strengthening, cooperatives management, gender sensitivity, legal and policy issues and values formation. The training also included discussions of methods for conserving fisheries resources and improving fisheries income as a result (Agbayani et al, 2000).

With the support of FAMI, the village council approved the establishment of a reef conservation area in which fishing would be banned, with FAMI members helping to monitor the area. FAMI were also able to substantially reduce destructive and illegal fishing practices, although many local fishermen were ambivalent about prohibitions of practices that they saw as the only way to obtain enough fish to feed their families.

The objective of promoting territorial use fishing rights was based on the premise that communities are most likely to become protective and judicious users of aquatic resources if they feel a sense of ownership and responsibility and have an opportunity for self-regulation based on sound empirical knowledge of local fishery ecosystems. The open access regime established in the 1970s was characterized by gear conflicts among Malalison fishermen as well as conflicts between local and commercial fishermen, with no workable mechanism for conflict reso-

lution or effective fisheries management. However, the devolution of administrative functions from the national to local governments under the Local
Government Code of 1991 provided an important step towards the establishment
of community fisheries management rights. The code provided municipalities the
exclusive right to grant fishery privileges to organizations and cooperatives of
marginal fisheries. What was needed in Malalison for this to occur were the motivation and capacity to organize and a full appreciation of the economic and
conservation benefits of doing so.

Following discussions with SEAFDEC researchers, the Culasi municipal
council decided to grant FAMI territorial fisheries rights to a 1 km² area between
Malalison Island and the mainland, but did not consult the fishermen of
Malalison and other coastal villages on the choice and size of the area. In 1995,
Executive Order 240 created a Fisheries and Aquatic Resources Management
Council (FARMC) in every coastal barangay (village) and municipality, setting the
stage for fisheries co-management at the village level, and FAMI formed a
FARMC for the village of Malalison. Under this arrangement the barangay
council enacts and implements fishery-related regulations with the advice of the
FARMC and with consultation as necessary with the national Bureau of Fisheries
and Aquatic Resources to determine whether a regulation is within the purview of
local government. FARMC members have been trained and deputized as fish
wardens to assist with the enforcement of regulation (Baticados and Agbayani,
2000).

A subsequent survey showed that the majority of local fishing families reported
higher incomes following the completion of the project as a result of catch
increases and opportunities for alternative employment in areas such as farming
and livestock raising. The survey also showed an increase in the abundance of fish
and a perception that there was now greater fairness in the control over fishery
resources, allocation of access rights and influence in fishery management.
Collective decision-making was easier and conflict resolution quicker.

Using marine protected areas to improve fishing livelihoods

The worldwide depletion of commercial fisheries has been due in large part to the
practice of heavily fishing one species until its populations start to disappear, then
moving on to another species or area and doing the same. In the past, the populations of many species were able to rebuild to some extent in natural refuges that were
either too deep or remote or dangerous to allow intensive fishing, but such areas have
become increasingly accessible with new fishing technologies. Establishing no-fish
areas to enable the restoration of vulnerable populations and ecosystems has become
an increasingly popular fisheries management technique in the past decade. Because
no-fish zones can contribute to fairly rapid population recoveries and hence to direct
economic benefits to fishermen and their communities, they may be an important
tool to promote sustainable livelihoods for fishing communities, especially in
southern countries.

Local fishermen often oppose the establishment of marine reserves because they
assume it means an immediate reduction in areas available for fishing. While this

may be true in the short term, there is increasing evidence that protecting a relatively small but well-chosen area can produce a 'spillover effect' that can fairly quickly result in fish population increases, and more productive fishing than before, in surrounding areas. Some recent studies suggest that fish in protected areas live longer and grow larger (Roberts and Hawkins, 2001). Larger fish not only produce more eggs but may also spawn more frequently. After a coral reef protected area was established as part of a cooperative community development project in the Philippines, a fish census four years later found that the abundance of surgeon fishes and fusiliers (the main species fished locally) was ten times higher than in non-protected areas, and that their biomass was 40 times greater (Agbayani et al, 2000). By increasing both population densities and the size of fish, reserves can greatly increase the number of young spawned, and the drifting of eggs and larvae into fishing grounds can help restock local fisheries. In addition, as the growth of protected fish populations produces crowding, migration of fish to outside areas also benefits fisheries.

Other scientists remain to be convinced of the effectiveness of protected areas as a fisheries management strategy and express concern that they may be little more than a scientific fad that has become a bandwagon of the ecological community. Yet another point of view is that fisheries don't fail because of the inability of local fishermen to manage catches but because of political pressures to prolong non-sustainable fisheries.[1] Consequently, what is chiefly needed is better communication to decision-making authorities about how protected areas work and how they can increase rather than decrease catches if given time. Clearly, protected areas should not be viewed as an alternative to catch restrictions for large-scale commercial fishing. Creation of protected areas may produce less dramatic results in areas where fish move over a wide range or where biodiversity is low than in coral reef chains or in tropical river systems, but the latter are likely to be the primary focus of agreements between indigenous and local communities. Already there are several promising examples of the use of protected areas to conserve fish populations and enhance local fisheries in such communities.

On the Caribbean island of St Lucia, life for fishermen had become increasingly difficult by the late 1980s. Catches had dwindled after decades of population growth led to an intensification of fishing along coral reefs. An initial attempt by the government to establish a country-wide system of 19 marine reserves failed because of inadequate funding and consultation with local fishermen. In the early 1990s, after catches had further deteriorated and fishermen were complaining about conflicts with tourists, the Fisheries Department set up a process of participatory community management around the town of Soufriere. The result was that local stakeholders, including fishermen, diving operators, hoteliers and boaters, agreed on a zoned management plan for 11 km of coastline. At the heart of the plan were four no-take zones, interspersed between fishing areas, to promote the build up of fish stocks while providing an attraction for divers.

The scepticism of local fishermen about the establishment of the protected areas disappeared five years later when it was found that not only had protected reef fish stocks tripled in number but also fish stocks in surrounding unprotected waters had doubled, resulting in a catch increase of close to 50 per cent. Moreover, biomass in one protected area where some trap fishing was later allowed was still higher than in sites with no protection, demonstrating that even partial protection can produce benefits (Roberts and Hawkins, 2001). While successes of this magnitude may not be expected in regions such as the North Atlantic, they can be very significant in coral reef ecosystems and in biodiversity rich river systems, provided that care is taken to involve all who have a direct stake in the local fishery.

SETTING THE STAGE FOR EFFECTIVE NEGOTIATIONS

In anticipation that benefit-sharing arrangements with communities are likely to become the norm in the future, and in keeping with the spirit of the CBD, some companies have already made it a practice to negotiate benefits whether or not the law requires it. Shaman Pharmaceuticals, for instance, developed the practice of not only making agreements with several South American countries but also arranging for any benefits to be shared with all communities in which it had been active. The company was praised by some for its innovative approach and criticized by others for presuming to decide what benefits were best for the communities it dealt with. The volatility of the pharmaceuticals market later forced the company to restructure and focus on botanicals, but its initiative set a precedent worthy of consideration.

Countries that already provide for community consent for access to genetic resources are discovering, perhaps to no one's great surprise, that legal requirements aren't worth much without an effective framework to support negotiations with and by communities. Case Study 5 describes the problems the Philippines has experienced in trying to ensure its Executive Order 247 facilitates rather than impedes access in communities. Case Study 3 describes the failure of negotiations for access to Arctic charr in Inuit communities of the Canadian north. The breakdown was a costly disappointment to a consortium that had spent considerable time and effort attempting to convince widely scattered communities. The failure was attributed to indigenous communities' concerns about interference with their spiritual connection with the fish, the proposed patenting of a genetic mapping process, and the potential for competition from the farming industry – despite the promise of joint ownership in the business. Everyone involved was breaking new ground – this was the first significant attempt in the country to develop an agreement with communities for access to aquatic genetic resources.

As illustrated by Case Study 6, two of the key differences between the Fijian and Canadian negotiations lay in the level of support for a negotiation framework and the variety of benefits on the table. There is no easy answer for what works and what doesn't in negotiations, but what the case studies do make clear is that access and benefit-sharing laws need to be supplemented by efforts – whether by government or by other organizations – to build sound negotiation frameworks. Key components of effective multiparty negotiations are likely to include ensuring that:

• Communities have the support they need to negotiate effectively.

- All stakeholders likely to be directly or indirectly affected by the outcome are included in the design and implementation of the negotiation agreement.
- Skilled facilitators or mediators are available to help identify stakeholder interests and explore options, including conditions for access and potential benefits.
- Sufficient relevant information is available to facilitate informed decision-making.

Obviously, the complexity of negotiations will depend very much on a variety of factors, including the magnitude of the stakes. Negotiations with a pharmaceutical company hoping to develop a product with significant commercial value are likely to be far more protracted than a deal with a fish farmer who wants to collect a few pairs of broodstock. The key point is that for prior informed consent to be meaningful, a community needs to have full information about the implications of providing consent before it decides whether and how to negotiate.

CASE STUDY 6. SHAPING NEGOTIATION TOOLS: A marine bioprospecting agreement in Fiji

One of the features distinguishing the British colonization of Fiji was the decision to reserve a large proportion of the land for indigenous Fijians, with the provision that the land not be sold or otherwise permanently alienated. Today, 83 per cent of the land in Fiji is communally owned by indigenous Fijians. Ownership of marine areas, including traditional fishing grounds, is governed by both national and customary law. The 1990 constitution recognizes indigenous rights over all resources located in fishing grounds, including the seabed; the state retains the right to collect royalties on resources extracted from the seabed. Family groups continue to manage lands in their territories, and often that control extends as far into the sea as local boats can go. Traditional authority is respected, and government is perceived as protecting traditional rights. It consults with chiefs on fishing licences and other resource use permits, and outsiders pay compensation to mataqali (land owning family groups) for local uses. The intensification of resource use by industries such as coral mining, logging and mining, and by a growing human population, has posed an increasing threat to both marine and forest biodiversity.

Since its founding in 1968, the chemistry department at the University of the South Pacific (USP) has been doing research on the isolation of natural products from plants used for medicinal purposes in Fiji. In the early 1990s, the department decided to expand into the marine area and to upgrade its facilities to add value to local samples. In 1995, USP reached agreement with the Biodiversity Conservation Network of the World Wildlife Fund (now the WWF) for funding of a bioprospecting research project with the understanding that the project would not only advance scientific knowledge but also promote community development and community-based conservation, adhering to CBD principles and emphasizing best practices for benefit sharing with communities. The project would include collection of both marine organisms and plants.

One of the selected source areas was the coastal community of Verata comprising eight villages with about 1600 people, whose traditional leaders had expressed concern about overfishing and coral mining. USP sought the support of Verata at an early stage of the project, holding community meetings to describe its purposes, encourage community participation in project activities, and make the link between conservation and community benefits. One of the objectives of the project was to establish protected areas where gathering would be prohibited, raising questions in the community about whether benefits from bioprospecting would adequately compensate for the loss of returns from *tabu* sites, and how long it would take to regenerate key species. The promise of benefits in addition to royalties was a key factor in winning over a community that in the past had received little or no return from bioprospecting by outsiders.

USP then approached Smith Kline Beecham (SB), a pharmaceutical company collecting marine samples, which responded positively to the request to extend its work to Fiji. Although the Fiji government had no policy on bioprospecting, a forward looking official from the Department of Environment (created specifically to deal with the implementation of the CBD and Agenda 21) formed a working group from relevant government ministries to set the parameters for the project and for bioprospecting in general. The government eventually decided to take a regulatory role to define the approval process and to ensure that the rights of communities were protected.

Following national government approval of the project, USP and its NGO partner, the South Pacific Action Committee for Human Ecology and Environment (SPACHEE), obtained project approval from the provincial department for native affairs with jurisdiction over Verata. The next step was to decide whether there should be a three-way agreement between SB, USP and Verata or separate contracts between SB and USP and between USP and Verata. Those in favour of a three-way agreement argued that Verata should be an equal partner in view of the role of the communities in conservation and as holders of traditional knowledge. However, legal constraints only allowed SB to make payments to legally constituted bodies. When SB closed down its natural products discovery division, USP found a new partner, Glasgow's Strathclyde Institute of Drug Research (SIDR).

Separate agreements were made between USP and SIDR and between USP and the community of Verata, in part because of SIDR's reluctance to contract directly with a community that was not a legal entity. While the USP–SIDR agreement recognized only the two parties as stakeholders, the draft agreement was put out for public discussion and suggestions for improvement, which were used where possible. In addition, the agreement implicitly acknowledged other stakeholders by requiring USP to obtain prior informed consent from resource owners for extraction and export of biological samples, and by noting that:

> one of the purposes of the agreement is to promote the conservation of bio-
> diversity in Fiji by creating incentives for species conservation and to

provide an equitable share of profits to the people of Fiji. In collecting extracts, cultural and ecological values will be respected.

The agreement between USP and Verata contained detailed procedures for prior informed consent by the community for any research activity. Applicants would be required to provide information on: all parties participating in the research and funding sources; the kind and amount of materials to be taken; the type and purpose of research; and the conservation status of species to be collected. In addition, USP agreed to involve the community in all phases of contract negotiations and subsequent activity, and to ensure that all draft agreements would be translated into the Fijian language and distributed to the community for its consideration. Any new potential commercial activity from an extract was to be fully discussed with the community at the beginning of research activities. Any subsequent disputes arising from the agreement were to be settled by the Permanent Arbitrator in Suva. The requirement for approval by the Paramount Chief of Verata and the *tikina* council was expected to reduce the likelihood of dispute.

The USP–SIDR and USP–Verata contracts did not address the issue of IPRs attached to ethnobiological knowledge because there was no reliance on traditional knowledge of marine species.

Benefits to the community covered by the agreement included:

- 100 per cent of the portion of extract licensing fees received by USP during the period of funding of the project, less the costs of extraction and transportation, to be held in a community trust (estimated at US$105,000).
- Equitable sharing of any further financial benefits between USP, Verata and the Fijian government.
- Training for community members in collection and preparation of samples and methods of biodiversity and socio-economic monitoring.
- Assistance with the development and the management of small, village-based enterprises.
- Community workshops in resource management and community development.

Other potential benefits not in the agreement included establishment of a marine conservation area and screening of biological compounds for activity against Pacific region diseases. Both the USP–SIDR and USP–Verata contracts stipulated that the collection of samples must not adversely affect the natural environment. In addition, the USP–Verata contract provided for community-based conservation projects to preserve species and habitats. One of these was for protected areas where extraction was banned to allow the recovery of species of commercial value. Preliminary biological monitoring indicated a substantial increase in the population of the kaikoso clam.

The comprehensive workshops subsequently organized in Verata by USP and SPACHEE led to the development of community action plans and resource management plans designed to ensure the sustainable commercial and subsistence use of renewable natural resources, including their protection and rehabilitation. Additional workshops provided training in biological monitoring, sample collection and preparation, and development of a community register of important plants (Aalbersberg, 1997; Aalbersberg et al, 1997; Columbia University, 1999; William Aalbersberg, personal communication).

The Fijian agreement illustrates several points that may be useful in planning future negotiations for access to aquatic genetic resources:

- Agreements with communities can contribute to the subsequent development of access policies by providing an opportunity to test the requirements for successful negotiation processes. Although the Fijian government was not directly involved in the negotiations, these were undertaken with proactive consultation with several government institutions, including the Department of Environment, which was created specifically to address the implementation of the CBD and Agenda 21. This consultation and the bioprospecting agreement helped in the formulation of Fiji's Sustainable Development Bill, which deals with access to genetic resources but hasn't been enacted.
- Funding and operational support from institutions or government greatly enhance the opportunity for successful negotiations. While this may seem obvious, the fact is that most small communities have neither the financial resources nor the skills needed to conduct protracted and complicated access and benefit-sharing negotiations. The agreement might be criticized because of USP's self-interest as a potential beneficiary of commercial benefits from discoveries made from collections. However, the agreement would not have occurred without NGO funding and the involvement of USP as an intermediary between the community and pharmaceutical organizations. Nor might it have occurred had the project team not provided a professional facilitator. Naturally, some communities may prefer to negotiate directly with collectors without intermediaries, and governments (or indigenous organizations) could develop programmes to train communities not only to conduct negotiations but also to negotiate a wide range of benefits acceptable to all parties. However, the general trend of emerging access laws is to require foreign collectors to collaborate with provider country universities or other institutions in negotiations involving communities. Direct negotiations with communities may be less complicated for collections of broodstock for aquaculture; however, the potential economic value of collections may also be less, limiting the ability of the collector to offer substantial or wide-ranging benefits.
- Government policy support for negotiations is crucial. In the Fiji case, government not only welcomed the project but saw it as an opportunity to advance its own efforts to develop workable access and benefit-sharing policies. This contrasts sharply with the situation described in Case Study 2, in which a Canadian salmon farmer was thwarted from collecting salmon broodstock in spawning streams or negotiating with indigenous communities because the fisheries department had not developed policies on community rights to consultation or on broodstock collection. Both types of policies are fundamental to the successful negotiation of agreements by communities.

- The legal status of a community may inhibit negotiations even when it has control over resources. In the Fiji project, the community did not have an opportunity to negotiate prior informed consent for commercial development by drug companies because it was not party to the agreement between USP and SIDR. Companies may balk at making agreements with communities that are not legal entities – that is, 'unorganized' villages as opposed to incorporated municipalities. Conversely, communities that are not treated as equal partners in negotiations are likely to have less incentive to consent to access. While some villages may be content to have their interests represented by municipal governments, others may be opposed to such an arrangement because it is inconsistent with traditional forms of government or simply because of distrust between government recognized municipalities and traditional communities.
- Broad stakeholder support for negotiations is critical. The Fiji project took great care not only to consult with community leaders but also to hold workshops, open to all members of the community, to define the nature and scope of negotiations. Translation of documents into the local language also helped to ensure the full involvement and understanding of local people. Especially when benefits are tied to conservation objectives, it is important that all community sectors (or stakeholders) are 'on side' to make agreements work.
- Traditional knowledge and IPRs are not necessarily vital components of successful agreements for access and benefit sharing. While this may seem like good news for fishing communities without a history of medicinal uses of aquatic genetic resources, problems are bound to arise. In the first place, the agreement with Verata was only possible because the national government had recognized indigenous ownership over lands and marine resources. Communities that have neither ownership rights nor relevant traditional knowledge may not have the opportunity to negotiate benefits unless national legislation permits it.

Chapter 7
Putting Principles into Practice

Artisanal fisherman and his family, São Francisco River, Brazil (Photo by Brian Harvey)

ACCESS AND BENEFIT-SHARING LAWS:
A work in slow progress

We have spent a considerable portion of this book examining the issue of access to aquatic genetic resources and the sharing of benefits derived from their use. The question of access and benefit sharing has been front and centre in international discussions about the trade in biological resources ever since the CBD acknowledged national sovereignty over biological diversity in 1992. Community rights have entered into the debate insofar as the CBD recognizes the importance of compensating communities for the contribution their traditional knowledge and practices may make to both the use of genetic resources and conservation of biological diversity.

Efforts to attain the lofty ideals of the CBD have hit a wide variety of stumbling blocks. Progress in the development of access and benefit-sharing laws has been slow. No developed countries have passed access and benefit-sharing laws (the US has pointedly declined to ratify the CBD), and developing countries are taking their time working out the details. This means not only learning from the experiences of early actors such as the Philippines but also determining how to address the impacts of the TRIPS agreement, which appears to have diminished the relevance of national sovereignty over genetic resources by strengthening the hand of genetic resources users – notably the corporations that hold the patents on inventions. Meanwhile, there are virtually no examples of actual benefits received by communities providing genetic resources.

Is access and benefit-sharing theory an emperor with no clothes? The frustration faced by researchers and the absence of benefits received by communities since the CBD came into force certainly raise questions about how access policies might work effectively in the future. The emperor may have very little on at the moment, but perhaps it's simply a question of taking the time and patience to find the clothes with the right fit.

Not everyone agrees that access and benefit-sharing laws are good things. Participants in the Crucible Group, a policy group representing a broad cross-section of interests, expressed very divided opinions: some commented that such laws create unrealistic expectations of economic rewards that are at best a long shot; others argued that well-constructed national access laws can ensure significant benefit sharing where none existed before and that, even if benefits are smaller than originally expected, it is still worthwhile to have them in place (Crucible Group, 2001). Indigenous groups appear to have mixed feelings about such laws. Some welcome the chance for a greater share of the pie, no matter how small. Others view access laws as merely a way of avoiding what they see as the real issue, namely ownership of lands and resources. Whatever their merits, access laws will increase in number as more and more countries move to meet their commitments under the CBD.

As this study has shown, the implementation of the CBD to date has been characterized by a preoccupation with plant genetic resources issues. As demands for access to aquatic genetic resources increase, especially in the field of food fish aquaculture, it will also become more important to take account of differences between plants and fish in the development of access laws. Most importantly, as discussed in Chapter 2, it will first be necessary to fill significant policy gaps in the *management* of aquatic genetic resources and aquatic biodiversity generally.

AQUATIC BIODIVERSITY MANAGEMENT:
Filling policy gaps

The preceding chapters have illustrated several key points about the management of aquatic biodiversity:

- The world is in the midst of a 'blue revolution' in which aquaculture is gradually catching up to capture fisheries as the primary source of the world's food fish supplies. The blue revolution is being fuelled by rapid progress in the science of genetics, with constant new developments in selective breeding and molecular biology. The blue revolution also includes bioprospecting for a marine organism that's genetic and chemical make-up hold clues for pharmaceutical and industrial applications.
- The genetic diversity of the world's aquatic life is the natural capital on which the blue revolution depends. An extraordinary range of aquatic species and subspecies have evolved to adapt to specific and localized habitat requirements. Scientific understanding of species adaptations will become increasingly important as the use of aquatic genetic resources expands and is refined. For example, a fish scientist wanting to develop a farmed salmon strain that is tolerant of warmer water conditions resulting from climate change might be able simply to select broodstock from a naturally occurring population – providing that the stock still exists and its special characteristics have been identified.
- The biological diversity of aquatic life and the genetic diversity within species continue to diminish at an alarming rate as a result of human activities. It is reasonable to assume that many aquatic species become extinct before science is even aware of their existence (an estimated 95 per cent of oceanic life forms remain unexplored). Funding for molecular biology is generally far more readily available than funding for the basic taxonomy that needs to be done in order to categorize aquatic species and populations. Ironically, the corporate (and hence academic) incentive to develop new techniques for using genetic resources far exceeds governmental incentives to promote the discovery and conservation of new species. The natural capital of the ocean, river, lake and wetland genetic resources is disappearing even before its magnitude is known.
- Most national aquatic resources policies remain fixated on the maintenance of current commercial fisheries or development of new ones. National policies on aquaculture tend to react to public concerns about environmental impacts rather than adopting a comprehensive and far-sighted approach to protecting ecosystems while at the same time exploring future opportunities, conserving the genetic diversity needed for productive and efficient aquaculture, and

ensuring that access to aquatic genetic resources, when required, will be facilitated and appropriately regulated.

- Parties to the CBD have acknowledged that indigenous and local communities have rights to fair treatment in negotiations for access to genetic resources and can play an important role in the conservation of aquatic biodiversity. While a few countries have taken steps to recognize certain rights of indigenous and local communities to negotiate access, most have been reluctant to address the issue, especially in light of concerns about impediments to academic and commercial research.

National policies on access and benefit sharing cannot be developed in a vacuum. As illustrated in Figure 7.1, effective policies for the management of aquatic genetic resources and the sustainable management of aquatic ecosystems are prerequisites for workable policies on access and benefit sharing. These secondary policy levels are far more developed for the plant than for the aquatic world. Moreover, plant genetic resources are generally collected from *ex situ* collections, while aquatic genetic resources are almost without exception collected from the wild.

Effective policies for the management of aquatic biological and genetic diversity depend in turn on a foundation of information (which again lags behind what is known about plants) and cooperation among policy makers and stakeholders. Each of the following components will be important in filling the policy gaps:

- Increasing scientific knowledge of the occurrence, distribution and genetic make-up of aquatic species; aquatic ecosystem relationships; and the human impacts on aquatic resources.
- Integrating traditional ecological knowledge with scientific research.
- Promoting effective systems for gathering, organizing, and sharing information about aquatic genetic resources.
- Increasing public and agency awareness about the importance of biological and genetic diversity, including aquatic genetic diversity, and of policies for sustainable use.
- Clearly defining and coordinating the responsibilities of government agencies involved in the management of aquatic resources.
- Ensuring the effective participation of stakeholders, including indigenous and local communities, in policy making.

Building information and understanding

Scientific knowledge

Without scientific understanding of biodiversity and ecosystem relationships, the development of aquatic resource management policies is likely to be shaped by the most influential stakeholders. In the past, the results have been overfishing, destruction of habitat, and loss of the biological and genetic diversity needed to sustain human uses of aquatic resources. Recognition of aquatic ecosystems as management units is very recent, and a high level of science is needed to support this management approach. The importance of expanding scientific knowledge to support policy making is still under-appreciated. The vast majority of aquatic species, both ocean and freshwater, haven't even been identified yet, and the impacts of human interventions (and disruptions such as global warming) on aquatic ecosystems aren't well understood.

The flow of scientific information is anything but guaranteed. Research institutions are struggling for government funding and increasingly must rely on corporate support. Aquatic resources policies must not only be guided by objective scientific knowledge, they also need to support its expansion. In particular, drafters of policies for access to aquatic genetic resources need to ensure that scientific research is encouraged rather than discouraged by regulatory requirements. Governments can't always wait for scientific certainty before making policy, but they need to be prepared to amend policy if research results clearly undermine outdated assumptions on which policy has been based.

Traditional ecological knowledge

Traditional knowledge needs to be considered and incorporated at the outset of policy making rather than being perceived simply as a resource that is traded for compensation.

Despite their contradictory approaches to learning, science and traditional knowledge can complement one another as a foundation for policy making. Science asks only those questions that can be answered and demands objective, verifiable proof, not belief. It attempts to reduce complex systems to their basic elements. Traditional knowledge takes the opposite approach. It sees nature as an integrated whole and incorporates that view into spiritual belief. Its lessons come from experience and anecdote, not analysis. The two systems can complement one another if mutual distrust can be overcome.

Indigenous peoples have become increasingly reluctant to share traditional knowledge, having seen it so often exploited and misused. Governments need to work with communities to build the trust needed to include traditional knowledge in policy making. Avenues for doing so may include strengthening understanding of cultural differences, ensuring legal protection against the unauthorized misuse of traditional knowledge, building co-management agreements with indigenous communities, and further expanding community rights over traditional lands and resources.

Gathering and collating information

The information needed for policy making goes far beyond the simple accumulation of scientific and traditional knowledge. Policy makers need to have access to that knowledge in order to identify what information they need and ensure that it is readily available at the local, national and international levels. Information systems for aquatic genetic resources are poorly developed. Significant gaps include assessments of fish stock distribution and abundance; tabulations of landings for all but the largest commercial fisheries; and searchable registers of genetic diversity information. The movement of fish between countries and through international waters increases the need for international collaboration in data collection and organization. Recent examples of such collaboration include the World Fish Center's FishBase database and the Aquatic Animal Diversity Information System (AADIS) being developed by FAO and World Fisheries Trust. Such registries need to include traditional knowledge where communities agree to provide it.

Public and professional awareness

Policies for aquatic resources management are unlikely to succeed without public awareness and support. People need to understand the reasons for developing a policy, its likely impact, and the consequences of doing nothing. At a more basic level, people need to understand the importance of sustaining biological and genetic diversity and the advantages and disadvantages of alternative management options. This is especially true for aquatic life because of the limitations of current scientific knowledge and because of uncertainties and potential conflicts about new uses of aquatic genetic resources. Tools such as the internet provide policy makers with an opportunity to increase public awareness. In addition, communications links enable an increased role for international and intergovernmental agencies to run public awareness programmes that can ease the way for national and local policy makers.

Communications with the public need to be clear, concise and free of jargon. As much as possible, it should also have the appearance of objectivity in order to build public trust in policy making, especially at a time of public scepticism about governance. For this reason too, public awareness should focus on informing rather than 'educating' the public, especially when dealing with controversial issues. It should also include an interactive component, ensuring ready access to information providers for citizens wishing to clarify issues. Finally, the scope of public awareness programmes should be broad enough to include commercial interests (eg small and large fisheries and other industries) and government agencies that may be directly or peripherally involved in policy making.

Professionals within agencies, including those charged with developing policy, are frequently poorly informed on aquatic issues peripheral to their own responsibility. Because of the interconnectedness of these issues, such a situation can cripple attempts at policy, and needs to be addressed through briefings within and between agencies and through greater contact with stakeholders.

Cooperative approaches to policy making

Agency coordination

Historically, government agencies have been defined by their responsibility for separate resources (agriculture, mining, forestry, fisheries), each operating in an insular manner. Both fisheries and aquaculture are often subsumed under larger departments such as agriculture, and agencies combined within a fisheries department may work at cross purposes or without integrated strategic plans. The need to address sustainable development issues has created complexities that require greater cooperation among existing resource agencies as well as the involvement of other agencies such as those that oversee municipal and indigenous affairs, environmental protection and marine protected areas, agriculture, forestry, water resources, and economic development.

The effectiveness of aquatic resources policies has too frequently been undermined by turf wars, lack of communication, and indecision over resource conflicts (eg between aquaculture and commercial fisheries, fisheries and forestry/mining, community and commercial fisheries). Governments need to take a stronger approach to promoting cooperation among all relevant agencies in the development, implementation and enforcement of aquatic resource policies, with clearly defined agency responsibilities at each level.

Stakeholder participation

The stability of policies is directly related to the extent of public 'buy in'. Clear and complete information is the first step towards building public support. In addition, policy makers need to anticipate and address the interests of the multiple stakeholders likely to be affected. In democratic societies, governments delegate decision-making authority to policy makers, and policies need to reflect the direction taken by government. However, 'public input' is not a token exercise. It not only provides a pool of information needed for sound decision-making but can also ensure to the greatest extent possible the fulfilment of apparently competing needs. Sustainable management policies based on inadequate consultation or heavily favouring individual sectors are unlikely to have long-term success. Moreover, as many governments are in the process of devolving management responsibilities to stakeholder partnerships (public and private sectors, NGOs, community fisheries organizations), intensive participation is required not only to shape government policies but also to work out the details of cooperative management. The very real risks of devolution, including a lowering of technical competence, loss of corporate memory, and loss of long-term funding need also to be recognized.

The list of stakeholders may include indigenous and local community fisheries, commercial fish farming and capture industries, sport fisheries, tourism, other industries such as forestry and agriculture, municipal governments, NGOs, and affected government agencies. Policy makers should, as much as possible, involve stakeholders directly in the policy making process through a cooperative and inclusive approach. The degree of involvement of indigenous and local communities should reflect the extent to which policies are likely to affect them. The benefits of stable and well-informed policies will almost certainly outweigh the costs of managing participation, and these costs are likely to diminish as effective participation mechanisms (including mediation where necessary) are fine-tuned.

Effective stakeholder participation is equally important at all policy levels, whether they relate to the management of aquatic biodiversity, uses of aquatic genetic resources, or access to genetic resources and the equitable sharing of benefits derived from their uses.

THE FOUR 'POLICY PILLARS' OF ABS LEGISLATION

The previous section describes the need for greater emphasis on the basic components needed for the development of aquatic resources policies. This section provides an overview of the policy levels needed to support access and benefit-sharing legislation that works for aquatic resources, illustrated by Figure 7.1.

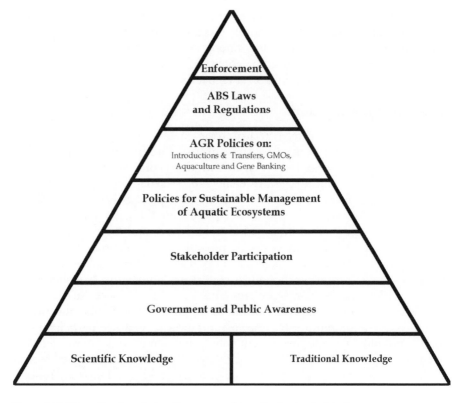

Figure 7.1 *The policy foundation for access and benefit-sharing legislation*

Pillar One: Management at the ecosystem level

Life was simpler for policy makers when fisheries management largely meant setting quotas and size limits. Today, policies for sustainable management of aquatic ecosystems need to follow a continuum of conservation and sustainable use, and policy makers' decisions are mightily complicated by changing scientific information, uncertainties about what makes ecosystems work and how human uses and natural events affect them, demands created by new uses of biological and genetic resources, increasing stakeholder conflicts, limited budgets and even climate change.

A coordinated approach to aquatic biodiversity management policies needs to take into consideration many factors that may not have been considered relevant to the development of earlier fisheries policies. The following are examples:

- Completeness of reliable information (science, traditional knowledge, stakeholder input).
- Integration of strategies for the conservation of aquatic biodiversity and wild fish populations (eg fish quotas, marine protected areas, habitat protection and restoration).
- Ecosystem relationships supporting not only commercially valuable fisheries but also those with potential commercial value, and the species in the food chain they depend on.
- Adherence to the precautionary principle of ecosystem management.
- Coordination of capture fishery and food fish aquaculture policies, addressing environmental and socio-economic impacts of each.
- Environmental effects of transgenic organisms, and introductions and transfers.
- Climate change and its effects on aquatic species.
- Land and access rights of indigenous peoples and their roles in ecosystem management.
- Promotion of community, small-scale fisheries, linking rights to use with responsibilities for conservation.
- Support for independent fish certification systems (such as MSC and Marine Aquarium Council) that apply objective standards to local operations and follow the chain of custody from original provider to end consumer.
- International cooperation in policy development and compliance with international agreements promoting conservation and sustainable use.

Pillar Two: Management of aquatic resources at the genetic level

All biological resources contain the functional units of heredity in every cell. The practical difference between aquatic biological resources and aquatic genetic resources lies in the manner in which they're used. New uses are proliferating in enhancement of farmed fish, the development of drugs and industrial products, and transfer of genes between unrelated species. Commercial uses for microbes from marine hydrothermal vents may be next.

Uses of aquatic genetic resources raise formidable social and environmental issues that need to be addressed. What are the implications of approving transplants of fish genes into a strawberry or of insect genes into a fish? Who owns or controls or even knows about material in a fish gene bank, and should there be any limitations on its use? If Florida ornamental fish breeders learn to culture new strains of cardinal tetra, what are the social and policy implications in the US and Brazil if the market for Rio Negro capture fisheries is wiped out? A few years ago, these applications of aquatic genetic resources would have been considered barely within the bounds of possibility; now each is a reality.

Governments need a set of policies specific to the management of aquatic genetic resources. Such species-specific policies are already well developed in the plant world. Policy makers on the aquatic side cannot afford to lag behind, because genetic uses are expanding quickly and bring with them complex social and environmental issues. Too often, governments have been too slow to act (eg policies on gene banking) or have jumped the gun (eg policies supporting net pen aquaculture without sufficient scientific information). A measured approach to policy making is needed not just for uses of aquatic genetic resources but also for their movement and handling. Under what conditions should transfers between watersheds and introductions of exotic species be permitted? Where should collectors be permitted to collect broodstock or other genetic material, and in what amounts?

Finally, governments need to address the thorny question of IPRs such as patents on fish genes. Whose property is a Super Salmon or Super Tilapia, and what rights does the owner have to protect it?

Pillar Three: Access and benefit sharing

Access and benefit-sharing policies cannot function in a vacuum. Collectors of aquatic genetic resources need clarity about whether the uses they propose will be permitted or can proceed without undue delay. One use of aquatic genetic resources might contribute positively to the sustainable management of aquatic biodiversity, another might have negative impacts – but the ground-rules need to be known. Collectors also need to know the rules for the handling and movement of genetic materials. Provider countries and communities have an interest in ensuring that benefits arising from access agreements contribute to sustainable ecosystem management and stable community economies. Sound policies for the management of aquatic biodiversity can be an important tool in the creation of sustainable fishing livelihoods and in decisions about appropriate transfer of technologies.

In addition to its access and benefit-sharing provisions, CBD lays the groundwork for national action in the development of policies on the management of aquatic biological diversity at the ecosystem and genetic levels. While both these levels of policy provide a foundation for access and benefit-sharing policy, all three levels are interdependent. For example, a primary purpose of access and benefit-sharing legislation is to contribute to sound biodiversity management and use of genetic resources. Unfortunately, national reports from CBD Parties, in sections dealing with aquatics, do not give a high priority to the development of access and benefit-sharing legislation.

Pillar Four: Enforcement

Access and benefit-sharing legislation is only as effective as the enforcement measures that accompany it, and the vast geographic scope of aquatic biodiversity means that enforcement is no easy matter. A variety of agencies may be involved in the administration of access and benefit-sharing legislation, and their efforts need to be clearly coordinated. Agencies' resources may be stretched by competing priorities.

Government needs to express its commitment to the effective functioning of access and benefit-sharing legislation. It needs to ensure that accompanying regulations are in place, clearly designate lead agencies and their responsibilities, and ensure that they have adequate resources to do the job. Efforts need to be made to ensure effective coordination not just among national agencies (or between them, when aquatic biodiversity crosses international boundaries) but also with their regional subsidiaries and with public sector groups that may be able to contribute to enforcement mechanisms. In addition, some countries may need to take steps to discourage bribery of local officials.

A CHECKLIST FOR DESIGNING ACCESS AND BENEFIT-SHARING POLICIES

National level

Access and benefit-sharing policies

- Ensure effective participation of stakeholders, including indigenous and local communities, in the development of ABS laws and policies.
- Clearly define aquatic genetic resources.
- Clearly define circumstances in which communities have the right to prior informed consent.
- Where relevant, clearly define the meaning of traditional knowledge associated with the use of genetic resources.
- Provide support for documentation of traditional fisheries knowledge.
- Clearly distinguish between requirements for commercial and academic users.
- Provide institutional support to build the capacity of communities to negotiate access agreements.
- Provide institutional support for benefit-sharing agreements, with a focus on sustainable livelihoods.
- Support development of international conflict resolution mechanism to resolve issues of equity in contractual agreements.

Community rights

- Develop *sui generis* policies for the protection of indigenous and local community rights.
- Address the question of indigenous rights to lands, waters, and control over aquatic genetic resources.

Uses of aquatic genetic resources

- Develop biosafety and transfer policies specific to aquatic genetic resources.
- Develop policies governing ex situ collections (gene banks).
- Develop policies governing food fish aquaculture, ornamental aquaculture and bioprospecting.

Community level

- Develop policies on ownership and control of aquatic genetic resources, co-management, and/or *sui generis* systems for protection of community resource and knowledge rights.
- Develop practical strategies and capabilities for co-management of aquatic genetic resources.
- Document traditional knowledge of aquatic genetic resources.
- Build capacity for participating in development of national/regional policies for biodiversity management, sustainable uses, and access and benefit sharing.
- Build capacity for negotiation of access agreements.
- Determine under what conditions and for what purposes consent for access to aquatic genetic resources will be provided.
- Determine information required from researchers regarding funding sources and their obligations to those sources.
- Analyse options for monetary and non-monetary benefits and their usefulness to fishing communities.
- Develop networks with other communities (including fisheries councils) and civil society organizations for development of consistent community policies.

Countries receiving genetic resources

- Direct a portion of foreign aid to building community capacity for negotiation of access agreements and for crafting of practical non-monetary benefits (eg low-tech sustainable fisheries livelihoods); support efforts of international development organizations to do the same.
- Promote industry and public awareness of independent certification systems applicable to access to aquatic genetic resources (eg MSC, MAC).
- Ensure that patent laws require declaration of origin of aquatic genetic resources and associated knowledge leading to inventions.
- Ensure that policies for aquaculture of exotic species take into account equitable sharing of benefits with source countries and communities and impacts on their capture fisheries, community cultures, and protection of fish habitat in source communities.

Notes

Chapter 1

1 K Davenport, Ornamental Aquatic Trade Association (OATA), UK, personal communication, 2000.
2 L Cruz, Marine Science Institute, University of the Philippines, personal communication, 2000.
3 S Dowd, New England Aquarium, personal communication, 2002.
4 NL Chao, Project Piaba, Universidade do Amazonia, personal communication, 1999.
5 Provisional Act No 2, 186–16 (2001).

Chapter 2

1 Dr David Narver, British Columbia Department of Fish and Wildlife, personal communication, 1993.
2 Sandy Johnson, Department of Fisheries and Oceans (DFO), Whitehorse, Yukon, personal communication, 1999.
3 Bill Vernon, President, Creative Salmon Ltd, personal communication, 1999.
4 Sandy Johnson, Department of Fisheries and Oceans (DFO), Whitehorse, personal communication, 1999.
5 Carl Sidney, Chair, Yukon Salmon Committee, personal communication, 1999.

Chapter 3

1 Dr Lourdes Cruz, Marine Science Institute, Quezon City, Philippines, personal communication, 2000.
2 Dr NL Chao, Universidade dos Amazonas, personal communication, 1999.
3 Timothy Fleming, Icy Waters Ltd, personal communication, 2001.
4 Timothy Fleming, Icy Waters Ltd, personal communication, 2001.

Chapter 4

1 Carol Cross, Fisheries and Oceans Canada, personal communication, 2002.

2 Modadugu Gupta, World Fish Center, Penang, Malaysia, personal communication, 2003.
3 Remedios Bolivar, Freshwater Aquaculture Center, Central State Luzon University, Philippines, personal communication, 2002.
4 Jiji Rodriguez, Executive Director, GIFT Foundation, personal communication, 2002.
5 www.genomar.com/tilapia.php

Chapter 5

1 Brazil: Provisional Act No. 2, 186–16 (2001); Costa Rica: Biodiversity Law (1998); India: Biological Diversity Bill (2000); Peru: Proposal of Regime of Protection of the Collective Knowledge of the Indigenous Peoples (1999); Philippines: Executive Order No. 247 (1995).
2 Sources include interviews with the following: Professor Gisela Concepcion; Professor Lourdes Cruz; Gil Jacinto, Director, Marine Science Institute, University of the Philippines; Neth Dano, Executive Director, Southeast Asia Regional Institute for Community Education; Amelia Guevara, Vice-Chancellor for Academic Affairs, University of the Philippines; Saturnino Halos, Natural Sciences Research Institute, University of the Philippines; Clarissa Marte, Head of Research Division, Aquaculture Department, Southeast Asian Fisheries Development Center; Mudjekeewis Santos, fishery biologist, Bureau of Fisheries and Aquatic Resources, Department of Agriculture; and Julita Ungson, Technical Consultant for Fisheries, Department of Agriculture; Ephraim Batungbacal, Coordinator, Anti-Biopiracy Program, Tambuyog Development Center.
3 The full title of EO247 is: 'Prescribing Guidelines and Establishing a Regulatory Framework for the Prospecting of Biological and Genetic Resources, Their By-Products and Derivatives, for Scientific and Commercial Purposes and for Other Purposes'.
4 Department of Environment and Natural Resources, Department Administrative Order No. 96–20: 'Implementing Rules and Regulations on the Prospecting of Biological and Genetic Resources', 1996.
5 In 1999, Senator Teresa Aquino-Oreta introduced for congressional approval a bill that was essentially a duplicate of EO247. However, Senate Bill 1645 did not proceed further. NGOs in particular criticized it for failing to improve on EO247 and for its omission of any mention of prior informed consent by non-indigenous communities.

Chapter 6

1 Ray Hilborn, School of Fisheries and Aquatic Sciences, University of Washington, broadcast radio interview, 'Quirks and Quarks', Canadian Broadcasting Corporation, 19 January 2002.

References

Aalbersberg, W (1997) 'Bioprospecting and its regulation by government in Fiji', Biodiversity Conservation Network, World Wildlife Fund, www.bcnet.org/whatsnew/fijigov.htm

Aalbersberg, W, Korovulavula, I, Parks, J and Russell, D (1997) 'The role of a Fijian community in a bioprospecting project', Access to Genetic Resources and Benefit-sharing Case Studies, Case Study 20, Convention on Biological Diversity, www.biodiv.org/doc/case-studies/cs-abs-fj.pdf

Abban, E (1999) 'Considerations for the conservation of African fish genetic resources for their sustainable exploitation' in R Pullin, Bartley, D and Kooiman, J (eds) *Towards Policies for Conservation and Sustainable Use of Aquatic Genetic Resources*, ICLARM Conference Proceedings 59, 14–18 April 1998, Manila

Abramovitz, J (1995) 'Freshwater failures: the crises on five continents', *World Watch*, September/October 1995, pp 27–35

Agbayani, R, Baticados, D and Siar, S (2000) 'Community fishery resources management on Malalison Island, Philippines: R & D framework, interventions, and policy implications', *Coastal Management*, vol 28, pp19–27

Appleton, C (2001) 'An African leech for use in microsurgery in Africa!', Science in Africa: Africa's First On-line Science Magazine, Archives page, Index to September 2001 issue, www.scienceinafrica.co.za/2001/september/leech2.htm

ASEAN (Association of South East Asian Nations) (2000) 'ASEAN framework agreement on access to biological and genetic resources (draft text)', ASEAN, http://216.15.202/docs/asean-access-2000/en.pdf

Axelrod, H (2001) 'Discovery of the cardinal tetra and beyond' in N Chao, Petry, P, Prang, G, Sonnieschien, L and Tlusty, M (eds) *Conservation and Management of Ornamental Fish Resources of the Rio Negro Basin, Amazonia, Brasil – Project Piaba*, Universidade do Amazonas and Bio-Amazonia Conservation International, Manaus, pp302

Baquero, J (1999) 'Marine ornamentals trade: quality and sustainability for the Pacific Region', Marine Aquarium Council, South Pacific Forum Secretariat and Marine Aquarium Council, www.aquariumcouncil.org

Barber, V and La Vina, A (1995) *Regulating Access to Genetic Resources: The Philippine Experience*, Presentation to the Global Biodiversity Forum, Jakarta, 4–5 November

Bardach, J, Ryther, J and McLarney, W (1972) *Aquaculture – The Farming and Husbandry of Freshwater and Marine Organisms*, John Wiley and Sons, New York, p868

Bartley, D (1997) 'Biodiversity and genetics' in *Review of the State of World Aquaculture*, FAO Fisheries Circular No. 886, FAO Fisheries Department, Rome, p163

Bartley, D (2000) 'Responsible ornamental fisheries', *FAO Aquaculture Newsletter*, vol 24, p10–14

Bartley, D and Pullin, R (1999) 'Towards policies for aquatic genetic resources' in R Pullin, Bartley, D and Kooiman, J (eds) *Towards Policies for Conservation and Sustainable Use of Aquatic Genetic Resources*, ICLARM Conference Proceedings 59, 14–18 April 1998, Manila, pp1–16

Barton, J (1991) *Relating Scientific and the Commercial Worlds in Genetic Resource Negotiation*, Paper presented at the Symposium on Property, Rights, Biotechnology, and Genetic Resources, African Centre for Technology Studies and World Resources Institute, Nairobi, Kenya

Baticados, D and Agbayani, R (2000) 'Co-management in marine fisheries on Malalison Island, central Philippines', *International Journal of Sustainable Development and World Ecology*, vol 7, pp1–13

Batungbacal, E (2000) *Marine Bioprospecting in the Philippines*, Tambuyog Development Center and Southeast Asia Regional Institute for Community Education, Quezon City, Philippines, p33

Bengwayan, M (2001) 'Companies rush to patent wildlife in the Philippines', *Earth Times*, 15 January 2001

Bensky, D and Gamble, A (compilers and translators) (1993) *Materia Medica: Chinese Herbal Medicine*, Eastland Press, Seattle, Washington DC

Berlin, S (1997) *Ways We Live: Exploring Community*, New Society Publishers, Gabriola Island, Canada, pp170

Bierer, D, Carlson, T and King S (1996) 'Shaman Pharmaceuticals: integrating indigenous knowledge, tropical medicinal plants, medicine, modern science and reciprocity into a novel drug discovery approach', The Science Center – Special Topics, Network Science, www.netsci.org/Science/Special/feature11.html

Blench, R (1998) 'Biodiversity conservation and its opponents', *Natural Resource Perspectives*, vol 32 (July), pp9

Brown, D and Greer, D (2001) *Forest Industry Certification in British Columbia: Issues and Options for Government Action*, BC Ministry of Forests, Victoria, Canada

Brummett, R (ed) (1994) *Aquaculture Policy Options for Integrated Resource Management in Subsaharan Africa*, International Center for Living Aquatic Resources Management, Manila and Deutsche Gesellschaft fur Technische Zusammenarbeit, Eschborn, Germany, pp38

Brush, S and Stabinsky, D (eds) (1996) *Valuing Local Knowledge: Indigenous People and Intellectual Property Rights*, Island Press, Washington DC

Bruton, M (1995) 'Have fishes had their chips? The dilemma of threatened fishes', *Environmental Biology of Fishes*, vol 43, no 1, pp1–27

CBD (Convention on Biological Diversity) (2002) 'Decision VI/24: Bonn Guidelines on access to genetic resources and fair and equitable sharing of the benefits arising from their utilization', COP Decisions – COP 6 – Decision VI/24, CBD, www.biodiv.org/decisions/ default.asp?lg=0&m=cop-06&d=24

Centeno, J (2000) 'Pirates plunder the tropics', *Protecting Knowledge: Articles of Interest*, 17 March 2000, www.members.home.nl/aeissing/00715.html

CGFRA (Commission on Genetic Resources for Food and Agriculture) (2002) 'International undertaking on plant genetic resources for food and agriculture', CGFRA Agriculture Section, United Nations Food and Agriculture Organization (FAO), http://www.fao.org/ag/cgrfa/IU.htm

CGIAR (Consultative Group on International Agricultural Research) SGRP (System-wide Genetic Resources Programme) (2001) 'Booklet of CGIAR centre policy instruments, guidelines and statements on genetic resources, biotechnology and intellectual property rights, version 1', System-wide Information Network for Genetic Resources website, Rome, http:/singer.cgiar.org/booklet.pdf

Chao, N (1998) 'A draft of Brazilian freshwater fishes for the hobby – a proposal to IBAMA', *Ornamental Fish International Journal*, vol 23, pp11–19

Chao, N, Prang, G and Petry, P (2001) 'Project Piaba – maintenance and sustainable development of ornamental fisheries in the Rio Negro basin, Amazonas, Brazil' in N Chao, Petry, P, Prang, G, Sonnieschien, L and Tlusty, M (eds) (2002) *Conservation and Management of Ornamental Fish Resources of the Rio Negro Basin, Amazonia, Brasil – Project Piaba*, Universidade do Amazonas and Bio-Amazonia Conservation International, Manaus, pp302

Columbia University, School of International and Public Affairs (1999) *Access to Genetic Resources: An Evaluation of the Development and Implementation of Recent Regulation and Access Agreements*, Environmental Policy Studies, Working Paper #4, The Tides Center – Biodiversity Action Network, Washington, DC, p101

Correa, C (1999) 'Intellectual property rights and aquatic genetic resources' in R Pullin, Bartley, D and Kooiman, J (eds) *Towards Policies for Conservation and Sustainable use of Aquatic Genetic Resources*, ICLARM Conference Proceedings 59, 14–18 April 1998, Manila

Crucible Group (1994) *People, Plants and Patents: The Impact of Intellectual Property on Trade, Plant Biodiversity, and Rural Society*, International Research Development Centre, Ottawa, p116

Crucible Group (2000) *Seeding Solutions, Volume 1: Policy Options for Genetic Resources*, IDRC, IPGRI and the Dag Hammarskjold Foundation, Ottawa, p120

Crucible Group (2001) *Seeding Solutions, Volume 2: Options for National Laws Governing Control Over Genetic Resources and Biological Innovations*, IDRC, IPGRI and the Dag Hammarskjold Foundation, Ottawa, p243

Dalton, R (2002) 'Bioprospectors turn their gaze to Canada', *Nature*, vol 419, p768

Dano, E (2001) 'Participation in the formulation of the Philippines Executive Order 247 on access to genetic resources, and priorities for implementation' in K Swiderska (ed) (2001) *Stakeholder Participation in Policy on Access to Genetic*

Resources, Traditional Knowledge and Benefit-sharing, International Institute for Environment and Development, London, p32

Delgado, C, Wada, M, Rosegrant, N, Meijer, S and Mahfuzuddin, A (2003) *Fish to 2020: Supply and Demand in Changing Local Markets*, International Food Policy Research Institute, Washington, DC, and World Fish Center, Penang, Malaysia

Dey, M (2000) 'The impact of genetically improved farmed Nile tilapia in Asia', *Aquaculture Economics and Management*, vol 4(1/2), pp109–26

Diversa Corporation (2000) 'Diversa signs first agreement granting legal access to biodiversity in Africa', www.diversa.com/presrele/2000/view_release.asp?id= 20001207

Dowd, S (2001) 'An aquarist's experience of Amazon River ecotour expeditions and hobbyist involvement in conservation' in N Chao, Petry, P, Prang, G, Sonnieschien, L and Tlusty, M (eds) (2002) *Conservation and Management of Ornamental Fish Resources of the Rio Negro Basin, Amazonia, Brasil – Project Piaba*, Universidade do Amazonas and Bio-Amazonia Conservation International, Manaus, p 302

Dutfield, G (1999) 'The public and private domains: intellectual property rights in traditional ecological knowledge', WP 03/99, OIPRC E-Journal of Intellectual Property Rights, Oxford Intellectual Property Research Centre, www.oiprc.ox.ac.uk/EJWP0399.html

Dutfield, G (n.d.) 'Biopiracy: the slavery of the new millennium? Surely not', http://users.ox.ac.uk/ wgtrr/slavery.htm

Ecotrust Canada (1997) *Seeing the Ocean Through the Trees: A Conservation-based Development Strategy for Clayoquot Sound*, Ecotrust Canada, Vancouver, p105

Edwards, P, Hiep, D, Anh P and Mair G (2000) 'Traditional culture of indigenous common carp in rice fields in northern Vietnam: does it have a future in poverty reduction?' *World Aquaculture*, December, pp34–40.

Eknath, A, Macaranas, J, Agustin, L, Velasco, R, Ablan, C, Pante, J and Pullin, R (1991) 'Biochemical and morphometric approaches to characterize farmed tilapias', *Naga*, vol 14(2) pp3–6

Eknath, A, Tayamen, M, Palada-de Vera, M, Danting, J, Reyes, R, Dionisio, E, Capili, J, Bolivar, H, Abella, T, Circa, A, Bentsen, H, Gjerde, B, Gjedrem, T and Pullin, R (1993) 'Genetic improvement of farmed tilapias: the growth performance of eight strains of *Oreochromis niloticus* tested in farmed environments', *Aquaculture*, vol 111, pp171–88

Environmental News Network (2001) 'Restaurants and grocers asked to avoid transgenic fish.' 22 October 2001. www.enn.com/news/enn-stories/2001/10/10222001/fish_45316.asp

FAO (Food and Agriculture Organization of the United Nations) (1997) *Aquaculture Development*, FAO, Rome, pp40

FAO (1998) *Aquaculture Newsletter*, December 1998, FAO, Rome

FAO (1999) 'Ornamental aquatic life: what's FAO got to do with it?, News & Highlights, 2 September 1999, FAO, www.fao.org/NEWS/1999/990901-e.htm

FAO (2000) *The State of World Fisheries and Aquaculture 2000*, FAO, Rome

FAO (2001) *Understanding the Cultures of Fishing Communities: A Key to Fishery Management and Food Security*, FAO Fisheries Technical Paper No. 401, FAO, Rome, pp304

Fletcher, G, Goddard, S and Wu, Y (1999) 'Antifreeze proteins and their genes: from basic research to business opportunity', *Chemtech*, vol 30(6), pp17–28

Froese, R and Torres, A (1999) 'Fishes under threat: an analysis of the fishes in the 1996 IUCN red list' in R Pullin, Batley, D and Kooiman, J (eds) *Towards Policies for Conservation and Sustainable use of Aquatic Genetic Resources*, ICLARM Conference Proceedings 59, 14–18 April 1998, Manila

Gardner, J and Peterson, D (2003) *Making Sense of the Salmon Aquaculture Debate: Analysis of Issues Related to Netcage Salmon Farming and Wild Salmon in British Columbia*, Pacific Fisheries Resource Conservation Council, Vancouver, Canada

Gjedrem, T (1997) 'Selective breeding to improve aquaculture production', *World Aquaculture*, vol 28, pp12–15

Glowka, L (1998a) *The Deepest of Ironies: Genetic Resources, Marine Scientific Research and the International Deep Sea-bed Area*, International Union for the Conservation of Nature, Bonn, pp22

Glowka, L (1998b) *A Guide to Designing Legal Frameworks to Determine Access to Genetic Resources*, IUCN (International Union for the Conservation of Nature), Gland, Switzerland, and Cambridge, pp97

Glowka, L (2001) *Towards a Certification System for Bioprospecting Activities*, Switzerland State Secretariat for Economic Affairs, Bern, pp119

Glowka, L, Plan, T and Stoll, P (1998) *Best Practices for Access to Genetic Resources*, Information paper for DG XI, European Commission and the German Federal Ministry of the Environment, Nature Conservation and Nuclear Safety, pp63

Gomez, E, Alcala, A and San Diego, A (1981) *Status of Philippine Coral Reefs*, Proceedings of the Fourth International Coral Reef Symposium, Manila

Gong, Z, Wan, H, Tay, T, Wang, H, Chen, M and Yan, T (2003) 'Development of transgenic fish for ornamental and bioreactor by strong expression of fluorescent proteins in the skeletal muscle', *Biochemical and Biophysical Research Communications* 308, pp58–63.

GRAIN (2002a) 'Overview of the BRL', Biodiversity Rights Legislation, GRAIN, www.grain.org/brl/overview-brl.cfm

Grajal, A (1999) 'Biodiversity and the nation state: regulating access to genetic resources limits biodiversity research in developing countries', *Conservation Biology*, vol 13(1), pp6–10

Grenier, L (1998) *Working with Indigenous Knowledge: A Guide for Researchers*, International Development Research Centre, Ottawa, pp115

Gupta, M, Acosta, B, Eknath, A and Dey, M (2000) 'Breakthrough in genetic improvement of tropical finfish through partnership between ICLARM, ASI and developing country NARS', Pools of Knowledge and Document Repository, Global Forum on Agricultural Research, www.egfar.org/documents/4_lines/Research_Partnerships/Genetic_Resources_Management/GRM_cases/3_8.PDF

Halewood, M (1999) 'Indigenous and local knowledge in international law: a preface to *sui generis* intellectual property protection', *McGill Law Journal*, vol 44(4), pp953–96

Harvey, B (1996) 'Banking fish genetic resources: the art of the possible', in F di Castri and Younes, T (eds) *Biodiversity, Science and Development: Towards a New Partnership*, CAB International, Wallingford

Harvey, B (1999) 'Fish genetic conservation in Canada and Brazil: field programs and policy development' in R Pullin, Bartley, D and Kooiman, J (eds) *Towards Policies for Conservation and Sustainable use of Aquatic Genetic Resources*, ICLARM Conference Proceedings 59, 14–18 April 1998, Manila, pp17–22

Harvey, B and Carolsfeld, J (1993) *Induced Breeding in Tropical Fish Culture*, International Development Research Centre, Ottawa, pp144

Harvey, B and Hoar, WS (1979) *The Theory and Practice of Induced Breeding in Tropical Fish Culture*, International Development Research Centre, Ottawa, pp48

Harvey, B and Macduffee, M (2002) *Ghost Runs: The Future of Wild Salmon on the North and Central Coasts of British Columbia*, Raincoast Conservation Society, Victoria, Canada

Harvey, B, Ross, C, Greer, D and Carolsfeld, J (1998) 'Action Before Extinction: An International Conference on Conservation of Fish Genetic Diversity', World Fisheries Trust, 16–18 February 1998, Victoria, Canada, pp259

Herrin, A and Racelis, R (1992) *Monitoring the Coverage of Public Programs on Low-income Families: Philippines 1992*, Integrated Development Planning Project, National Economic Development Authority, Manila

Hew, C and Fletcher, D (1997) 'Transgenic fish for aquaculture', *Chemistry & Industry*, vol 21 (April), pp311–14

Heywood, VH (ed) (1995) *Global Biodiversity Assessment*, United Nations Environment Programme, Cambridge University Press, Cambridge

Hobbelink, H (1991) *Biotechnology and the Future of World Agriculture*, Zed Books, London

Hodgkin, T and Ouedraogo, A (1996) 'Forestry, fish and crop genetic resources: commonalities and differences for effective conservation, sustainable management and use', In R Pullin and Casal, C (eds) *Consultation on Fish Genetic Resources*, International Center for Living Aquatic Resources, Makati City, Philippines

Holman Hunters and Trappers, Fisheries Joint Management Committee, and Canada Department of Fisheries and Oceans (1994) *Plan for Recovery of the Kuujjua River Charr Stock*, Brochure

ICLARM (International Center for Living Aquatic Resources Management) (1992) *Recommendations of the Meeting on International Concerns in the use of Aquatic Germplasm*, 1–5 June 1992, ICLARM, Manila

ICLARM (1996) *Draft Policy for Intellectual Property Rights on Fish Genetic Resources*, ICLARM, Manila

ICLARM (1999) *Operational Plan*, Biodiversity and Genetic Resources Program, ICLARM, Manila

ICLARM (2002) *Medium Term Plan 2002–2004*, ICLARM, Penang, Malaysia, pp102

IFPRI (International Food Policy Research Institute) and World Fish Center (2003) *Outlook for Fish to 2020: Meeting Global Demand*, IFPRI and WFC, pp36

IIFB (International Indigenous Forum on Biodiversity) (2001) 'Statement of international indigenous forum on biodiversity to the CBD ad-hoc open-ended working group on access and benefit-sharing', Convention on Biological Diversity, 22–26 October 2001, Bonn, www.nciv.net/engels/IIFB/ statementengels.htm

Illo, J and Polo, J (1990) *Fishers, Traders, Farmers, Wives: The Life Stories of Ten Women in a Fishing Village*, Institute of Philippine Culture, Ateneo de Manila University, Quezon City, Philippines

IRRI (International Rice Research Institute) (2004) 'International rice genebank: Sharing the seeds', www.irri.org/GRC/irg/biodiv-genebank.htm

IUCN (International Union for the Conservation of Nature) (2001) 'Achieving the benefit-sharing objective of the Convention on Biological Diversity', Preliminary recommendations to the CBD Ad-Hoc Open-ended Working Group on Access and Benefit-sharing, October 2001, pp7, www.iucn.org/themes/pmns/topics/absmaria.html

Jain, H (1994) 'The biodiversity convention: more losers than winners', *Biotechnology and Development Monitor*, vol 21 (December)

Johannes, R and Ruddle, K (1993) 'Human interactions in tropical coastal and marine areas: lessons from traditional resource use' in A Price and Humphrey, S (eds) *Application of the Biosphere Reserve Concept to Coastal Marine Areas*, IUCN, Gland, Switzerland, pp21–7

Khalil, M (1995) 'Biodiversity and the conservation of medicinal plants: issues from the perspective of the developing world' in T Swanson, (ed) *Intellectual Property Rights and Biodiversity Conservation: An Interdisciplinary Analysis of the Values of Medicinal Plants*, Cambridge University Press, Cambridge

Kneen, B (1999) *Farmageddon: Food and the Culture of Biotechnology*, New Society Publishers, Gabriola Island, BC, Canada

Laird, S (ed) (2002) *Biodiversity and Traditional Knowledge: Equitable Partnerships in Practice*, Earthscan Publications, London, pp504

Lewis, D, Wood, G and Gregory, R (1996) *Trading the Silver Seed: Local Knowledge and Market Moralities in Aquacultural Development*, Intermediate Technology Publications, London

Lynch, O and Maggio, G (1997) 'Human rights, environment and economic development: existing and emerging standards in international law and global society', Background – Relevant Documents, International Ombudsman Centre for the Environment and Development, www.omced.org/wri/om_wri.htm

Madeley, J (2000) 'Trade and hunger', *Seedling: The Quarterly Newsletter of Genetic Resources Action International*, December 2000, GRAIN publications, Seedling in 2000, www.grain.org/publications/dec002-en.cfm

Mann, H (1997) *Indigenous Peoples and the Use of Intellectual Property Rights in Canada: Case Studies Relating to Intellectual Property Rights and the Protection of Biodiversity*, Industry Canada, Ottawa

Marine Aquarium Council (2001) 'Fast Facts, No 1, 22 May 2001, Marine Aquarium Council, www.aquariumcouncil.org

Martinez, A (2002) *The Impact of TRIPS and the CBD on Coastal Communities*, International Collective in Support of Fishworkers, Barcelona

May, R (1988) 'How many species are there on earth?', *Science*, vol 241, pp1441–9

McAllister, D, Hamilton, A and Harvey, B (1997) 'Global freshwater biodiversity: striving for the integrity of freshwater systems', *Sea Wind: Bulletin of Ocean Voice International*, vol 11(3), Ocean Voice International Inc, Ottawa, pp140

McChesney, J (1992) *Biological Diversity, Chemical Diversity and the Search for New Pharmaceuticals*, Paper presented at the Symposium on Tropical Forest Medical Resources and the Conservation of Biodiversity, January 1992, Rainforest Alliance, New York

Moore, R (2000) 'The spawning of a new era: GM super salmon and the wisdom of tinkering with fish', *University of Minnesota Kiosk Newspaper*, December 2000, About U of M – News and Publications – University Newsletters – Kiosk, University of Minnesota, www1.umn.edu/urelate/kiosk/12.00text/salmon.html

Nelson, J (1994) *Fishes of the World, 3rd Edition*, John Wiley and Sons Inc, New York, pp600

Norse, E (1993) *Global Marine Biological Biodiversity*, Island Press, Washington, DC

Nunavut Wildlife Management Board (1998) *Minutes: Meeting No. 18*, 12–14 May 1998, Broughton Island, Nunavut Territory, Canada

Organization of African Unity (2000) 'African model legislation for the protection of the rights of local communities, farmers and breeders, and for the regulation of access to biological resources', Geneva, http://r0.unctad.org/trade_env/docs/oaulaw.pdf

Pauly, D (2003) 'The future for fisheries', *Science,* vol 241, pp1359–61

Penman, D (1999) 'Biotechnology and aquatic genetic resources: genes and genetically modified organisms' in R Pullin, Bartley, D and Kooiman, J (eds) *Towards Policies for Conservation and Sustainable Use of Aquatic Genetic Resources*, ICLARM Conference Proceedings 59, 14–18 April 1998, Manila

Peria, E (2002) *The Way We Were, as We Are Now: Access and Benefit-sharing in the Philippines*, South East Asia Regional Initiatives for Community Empowerment (SEARICE), Quezon City, Philippines

Plotkin, M (2000) *Medicine Quest*, Penguin Books, Harmondsworth, Middlesex

Posey, D (1993) 'Indigenous knowledge in the conservation and use of world forests' in K Ramakrishna and Woodwell, G (eds) *World Forests for the Future: Their Use and Conservation*, Yale University Press, New Haven, pp59–77

Posey, D (1999) 'Developing *sui generis* options for the protection of living aquatic resources of indigenous and local communities' in R Pullin, Bartley, D and Kooiman, J (eds) *Towards Policies for Conservation and Sustainable Use of*

Aquatic Genetic Resources, ICLARM Conference Proceedings 59, 14–18 April 1998, Manila

Posey, D and Dutfield, G (1996) *Beyond Intellectual Property: Toward Traditional Resource Rights for Indigenous Peoples and Local Communities*, International Development Research Centre, Ottawa

Prang, G (2001) 'Aviamento and the ornamental fishery of the Rio Negro, Brazil: implications for sustainable resource use' In N Chao, Petry, P, Prang, G, Sonnieschien, L and Tlusty, M (eds) (2002) *Conservation and Management of Ornamental Fish Resources of the Rio Negro Basin, Amazonia, Brasil – Project Piaba*, Universidade do Amazonas and Bio-Amazonia Conservation International, Manaus, pp302

Primavera, J and Agbayani, R (1997) 'Comparative strategies in community-based mangrove rehabilitation programmes in the Philippines', in P Hong, Ishwaran, N, San, H, Tri, N and Tuan, M (eds), *Proceedings of Ecotone V, Community Participation in Conservation, Sustainable Use and Rehabilitation of Mangroves in Southeast Asia*. UNESCO, Japanese Man and the Biosphere National Committee and Mangrove Ecosystem Research Centre, Vietnam, pp229–43

Project Seahorse (1998) 'Managing fisheries and adjusting supply', About the Project – Programs, Seahorse Project: Advancing Marine Conservation, http://seahorse.fisheries.ubc.ca/programs.html

Project Seahorse (2000) 'Seahorse conservation and management in Bohol, Philippines', About the Project – Programs, Seahorse Project: Advancing Marine Conservation, http://seahorse.fisheries.ubc.ca/programs.html

Pullin, R (1993) 'Ex-situ conservation of the germplasm of aquatic organisms', *Naga*, July, 15–17

Pullin, R, Bartley, D and Kooiman, J (eds) (1999) *Towards Policies for Conservation and Sustainable Use of Aquatic Genetic Resources*, ICLARM Conference Proceedings 59, Manila

Pullin, R and Casal, C (eds) (1996) *Consultation on Fish Genetic Resources*, International Center for Living Aquatic Resources, Makati City, Philippines

Pullin, R, Eknath, A, Gjedrem T, Tayamen, M, Macaranas, J and Abella, T (1991) 'The genetic improvement of farmed tilapias (GIFT) project: the story so far', *Naga*, vol 14(2), pp3–6

Rajapakse, M (1998) 'The ornamental aquatic industry in Sri Lanka', *OFI Journal*, 24 August

Raymond, R (1999) 'Agricultural research and the art of public awareness' in R. Pullin, Bartley, D and Kooiman, J (eds) *Towards Policies for Conservation and Sustainable Use of Aquatic Genetic Resources*, ICLARM Conference Proceedings 59, 14–18 April 1998, Manila

Reid, W, Laird, S, Meyer, C, Gamez, R, Sittenfeld, A, Janzen, D, Gollin, M and Juma, C (1993) *Biodiversity Prospecting: Using Genetic Resources for Sustainable Development*, World Resources Institute, pp341

Revenga, C, Brunner, J, Henninger, N, Kassem, K and Payne, R (2000) *Pilot Analysis of Global Ecosystems: Freshwater Ecosystems*, World Resources Institute, Washington, DC, 83pp

Ricciardi, A and Rasmussen, J (1999) 'Extinction rates of North American fresh-water fauna', *Conservation Biology*, vol 13(5), pp1220–2

Rifkin, J (1998) *The Biotech Century*, Penguin Putnam Inc, New York, pp271

Roberts, C and Hawkins, J (2001) 'Fully protected marine reserves', Worldwide Fund for Nature, www.panda.org/resources/publications/water/mpreserves/mar_index.htm

Rohter, L (2001) 'A collector's item costs Brazilian divers dearly', *New York Times*, 5 November, ppA4

Rosendal, K (1992) 'Blue revolution could avoid failures of green predecessor', *Biotechnology and Development Monitor*, vol 12 (September), pp10

Ruiz, M (1998) 'When science, law and politics collide: the inevitable suffering of basic science', ENVIS (Environmental Information System Centre – Biodiversity, Indian Institute of Science Center for Ecological Sciences, www.ces.iisc.ernet.in/hpg/envis/doc98html/biodsc95.html

Schumacher, E (1973) *Small Is Beautiful: Economics as if People Mattered*, Harper and Row, New York

SEDA (Department of Economic and Social Affairs), United Nations (2000) *World Population Prospects: The 2000 Revision*, United Nations, New York, www.un.org/esa/population/publications/wpp2000/highlights.pdf

Seiler, A and Dutfield, G (2002) 'Regulating access and benefit-sharing', *Biotechnology and Development Monitor*, vol 49, pp3–7

Shiva, V (1997) *Biopiracy: The Plunder of Nature and Knowledge*, Between The Lines, Toronto, Canada, pp148

Shiva, V (1999) 'Who pays the price? The shrimp industry, rich consumers, and poor coastal communities' In N Svennevig, Reinertsen, H and New, M (eds) *Sustainable Aquaculture: Food for the Future?*, AA Balkema, Rotterdam

Shiva, V (2000) *Poverty and Globalisation*, British Broadcasting Corporation Reith Lectures 2000, http://news.bbc.co.uk/hi/english/static/events/reith_2000/lecture5.stm

Singh, S (2000a) 'Indigenous community bans TNC researchers', *South-North Development Monitor*, 24 February, www.twnside.org.sg/title/bans.htm

Singh, S (2000b) 'Rampant biopiracy of South's biodiversity', *Third World Network*, 20 July, www.twnside.org.sg/title/rampant.htm

Singh Nijar, G (1998) 'Community intellectual property rights protect indigenous knowledge'. *Biotechnology and Development Monitor*, no 36, pp11–12

Specter, M (2000) 'The Pharmageddon riddle', *The New Yorker*, 10 April, pp58–71, www.michaelspecter.com/ny/2000/2000_04_10_monsanto.html.

Swiderska, K (2001) *Stakeholder Participation in Policy on Access to Genetic Resources, Traditional Knowledge and Benefit-sharing*, International Institute for Environment and Development, London, pp32

Tauli-Corpuz, V (1999) *Impacts of WTO on the Environment, Cultures and Indigenous Peoples*, Presentation to workshop on Human Face of Trade: Health and Environment, 27 November, Tebtebba Foundation (Indigenous Peoples' International Centre for Policy Research and Education), Seattle, www.ratical.org/co-globalize/impactsofWTO.html

ten Kate, K and Laird, S (1999) *The Commercial Use of Biodiversity*, Earthscan Publications, London, pp398

Tlusty, M (2002) 'The benefits and risks of aquacultural production for the aquarium trade', *Aquaculture*, vol 205, pp203–19

Toledo, V (1991) 'Patzcuaro's lesson: nature, production and culture in an indigenous region of Mexico' in M Oldfield and Alcorn, J (eds) *Biodiversity: Culture, Conservation and Ecodevelopment*, Westview Press, Boulder, Colorado

Touch, C and Griffiths, D (2001) 'Small-scale fish production – a success in Cambodia', *Catch and Culture: Fisheries Research and Development in the Mekong Region*, vol 7:2 (December), Mekong River Commission, www.mrcmekong.org

Townsend, P (1998*) Social Issues in Fisheries*, FAO Fisheries Technical Paper 375, FAO, Rome, pp93

Turner, N (1975) *Food Plants of British Columbia Indians: Part 1/Coastal Peoples*, British Columbia Provincial Museum, Victoria, Canada, pp264

Turner, N (2000) *Coastal Peoples and Marine Plants on the Northwest Coast*, Presentation to 26th Annual International Association of Marine Science Information Specialists and Librarians Conference

Turner, N (2002) *The Forest and the Seaweed: Gitga'at Seaweed, Traditional Ecological Knowledge and Community Survival*, Presentation to workshop on Local Knowledge, Natural Resources and Community Survival: Charting a Way Forward, 1–2 February, Prince Rupert, BC, Canada

UNCTAD (United Nations Conference on Trade and Development) Secretariat (2000) *Systems and National Experiences for Protecting Traditional, Knowledge, Innovations and Practices*, UNCTAD, Geneva

US Department of State (2002) Fact Sheet: Guidelines for Collecting Genetic Materials Abroad, 6 May, US Department of State, Washington, DC

Veash, N (2000) 'Biopiracy – a new threat to Amazon rainforest's treasures', *The Independent*, 16 October, London

Virchow, D (1999) 'Economic value of genetic resources: an agenda for research', *AgBiotechNet*, vol 1 (February), www.agbiotechnet.com

Warren, D, Slikkerveer, L and Brokenshaw, D (eds) (1995) *The Cultural Dimension of Development: Indigenous Knowledge Systems*, Intermediate Technology Publications, London

Watson, I (2000) *The Role of the Ornamental Fish Industry in Poverty Alleviation*, Natural Resources Institute, Kent, UK, Project No V0120, pp66

WCED (World Commission on Environment and Development) (1987) *Our Common Future* [The Brundtland Report], Oxford University Press, Oxford, pp383

Welcomme, R (1999) 'Institutional factors relating to aquatic genetic resources' in R Pullen, Bartley, D and Kooiman, J (eds), *Towards Policies for Conservation and Sustainable Use of Aquatic Genetic Resources*, ICLARM Conference Proceedings 59, Manila, Philippines, pp207–16

White, S (1992) *Arguing with the Crocodile: Gender and Class in Bangladesh*, The University Press Ltd, Dhaka

Wilson, E (1988) *Biodiversity*, National Academy Press, Washington, DC

Wilson, E (1999) *The Diversity of Life*, WW Norton, New York, pp424

Wiser, G (1999) *PTO Rejection of the 'Atahuasca Patent Claim'*, Center for International Environmental Law, Washington, DC

World Fisheries Trust (2002a) Integration of Biodiversity into National Fishery Sectors. UNEP-BPSP Thematic Studies, www.unep.org/bpsp/ HTML% 20files/TS-Fisheries.html

World Fisheries Trust (2002b) *Progress in Implementing the Programme of Work on Inland Waters*, Convention on Biological Diversity Secretariat, Montreal

WWF (World Wide Fund for Nature) (2000) *Indigenous and Traditional Peoples of the World and Ecoregion Conservation: An Integrated Approach to Conserving the World's Biological and Cultural Diversity*, WWF International – People and Conservation Unit and Terralingua: partnerships for linguistic and biological diversity, Discussion Document, Draft, July 2000, www.terralingua.org/ WWFExecSummary.html

Yaakob, W and Ali, A (1992) 'Simple Method for backyard production of snakehead fry', *Naga*, April, pp22–3

Index

Law of the Sea
 see UN Convention on the Law of
 the Sea
leech 52

Marine Aquarium Council 56, 164,
 165
marine protected areas 129, 192–5,
 197–8
Marine Science Institute 107, 168
Marine Stewardship Council 83, 164
medicinal uses of plants and animals
 52
micro-organisms 25, 29, 181

National Biodiversity Strategies (CBD)
 83–4
National Cancer Institute 109, 169
National Museum of the Philippines
 169, 170
national sovereignty 91
negotiation framework 195–6
Network of Aquaculture Centers in
 Asia 71
Neurex Inc 106
New Zealand 36
North American Free Trade Agreement
 100
Northwest Territories Scientists Act
 110
Norway 67
Nunavut Land Claims Agreement 110
Nuu-chah-nulth First Nation 52, 115

ocean warming 28
Organization of African Unity model
 law 101, 140, 149–60, 185
ornamental fishery 15–16, 43–6,
 54–9, 130–1, 162, 183

patent law 162
 history 100–1

traditional knowledge 104
 see also intellectual property rights;
 TRIPS
Peru 134, 150, 153, 154, 159, 161
pharmaceutical industry 2, 46–52,
 98–9, 105–10, 130, 181–2,
 196–200
Philippines 8, 20, 48, 94, 104, 106–7,
 116, 134, 135, 136, 137, 138,
 149–51, 185, 190–5
 Executive Order 247 48, 107,
 149–61, 166–76
Plan of Work on Inland Waters (CBD)
 82
Plant Breeders' Rights 97, 100–1
policy gaps
 managing aquatic biodiversity 2–3,
 75–81, 203–10
 access and benefit-sharing 87,
 208–11
 policy checklist 211
pond farming 39, 116, 119, 135, 142
poverty in fishing communities 6,
 115–7, 167, 184, 190
precautionary principle 3, 39, 209
prior informed consent 9, 107, 134,
 141, 148, 153–4, 170–2, 176,
 184
 negotiation tools 195–6, 199–200
PROCESS Foundation 192
Project Piaba 11, 15, 59–60
Project Seahorse 11, 174, 190–1
protected areas
 see marine protected areas
public and professional awareness
 206
Ramsar Convention on Wetlands 82

research
 academic vs commercial research 9,
 140–1, 157–8, 168–70
 Law of the Sea 92

ALSO AVAILABLE FROM EARTHSCAN

MANAGING NATURAL RESOURCES FOR SUSTAINABLE LIVELIHOODS

Uniting Science and Participation
Edited by Barry Pound, Sieglinde Snapp, Cynthia McDougall and Ann Braun

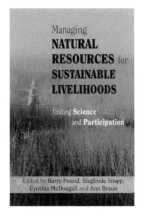

Management of local resources has a greater chance of a sustainable outcome when there is partnership between local people and external agencies, and agendas relevant to their aspirations and circumstances. Managing Natural Resources for Sustainable Livelihoods analyses and extends this premise to show unequivocally that the process of research for improving natural resource management must incorporate participatory and user-focused approaches, leading to development based on the needs and knowledge of local resource users.

Drawing on extensive and highly relevant case studies, this book:

- Presents innovative approaches for establishing and sustaining participation and collective decision-making, good practice for research, and challenges for future developments.

- Covers a wide range of natural resources - including forests and soils, and water and management units, such as watersheds and common property areas - and provides practical lessons from analysis and meta-analysis of cases from Asia, Africa and Latin America.

- Offers insights on how to make research participatory while maintaining rigour and high-quality biological science, different forms of participation, and ways to scale up and extend participatory approaches and successful initiatives.

This book will be invaluable for those professionally involved in natural resource management for sustainable development and an essential resource for teachers and students of both the biophysical and social science aspects of natural resource management.

Paperback £22.95 1-84407-026-3 ● Hardback £65.00 1-84407-025-5

Order on-line at www.earthscan.co.uk

Or send your order to:
James & James/Earthscan
FREEPOST NAT12094
8-12 Camden High Street
London NW1 0YA UK
Tel +44 (0)20 7387 8558
Email earthinfo@earthscan.co.uk